Shepherding the Flock of God

American University Studies

Series VII
Theology and Religion

Vol. 101

PETER LANG
New York · San Francisco · Bern
Frankfurt am Main · Paris · London

R.A. Krupp

Shepherding the Flock of God

The Pastoral Theology of John Chrysostom

PETER LANG
New York · San Francisco · Bern
Frankfurt am Main · Paris · London

G

Library of Congress Cataloging-in-Publication Data

Krupp, Robert Allen.
   Shepherding the flock of God: the pastoral theology
of John Chrysostom / R.A. Krupp.
     p. cm. – (American university studies. Series VII,
Theology and religion ; vol. 101)
   Includes bibliographical references.
   1. John Chrysostom, Saint, d. 407–Contributions in
pastoral theology. 2. Bishops–History. 3. Pastoral
theology–History of doctrines–Early church, ca. 30-600.
   I. Title. II. Series. American university, Series VII.
Theology and religion: v. 101.
BR65.C46K78   1991   253'.092–dc20   91-17583
ISBN 0-8204-1515-4   CIP
ISSN 0740-0446

Die Deutsche Bibliothek-CIP-Einheitsaufnahme

Krupp, Robert A.:
Shepherding the flock of God : the pastoral theology of
John Chrysostom / R.A.Krupp.– New York; Berlin;
Bern; Frankfurt/M.; Wien; Paris: Lang, 1991
   (American university studies : Ser. 7, Theology and
religion ; Vol. 101)
   ISBN 0-8204-1515-4
NE: American university studies / 07

The paper in this book meets the guidelines for permanence and durability
of the Committee on Production Guidelines for Book Longevity of the
Council on Library Resources.

Printed in the United States of America.

92-01928

To Collette

TABLE OF CONTENTS

PREFACE

I believe it is time to venture forth with an introduction to the thought of John Chrysostom. His pivotal ministry has not received the attention it deserves in works that are accessible to an audience broader than the scholarly community. The current biography by Baur is sixty years old and numerous critical editions and new translations of Chrysostom's works have come on the scene since its publication.

This work is introductory but should serve as a gateway into the vast Chrysostom corpus for those who would seek to use his literary legacy as a vantage point to view life in the Church at a critical juncture in its history. This volume has benefitted from the research of numerous specialists and seeks to integrate their work and put forth a concise statement of Chrysostom's pastoral theology.

Many segments of Christendom are currently wandering without theological moorings and the wisdom of those who have attempted to live for Christ and serve Him in previous eras will provide some badly needed guidance. Issues such as congregational indifference, ecclesiastical power struggles, pastoral accountability, individual freedom, and church-state relations which plague the church today were problems in John's era as well. C.S. Lewis noted in his introduction to an edition of Athanasius that "two heads are better than one, not because either is infallible, but because they are unlikely to go wrong in the same direction."[1] Lewis made the case in his introduction that the books of the past can help students because they can challenge their presuppositions from a perspective outside their cultural and historical framework. Chrysostom was a preacher and bishop who can critique and challenge modern ministry by his words and actions.

Two of the chapters of this work were in seed form in seminar papers and a theses at the University of Portland under Dr. Loretta Zimmerman. Her care of her students and the time she invested in each thesis under her tutorage is an example that has challenged me as I now serve as an advisor to students' research.

I have served on the staffs of the University of Portland, Houston Public Library, and Western Seminary. The interlibrary loans departments of these libraries have been helpful in procuring the necessary resources for my work. A sabbatical spent at the Bodleian Library at Oxford University gave me access to materials not available elsewhere. For my seat in Duke Humphrey's Library and the patience of the staff who daily found requests for theses, dissertations and other items on their desks and always responded cheerfully, I also give thanks.

Miss Audrey Arnst who works with in the library at Western Seminary has handled many difficult interlibrary loan requests and has saved me much time.

While I have served as Library Director and Vice President for Administration at Western Seminary, Mrs. Bonnie Liljenberg, Mrs. Lita Norsworthy, and Mrs. Lori Einfalt have served as my administrative assistants or secretaries. They have often used their administrative skills to free my time for study. They have also provided editorial help in the various drafts of this work.

I am also thankful for the students at Western Seminary who have responded to my lectures on Chrysostom in various classes or participated in seminars I've offered. They have often challenged my thinking and interpretations.

Many colleagues and friends have read drafts of this volume and I am thankful for their criticism and encouragement.

My wife Collette has endured and apparently enjoyed vacations built around trips to libraries and historical sites and I am always indebted to her for her support and encouragement.

1.C.S. Lewis. Introduction to Athanasius. *On the Incarnation.* Translated and edited by a Religious of C.S.M.V. (Crestwood, New York: St. Vladimir's Seminary Press, 1982) 5.

ABBREVIATIONS

| NPNF | *Nicene and Post Nicene Fathers, Second Series.* |

John Chrysostom's Works

Ad Dem de comp	Ad Demetrium de compunctione libre 1
Ad pop Anti	Ad populum Antiochenum homiliae 1-21
Ad Stag a dae	Ad Stagirium a daemone vexatum libre 1-3
Ad Theo	Ad Theodorum lapsum libri 1-2
Ad vid jun	Ad viduam juniorem
Adv Jud	Adversus Judaeos orationes 1-8[1]
Adv op	Adversus oppugnatores vitae monasticae libri 1-3
Cat ill	Catecheses ad illuminandos[2]
Con Anom	Contra Anomoeos homilia 11
Con e q sub	Contra eos qui subintroductas habent virgines
Con Jud et gen	Contra Judaeos et gentiles quod Christus sit deus
De Anna	De Anna sermones 1-5
De b Phil	De beato Philogonio
De bap Chris	De baptismo Christi
De Chris divin	De Christi divinitate
De Chris prec	De Christi precibus
De Consub	De Consubstantiali
De diab tent	De diabolo tentatore homiliae 1-3
De inani gloria	De inani gloria et de educandis liberis
De incomp dei	De incomprehensibili dei natura homiliae 1-5
De laud s Paul	De laudibus sancti Pauli apostoli homiliae 1-7
De Laz	De Lazaro conciones 1-7
De mut nom	De mutatione nominum homiliae 1-4
De n iter	De non iterando convigio
De pet mat	De petitione matris feiliorum Zebedaei
De prod Jud	De proditione Judae homiliae 1-2
De proph obscur	De prophetiarum obscuritate homiliae 1-2
De s Bab c Iul	De s. Babyla contra Iulianum et gentiles
De s Dros	De s. Droside martyre
De s h Bab	De s. hieromartyre Bablya

De sac	De sacerdotio libri 1-6
De san pent	De sancta pentecoste homiliae 1-2
De ter motu	De terrae motu
De vir	De virginitate
Ep	Epistulae 1-242
Ep ad I	Epistula ad Innocentium papam 1-2
Ep ad Olym	Epistula ad Olympias
Ex in ps	Expositiones in psalmos 4-12, 41, 43-49, 103-106, 108-117, 119, 150
In Acta	In Acta apostolorum homiliae 1-55
In Col	In Colossenses homiliae 1-12
In 1 Cor	In epistulam i ad Corinthios argumentum et homiliae 1-44
In 2 Cor	In epistulam ii ad Corinthios argumentum et homiliae 1-30
In diem nat	In diem natalem
In Eph	In epistulam ad Ephesios argumentum
In Eut	In Eutropium
In Gal	In epistulam as Galatas Commentarius
In Gen	Homiliae 1-67 in Genesim
In Heb	In epistulam ad Hebraeos argumentum et homiliae 1-34
In il Pater s p	In illud: Pater si possible est transeat (Mat 26:39)
In il Prop	In illud: Propter fornicationes uxorem (1 Cor 7:2)
In il Si esur	In illud: Si esurierit inimicus (Rom 12:20)
In il Vid elig	In illud: Vidua eligatur (1 Tim 5:9)
In il Vidi dom	In illud: Vidi dominum (Is 6:1) homiliae 1-6
In Jn	In Johannem homiliae 1-88
In Kal	In kalendas
In Mat	In Matthaeum homiliae 1-89[3]
In para	In paralyticum demissum per tectum
In Phil	In epistulam ad Philippenses argumentum et homiliae 1-15
In Philemon	In epistulam ad Philemonem argumentum et homiliae 1-3
In princ Act	In principium Actorum homiliae 1-4

In quat Laz A	In quatriduanum Lazarum (PG 48,779-784)
In Rom	In epistulam ad Romanos homiliae 1-32
In s Igna	In s. Ignatium martyrem
In 1 Thess	In epistulam i ad Thessalonicenses homiliae 1-11
In 2 Thess	In epistulam ii ad Thessalonicenses homiliae 1-5
In 1 Tim	In epistulam i ad Timetheum argumentum et homiliae 1-18
In 2 Tim	In epistulam ii ad Timotheum argumentum at homiliae 1-10
In Tit	In epistulam ad Titum homiliae 1-6
Q nemo	Quod nemo laeditur nisi a se ipso
S Gen	Sermones 1-9 in Genesim

1.In *Adversus Judaeos orationes* the numbering system employed by Harkins in his translation (*Discourses Against Judaizing Christians*. Washington: Catholic University of America Press, 1979) has been adopted because of the addition of a third numeral in the notation breaks the text into smaller units making location simpler.

2.In *Catecheses ad illuminandos* the various homilies from the different series have been ordered as follows:

i	Stavronikita	1
ii	"	2
iii	"	3 and Papadopoulos - Kerameus 4
iv	"	4
v	"	5
vi	"	6
vii	"	7
viii	"	8
ix	Montfaucon 1 and Papadopoulos - Kerameus 1	
x		" 2
xi		" 3
xii	Montfaucon 2	

This appears to be the best reconstruction of the homilies and agrees with Harkins' translation (*Baptismal Instructions*. New York: Newman Press, 1963).

3.In *In Matthaeum homiliae 1-89* the numbering of the Greek homilies is used; the Latin translation is numbered 1-90. The difference occurs when Homily 19 in the Greek text is divided at paragraph 6 into two homilies affecting the numbering of the remaining sermons.

CHAPTER 1
INTRODUCTION

John Chrysostom considered the priesthood the highest calling on earth but avoided ordination by deceit. His voice could move the masses of the capital city, but he died alone in exile at the edge of the known world. He wrote in exile that no one can harm the man who does not harm himself, but he was deposed and exiled by a young and inexperienced emperor. That emperor's son wept for his parents' forgiveness on Chrysostom's coffin thirty years later. Chrysostom praised the virtues of the solitary life but admitted from the pulpit that he could not live without his congregation. His enemies could not tolerate the forgiveness he offered for all sinners, but his homilies against Christians with Judaizing tendencies are considered among the most embarrassing examples of anti-Semitism in Christian history. He was a chauvinist raised by a woman and an ethnocentric Greek of the city spiritually nurtured by ascetic hermits. He was a small man with health permanently impaired through the monastic rigor of his youth, but he preached with such power that he became Chrysostom, the golden mouth. The life and ministry of John Chrysostom, priest and bishop of the late fourth and early fifth century, is a study in contrasts.

This work attempts to walk a couple of difficult tightropes at the same time. It is an integrative study and will undoubtedly offend specialists whose disciplines have not been handled to their expectations. It shall fall victim to the barbs noted by Will Durant: "The man who sells his soul to synthesis becomes the tragic target of a myriad merry darts of specialist critique."[1] It also attempts to benefit from the vast array of research into the life and writing of John Chrysostom but wishes for him to speak in his own words whenever possible. Most of the analysis of secondary sources will take place in the notes.

In 1967 Robert Carter reported to the International Conference on

Patristic Studies on the state and future of Chrysostom studies.   He
concluded that the present agenda for Chrysostom scholars should put
manuscript studies at the highest priority, resulting in the issuing of critical
editions as well as new translations of works not yet readily available in
contemporary and readable editions. He concluded that even though studies
of Chrysostom's thought would be of the highest value they would have to
be postponed until these other tasks are completed.[2] We still do not have
critical texts of all of the Chrysostom corpus, and there are significant works,
especially among John's discourses on the Old Testament books, where the
English-speaking scholar is without the aid of a translation. However, even
with these limitations, I shall venture forth into a study of the thought and
contribution of John Chrysostom. Occasionally John has been dismissed as
making no theological contribution, but a study of his homiletical legacy
reveals that this pivotal ministry of the late fourth and early fifth century was
shaped by strong convictions rooted in a coherent theology of the Christian
life.[3] To be sure, John presents a formidable challenge because his style in
the pulpit and as a correspondent utilized a rhetorical flourish that can easily
frustrate most exegetes.[4]

     This study is built on the work of many scholars and is a preliminary
analysis of John's thought.   It seeks to expound and contextualize his
contribution to significant areas of Christian reflection in the theology of the
godly life, the Christian ministry, the task of the preacher, and the apologetic
mission of the church.

     Carter's caution not to proceed with studies of John's thought without
the base of manuscript and other foundational studies confronted this author
in a personal way. The goal of this study was set in the mid-1970s but a five-
year delay occurred when I realized that I could not proceed without a more
faithful guide to Chrysostom's use of Scripture. The various indices of the
different editions and translations, each keyed to a specific volume, were not
helpful as one moved from one edition of a work to another. This need was

filled with *Saint John Chrysostom: A Scripture Index*, enabling work on this project to proceed.[5]

In addition to the need for further foundational research, the student of Chrysostom is confronted with a more pleasurable but potentially more frustrating challenge. The organization of John's thought, as revealed in the vast Chrysostom corpus, into a coherent and communicable whole is an ever-present obstacle. The organization must be faithful to Chrysostom's theological context and emphases or anachronistic prooftexting will result. It must also present the interrelationships and priorities of John's pastoral theology or the reader will not appreciate the coherence of his thought.

There are many motifs of the Christian life that emerge from Chrysostom's literary legacy in sermon, letter, and treatise. Three, however, are central to his understanding of Christian ministry and spiritual life: the desert father, the martyr, and the bishop.[6] When one views John's historical context these are likely emphases of his preaching and writing. He lived in an era still vividly in touch with the age of martyrs and at a time when the theology of martyrs and martyrdom was undergoing significant development. That age also saw the flowering of the flight to the white martyrdom of the desert, a life wholly devoted to God without the shedding of blood. Finally, he was a bishop who wrote eloquently and soberly about the role of the Christian shepherd. Jaroslav Pelikan cogently observes concerning the role of vocation in the development of Christian theology that "during the years 100 to 600, most theologians were bishops; from 600 to 1500 in the West, they were monks; since 1500, they have been university professors."[7] John was a transitional figure. He was a bishop with the heart of monk. He linked a pride in the polis as the center of a Christianized Hellenism with a vision of the encounter with God that only occurs in solitude.

The images of the desert father, bishop, and martyr as idealizations of the Christian are not unique to John. They have played a significant role in influencing the Christian spirituality of others, but John exemplified a period when these images were central in the prevailing concepts of piety. It would be unfair and inaccurate to consider these motifs to be stages in John's development. They are all strong throughout his life and when viewed both in isolation and in composite give great insight into John and his era.

This work will focus on the image of the bishop in John's life and thought and will seek to articulate the theology of the Christian life and the pastoral ministry through his eyes. If this is accomplished, he can instruct those who seek to understand the dynamics of Christian piety in an historical perspective. His views can also shed light on how Christians sought to live for Jesus Christ in a period that has emerged as critical in the history of the Church.

1.Quoted in John H. D'Arms, "Facing the Future of Graduate Education," *Rackham Reports* 1986-1987. 11.

2.Robert E. Carter, "The Future of Chrysostom Studies: Theology and Nachleben," *Studia Patristica* 10 (1970): 20.

3.F.X. Murphy,"The Moral Doctrine of Saint John Chrysostom," *Studia Patristica* 11 (1972): 52-53.

4.Charles Kannengiesser, "Le mystére pascal du Christ mort et ressusitè selon Jean Chrysostome," *Jean Chrysostom et Augustine* (Paris: Éditions Beauchesne, 1975), 221.

5.R.A. Krupp, *Saint John Chrysostom: A Scripture Index* (Lanham, MD: University Press of America, 1984).

6.An approach similar to the one taken in this volume is seen in *Jesus Through the Centuries* by Jaroslav Pelikan (New Haven: Yale University Press, 1985.). He illustrates the development of Christian thought in the conceptions of Christ in the history of the Church. He has been envision-ed as a monk, rabbi, or soldier by sincere followers. James Houston, Chancellor of Regent College, in a conversation with the author, indicated that an emphasis in his research views the history of Christian spirituality through the pictures of the ideal Christian. The ideal Christian has been conceived of as a monk, soldier, pilgrim, or child in different eras. Cer-tainly these sets of pictures are interrelated. Christlikeness has been a consistent goal of the Christian community. Secondly, these pictures are all, when viewed individually, reductionistic. However, when they are viewed with balance and in an integrative manner, this approach can serve to illustrate the way in which theological truths are formulated and de-velop.

7.Jaroslav Pelikan, *The Emergence of the Catholic Tradition (100-600)* (Chicago: The University of Chicago Press, 1971), 5.

CHAPTER 2
THE CONTEXT OF JOHN'S MINISTRY

The Political Context

The last third of the fourth century, when John entered the service of the church[1] at Antioch, gave no assurance that Christianity had emerged as the victorious faith of the empire. Julian the Apostate had abandoned the Christian faith. He recent reign and government vacillations between the Arian and Trinitarian versions of orthodoxy had exiled and recalled bishops with disruptive regularity. John could not bring himself to believe that he was living in a Christian era and that the pagans would not rule again.[2]

His description of his perilous times was given poignantly to a young widow, a woman whose distress must have touched him personally because his mother had suffered a similar fate. John's widowed mother, Anthusa, lost her husband, a government official of standing, when she was barely twenty years old with two young children. John began the letter by acknowledging the depths of the woman's sorrow and advised her to pursue the vocation of widowhood within the Church, but soon his words turned to the political situation of their day. He said he was led to do so because her recently deceased husband had been considered for the office of Prefect.[3] He consoled the widow, extolling the character of her late husband.

> I grant you that all the world over among men engaged in secular affairs there have been few like him, so affectionate, so gentle, so humble, so sincere, so understanding, so devout.[4]

In discussing the political climate of the previous half-century he contrasted the fate of her husband, dying peacefully while speaking his last words with her and then being granted a funeral with great honor, with the fate of recent emperors and their widows.

> Now passing over ancient times, of those who have reigned in our own generation, nine in all, only two have ended their life by a natural death; and of the others one was slain by a usurper, one

in battle, one by a conspiracy of his household guards, one by the very man who elected him and invested him with the purple, and of their wives some, as it is reported, perished by poison, others died of mere sorrow; while some of those who still survive, one, who has an orphaned son, is trembling with alarm lest any of those who are in power, dreading what may happen in the future, should destroy him; another has reluctantly yielded to much entreaty to return from exile into which she had been driven by him who held the chief power. And of the wives of the present rulers the one who has recovered a little from her sorrow mingled with her joy because the possessor of power is still young and inexperienced and has many designing men on all sides of him; and the other is ready to die of fear, and spends her time more miserably than criminals condemned to death because her husband, ever since he assumed the crown up to the present day, has been constantly engaged in warfare and fighting, and is more exhausted by the shame and the reproaches which assail him on all sides than by actual calamities. For that which has never taken place has now come to pass, the barbarians leaving their own country have overrun an infinite space of our territory, and that many times over, and having set fire to the land, and captured the towns they are not minded to return home again, but after the manner of men who are keeping holiday rather than making war, they laugh us all to scorn.[5]

Neither the faith nor the empire was secure.[6]   John's theology embraced a role for the state and he welcomed the Christianization of the imperial purple, but he entered the priesthood in a climate where neither the commitments of the emperor nor the security of the empire could be accepted without reservations and concern.

The Religious Climate

Even though John was ordained to the priesthood after the decree of Theodosius, which gave more security to the Trinitarian faith within the empire, he often longed for the primitive purity of the early Church. As he preached in the capital city he could long for a time when Christianity was a little-known sect.   John looked at the spiritual dynamic of the first

Christians and found that power lacking in the Church of his day.

> What now can be more awful than these things? For in truth the
> Church was a heaven then, the Spirit governing all things, and
> moving each one of the rulers and making him inspired. But now
> we retain only the symbols of those gifts. For now also we speak
> two or three, and in turn, and when one is silent, another begins.
> But these are only signs and memorials of those things. Where-
> fore when we begin to speak, the people respond, "with thy
> Spirit," indicating that of old they thus used to speak, not of their
> own wisdom, but moved by the Spirit. But not so now: (I speak
> of my own case so far.) But the present Church is like a woman
> who has fallen from her former prosperous days, and in many
> respects retains the symbols only of that ancient prosperity;
> displaying indeed the repositories and caskets of her golden
> ornaments, but bereft of her wealth; such a one does the Church
> resemble. And I say this not in respect of gifts: for it were
> nothing marvelous if it were this only: but also in respect to life
> and virtue.... For then instead of gold they were clothed with the
> fair array of almsgiving: but now, having left this off, they are
> decked out on every side with cords of gold woven of the chain
> of their sins.

> Then the very houses were churches: but now the church itself
> is a house, or rather worse than any house.... But here great is
> the tumult, great the confusion, and our assemblies differ in
> nothing from a vintner's shop, so loud is the laughter, so great
> the disturbance; as in baths, as in markets, the cry and tumult is
> universal.

> Does it make your flesh creep to be told of these things? No
> then, much rather let it creep when you do them.[7]

The fourth century brought a new consciousness to the empire. The
Christianization of the empire, leading to such expressions of piety as the
quest for relics by members of the imperial household, stood in marked
contrast to an incident a few decades earlier. Eusebius recounts the
questioning of some Christians before the governor, Firmilianus, in Caesarea,

Palestine, in the first years of the fourth century. When the official asked where they were from they responded that they were from Jerusalem, a reference to the heavenly city because they were actually from Egypt. The governor believed that this was a Persian city even though the former Jewish capital, now called Aelia Capitolina, was under his jurisdiction.[8]

The religious climate of the empire certainly changed in the fourth century, even taking Chrysostom's reservations into account. In the course of the struggle that brought him to sole authority, Constantine had his famous vision of the cross and declared himself a Christian. The very manner of his conversion affected his relationship with the Church. Faith in Christ did not come to him through the Church or any other human agency. God revealed Himself to Constantine in the sign of the cross as he prepared for battle. This direct call of God created an imperial consciousness that saw the Church and throne as coagents of God in the government of His creation.[9] Constantine was a unique Christian. He was neither a bishop nor an ordinary layman. He did not vote as a cleric in councils, but he convened councils and intervened in the appointment of bishops at will.[10] Constantine's religious agenda was more that of acting out his own convictions rather than a submission of the empire to the faith of the Church. Many of his legal changes were inconsistent and incomplete and did not lead to a formal revision of the empire's legal code.[11]

During this transitional period there were many pagan vestiges, and John wrestled with his stance of toleration for pagans and the avoidance of force in their conversion.[12] Many German officers in the imperial service such as the Frank Arbogast and the Gothic leaders Fravitta and Generid retained their non-Christian beliefs.[13] However, pagan religion quickly sunk to the point where in August, 362, when Julian went to the festival of Apollo at Daphne, the priest was going to sacrifice a goose, which the emperor viewed as an insult. This humiliation of pagan practice was soon after the triumphant return of the body of the martyred Antiochene bishop Saint

Babylas accompanied by a great hymn-singing procession.[14] The toleration of Valentinian I further complicated the religious climate for he chose not to abolish the state cult and to broadly extend toleration to all Christian sects.[15]

A set of important subtle changes took place during the period of the ascension of Christianity and the decline of the influence of the traditional pagan cults during the fourth century. Civic liberality tied civic life to various cults before Constantine's conversion. This changed under state-supported Christianity and led both to centralized authority and a new concept of transcendence in government.[16] Power moved from the city to the imperial throne, and a despotism involving quasi-divine attributes in an emperor who was called and supported by God, characterized the Christian empire. This development began with Constantine and continued through the Byzantine era. In the context of the emergence of this trend, Christianity became the official faith of the empire and after the unifying Council of Constantinople in 381 Trinitarian orthodoxy was, at least in name, the accepted version of the faith.

Antioch

In addition to being a product of his century, Chrysostom was also a son of Antioch, one of the cultural centers of the ancient world. The position of Antioch near the Persian frontier and many days' journey from the capital in Constantinople contributed to the climate that bred John's uneasiness with the political situation and also brought the city into closer contact with the orient than was true of most of the rest of the empire. It was a point of confluence of many cultures and theologies. Its long Christian heritage was a source of pride to John. As he preached he reminded his audience that their city was the place where the followers of Jesus were first called Christians.[17] He also exhorted the people that they were of the same culture as the Apostle Paul and therefore could imitate his spiritual feats.[18]

Antioch may have been the first place for the name Christian, but Fortune was the god of the city, and the city was the home of a complex religious climate.[19] Not only was its paganism not dead but its Christianity was divided during John's ministry in that city. The different sects and their infighting over the doctrinal differences among their various understandings of orthodoxy were a scandal to those outside the Church. It served, along with the rampant materialism he saw among Antiochene Christians, to diminish the influence of the Church in that city.[20]

Adorning this Christian community were two great monuments to the faith, the "Great Church" and the "Old Church." The Christians of Antioch clung to their "Old Church" with much love and veneration for a long time after a new edifice was begun under Constantine and dedicated in 341. This new octagonal church was the most famous of its style in northern Syria where octagonal churches were rare.[21] Chrysostom, on an occasion when divine service could not be held in the new "Great Church," probably because of alterations in the building, spoke of the congregation's attachment to and veneration of the older building.[22] This church was constructed before the era of persecution and reminded the congregation of the great history and steadfastness of the Christian community in Antioch.

Also adorning Antioch was the memory of Saint Babylas. There has been confusion about the details of his life and the form of his final confession because of the paucity of sources.[23] However, his defiance of an emperor and his subsequent execution were a source of pride to the Antiochene church. Also testifying to the position of this church in Christendom were the ministries of the Apostle Peter and Ignatius in the city. Ignatius the second-century bishop was martyred, "having heard Christ saying, the good shepherd lays down his life for the sheep, with all courage he [Ignatius] lay it down for the sheep."[24]

John was proud of Antioch's place in secular and religious history.[25] As he corrected the conduct of his congregation as a priest in the city he chided their lack of generosity and concluded with the following praise of their city's Christian heritage.

And all this in Antioch, where men were first called Christians, wherein are bred the most civilized of mankind, where in old time the fruit of charity flourished so abundantly. For not only to those at hand but also to those very far off, they used to send, and this when famine was expected.[26]

Antioch was a wealthy city and its wealth figured often in John's preaching.[27] The pride of Antiochenes in their self-sufficiency and stature was seen when they felt dishonored by another city's entreaty for them at the time of their rebellion.[28]

Such a city provided tremendous educational and cultural advantages. Centuries before John, Cicero praised the city as the "Queen of the East" and held its cultural and education community in high regard.[29] Being an Antiochene of John's social class meant being a product of a culture that was essentially Greek. John characterized other languages as unbeautiful when compared to his mother tongue. John depreciated Hebrew and Syriac in one of his descriptions of the Apostle Paul.

He was a Cilician and the difference between Rome and Cilicia all know. He was a tent-maker, a poor man, unskilled in the wisdom of those without, knowing only the Hebrew tongue, a language despised by all, especially the Italians. For they do not so much despise the barbarian, the Greek or any other tongue as the Syriac, and this has an affinity with the Hebrew. Nor wonder at this, for if they despised the Greek, which is so admirable and beautiful, much more than Hebrew.[30]

John's ethnocentrism was also revealed as he interpreted Christ's words in the Olivet Discourse about the preaching of the Gospel to the end of the earth before His return and contended that Paul had covered the entire earth during his lifetime.[31] His class consciousness surfaces a number of times in his sermons. He speaks of women of "good breeding" and notes that friends should be of the same class.[32] Another prejudice of John's class was seen in his attitude toward servants. Even though he preached that they should receive better treatment, when he taught on Genesis he noted that

Hagar despised Sarah after Hagar became pregnant through Abraham. As he preached on this passage he said, "This, you see, is the way with servants; if they happen to gain some slight advantage, they can't bear to stay within the limits of their station but immediately forget their place and fall into an ungrateful attitude."[33]

John's life in Antioch[34]

John was born in Antioch-on-the-Orontes around the midpoint of the fourth century.[35] His father, Secundus, was a government official and died when John was very young. His mother, Anthusa, did not remarry but preserved her husband's estate and used her dowry to pay for John's education. John's aunt was a deaconess.[36]

John used very few illustrations from his early life but, when he was preaching on the grace of God from the book of Acts to the people of Constantinople in the final years of his ministry, he recounted an incident involving a magic book which illustrated the military presence in his native Antioch.

> Once upon a time a suspicion of tyrants was raised in our city. At that time I was but a youth and all the soldiers being set to watch the city as it chanced, they were making strict inquisition after books of sorcery and magic. And the person who had written the book had flung it unbound into the river, and was taken, and when asked for it, was not able to give it up, but was carried all around the city in bonds. When, however, the evidence being brought home to him, he suffered punishment. Just then it chanced that I, wishing to go to the Martyrs' Church, was returning through the gardens by the riverside in company with another person. He, seeing the book floating on the water at first thought it was a linen cloth, but when he got near perceived it was a book, so he went down and took it up. I however called shares in the booty and laughed about it. But let us see, says he, what in the world it is. So he turns back a part of the page, and finds the contents to be magic. At that very moment it chanced that a soldier came by, after having paced backward and forward he went off. There we were congealed with fear. For who would

have believed our story that we had picked it up from the river, when all were at that time even the unsuspected, under strict watch? And we did not dare cast it away, lest we should be seen, and there was a like danger to us in tearing it to pieces. God gave us means, and we cast it away and, at last, we were free for that time from the extreme peril.[37]

John studied under the pagan rhetor, Libanius, who had previously taught the future emperor Julian, know as the Apostate. He probably began his formal education at five years old and finished his studies at eighteen.[38]

When John explained his escape from ordination to Basil, one of the reasons he gave was his inexperience in service in the church and his devotion to "vain" secular learning. He complained that the selectors had been attracted to the wrong person.

Christ called fisherman, tentmakers and publicans to this dignity, whereas these men reject those who support themselves by daily labor but if there be any one who devotes himself to secular learning and is brought up in idleness, him they receive and admire. For why, pray, have they passed by men who have undergone innumerable toils in the service of the Church, and suddenly dragged into this dignity one who has never experienced any labors of this kind, but has spent all his youth in the vain study of secular learning. These things and more they might have said had I accepted the office but not so now.[39]

The church historian Sozomen reported that when Libanius was on his deathbed, he was asked who would be his successor as the rhetor of Antioch. He replied, "It would have been John had the Christians not taken him from us."[40]

John's comments about Libanius are few. This may seem surprising in light of their relationship during John's days as a student and their activity in Antioch during John's decade and a half of service in the church there. However, Libanius' influence had declined after the death of Julian. In his letter to a young widow John refers to his teacher as "the most god-fearing of all the pagans."[41]

John's view of the world was shaped by his schooling and was typical of an educated man in his day. He uses the gusts of the Aegean Sea and the dangers of sea travel as an illustration of the seas of life.[42] In the sphere of medicine, he believed that the human body contained four special elements: the warm element of the blood, the sluggish element of the yellow bile, the moist element of the mucus, and the cold element of the black bile. Such was the physical foundation for the four temperaments, the sanguine, the choleric, the phlegmatic, and the melancholic.[43] He believed that the heavenly bodies orbited the earth in a fixed path.[44] He divided the human race into Greek and barbarian and among the barbarians he knew of the Italians, the Sythians (Goths), Thracians, Persians, Parthians, and Medes, natives of India, the inhabitants of the British Isles, the Saracens, and the Chinese.[45] His knowledge of geography included the Euphrates, Tigris, Nile, and Ganges rivers.[46] But, as would be expected from a student of Libanius his greatest skill was that of rhetoric and he watched and enjoyed the practice of this skill in the lawcourts.[47]

John was baptized by the Archbishop, Meletius, about 367. After the death of his mother, he pursued a time of monastic rigor. He was ordained a deacon by Meletius before the archbishop left for the Council of Constantinople in 381. In 386 he became a priest under Meletius' successor, Flavian. During his twelve year priesthood in Antioch his fame spread as he preached regularly for the aged archbishop.

John as Archbishop of Constantinople

John was elevated to the Archbishopric of Constantinople in 398 partially through the influence of the eunuch, Eutropius, who held power over the young and inexperienced emperor, Arcadius. He was brought to the capital city because of his fame as a preacher. His sermons immediately attracted large crowds and his second sermon, which was against the Arians, was a great success.[48] His moralistic preaching soon disturbed the upper classes of the city as well as some of the clergy who had enjoyed looser standards under his predecessor, the aged Nectarius.[49] John conducted an investigation into clerical simony in Asia Minor which further alienated some of the clergy.[50]

The incident which led to John's exile began as a dispute in the church at Alexandria over the teaching of the Church Father, Origen. This Alexandrian theologian who died in the middle of the third century, held a following among the monks of Egypt. The Archbishop of Alexandria, Theophilus, who had consecrated John as Archbishop of Constantinople against his will, turned against Origen's theology and the monks fled, eventually reaching Constantinople. John delayed a decision on their orthodoxy and thus enraged Theophilus. Theophilus still resented the elevation of the see of Constantinople to the second position of honor behind Rome at the Council of Constantinople in 381 and used the monks as an excuse to move against John. He sailed for the capital city with a contingent of Egyptian bishops who seized the resentment of the court and some of the clergy toward the rigorist John. He conducted the Synod of the Oak at an estate at Chalcedon against John who refused to attend. John was exiled by the emperor and after riots in the city was quickly recalled. Theophilus pardoned the monks and rapidly departed for Alexandria.[51]

John returned victorious to the city and resumed his ministry. He was exiled again in 404 and died three years later on the eastern shore of the Black Sea. He carried on an extensive correspondence in exile, including a letter to Pope Innocent trying to convene a council to clear his name. His body was returned to the capital city in the reign of Arcadius' son Theodosius II.[52]

1.In this study "church" will be used to designate a particular Christian community. "Church" will be used for a broader manifestation of Christianity or Christians generally.

2.Adv op 2,9. For a discussion of the incomplete moral triumph as seen in John's preaching see Jaroslav Pelikan, *The Excellent Empire: The Fall of Rome and the Triumph of the Church* (San Francisco: Harper and Row, 1987) 21.

3.Ad vid jun 4.

4.Ad vid jun 3. (NPNF 9, 123).

5.Ad vid jun 4 (NPNF 9, 124-125); Although it is not a major theme in John's works, there was great political and economic corruption in addition to the imperial intrigue he focused on in this description. For an extended development of this theme see Ramsey Macmullen's *Corruption and the Decline of Rome* (New Haven: Yale University Press, 1988).

6.However, it should be noted that John's homilies revealed prosperity amid the political instability. For example in In Phil 10,3 he describes the beautiful building projects of Antioch during his priesthood.

7.In 1 Cor 36, 7-8. (NPNF 12, 219-220). Other passages that speak of the Church in John's day as a shadow of the Church in the apostolic age are In Acta 40,2 and In 1 Cor 43,2.

8.De Martyr Palestinae 11, 9-10. This incident is discussed in M. Avi-Yonah, *The Jews of Palestine: a political history from the Bar Kokhba War to the Arab conquest* (New York: Schocken Books, 1976), 160.

9.This point is discussed more fully in Alexander Schmemann. *The Historical Road of Eastern Orthodoxy* (New York: Holt, Rinehart and Winston, 1963) 66. Further speculations on the supernatural nature and implications of the manner of Constantine's conversion are made by Norman H. Baynes in "Constantine the Great and the Christian Church." *Proceedings of the British Academy* (1930): 1-8. The results of this relationship between the

Church and the emperor in patronage is discussed in Deno John Geanako-polos, "Church Building and Caesaropapism AD 312-565." *Greek, Roman and Byzantine Studies* 7 (1966): 167-186. A discussion of the social factors that support the trend toward Caesaropapism is contained in Robert M. Grant, *Early Christianity and Society* (New York: Harper and Row, 1977) 13-43.

10.Socrates, *Ecclesiastical History*. 1,10. Eusebius, *Life of Constantine* 2,51-73; 4,24; 4,41. Cf J.B. Bury, *History of the Later Roman Empire* (New York: Dover, 1958) I, 63-64.

11.The implications of these changes for the Jewish people of the empire is discussed in M. Avi-Yonah, *The Jews of Palestine: a political history from the Bar Kokhba War to the Arab conquest* (New York: Schocken Books, 1976), 172.

12.De s Bab c Jul 13; De s Dros 2; and De sac 2,3. This point is dis-cussed in F. Dvornik, *Early Christian and Byzantine Political Philosophy: Origins and Background*. (Dunbarton Oaks Studies, 9.) Washington, D.C, 1966. 694, 696-7. M.L. W. Laistner, *Christianity and Pagan Culture in the Later Roman Empire, with John Chrysostom's Address on Vainglory and the Right Way for Parents to Bring Up Their Children* (Ithica: Cornell University Press, 1967) 7-8.

13.A.H.M. Jones, "The Social Background of the Struggle Between Pagani-sm and Christianity." In *The Conflict Between Pagan and Christianity in the Fourth Century*. ed by Arnaldo Momigliano, (Oxford: Clarendon, 1963) 31. Zosimus. *Historia Nova* 5,20; 5,46; Paulinus *Vita Ambrosii* 26; 31.

14.De s h Bab 67, 81, 87, and 93 Bowder, Diana. "Paganism and Pagan Revival: Constantius II to Julian." D. Phil. diss. Oxford University, 1976. 519.

15.Tomlin, R.S.O. "The Emperor Valentinian I." D. Phil. diss. Oxford University, 1973. 401.

16.Davis, R.P. "The Value of *Liber Pontificalis* as Comparative Evidence for Territorial Estates and Church Property from the Fourth to the Sixth Century." D. Phil. diss. Oxford University, 1976. 30.

17.In 1 Cor 21,9.

18.De laud s Paul 2.

19.Bruce Metzger, "Antioch on the Orontes." *Biblical Archaeologist* 11 (1948): 75 and A. F. Norman, *Libanius. Works: The Julianic Orations* (Cambridge: Harvard University Press, 1969), xviii.

20.In Mat 85,4.

21.Butler, Howard Crosby. *Early Churches in Syria*. Princeton: The Department of Art and Archaeology of Princeton University, 1929. 192-193

22.In princ Act 2.

23.The basic sources are Chrysostom's homily De s Bab c Jul and Eusebius, *Ecclesiastical History* 6,29,1-4. There is an overview of the critical and historical issues in dating Babylas and his martyrdom in Schatkin and Harkins, (*Saint John Chrysostom: Apologist*, 46-59). Later sources on the bishop are most probably derivative.

24.In s Igna 1. (NPNF 9, 136). The words of Christ are recorded in John 10:11.

25.The complex history and formation of Antiochene identity and an overview of dominant cultural characteristics is given in George Haddad, *Aspects of Social Life in Antioch in the Hellenistic-Roman Period* (New York: Hafner, 1949).

26.In 1 Cor 21,9-10. (NPNF 12, 124). When John preached to the city after the rebellion that led to the desecration of the statues of the emperor and his wife, he played on the civic pride of the people. (Ad pop Anti 3,1-2; 14,6; 17,2.). He even reflected with pride on Antioch from the pulpit when he was Archbishop of Constantinople. In his second sermon after his elevation to the see in the capital city he told the congregation that "I love you no less than I love the church in which I was born, nurtured and reared.... If the church of Antioch is older in terms of time, this church of Constantinople is more fervent in its faith. The congregation at Antioch is larger and its theater more famous, but your patience and endurance are greater." Con Anom 2 (Harkins, *Saint John Chrysostom: On the Incomprehensible Nature of God*. 270-271).

27.In Mat 28,5 and In Kal are examples. In De inani gloria the public sponsorship of theatre was seen as a function of this wealth.

28.In Col 7.

29.Pro A. Licinio Archia, chapter 3. cited in C. Baur, *John Chrysostom and His Time*. (Westminster, Maryland: Newman, 1960), I, 16,21.

30.In 2 Tim 4. (NPNF 13, 490).

31.In Mat 75,2f.

32.In Acta 27,2 and De sac 1,1.

33.In Gen 38,12. (Hill. *Saint John Chrysostom: Homilies on Genesis 18-45.* 363).

34.The next two sections are a very brief overview of the events of John's life. The most complete biography is C. Baur's *Johannes Chrysostomus und Seine Zeit* (Munich: Hueber, 1930. 2v.) (English translation: *John Chrysostom and His Time*. Westminster, Maryland: Newman, 1960. 2v.).

35.Suggestions for his birth date range from 347 to 353 B.C. This is discussed in Robert E. Carter, "The Chronology of Saint John Chrysostom's Early Life." *Traditio* 18 (1962): 357-364; A.H.M. Jones, "Saint John Chrysostom's Parentage and Education." *Harvard Theological Review* 46 (1953): 171-173, and Gerard H. Ettlinger, "Some Historical Evidences for the Date of Saint John Chrysostom's Birth in the Treatise *Ad Viduam Iuniorem*." *Traditio* 16 (1960): 373-380.

36.Palladius. *The Lausiac History of Palladius.* 142.

37.In Acta 38,4 fin.

38.De mut nom 2,1. Palladius, *Dialogue*, 5. Baur discusses John's education in *John Chrysostom and his Time*, I,11-12. For an overview of education in this era see Werner Jaeger, *Early Christianity and Greek Paideia* (Oxford: Oxford University Press, 1961) and *Paideia: the Ideals of Greek*

Culture (Oxford: Oxford University Press, 1943), 3 vols., and Edwin Hatch, *The Influence of Greek Ideas and Usages upon the Christian Church* (London: Williams and Norgate, 1904), 40-42. Libanius maintained a correspondence with the Christian theologian Basil the Great which is discussed in Toivo Harjunpaa, "Saint John Chrysostom in the Light of His Catechetical and Baptismal Homilies." *Lutheran Quarterly*, 29 (1977): 167-195. The letters are found in *Letters of Saint Basil II*, (Father of the Church v 28), 318-336.

39.De sac 2,8.

40.Sozomen. *Ecclesiastical History*. 8,2.

41.Ad vid jun 2.

42.In Mat 81,5.

43.Ad pop Antioch 10,2; In 1 Cor 38,1.

44.Ad pop Antioch 12,2.

45.Adv Jud 4,7,12; De laud s Paul 4; In Mat 3,2; De incomp die 2; In 1 Tim 17.

46.In princ Act 3,1.

47.De sac 1,1-4. Augustine confessed a similar youthful focus in *Confessions* 3,3.

48.Paul Harkins, *Saint John Chrysostom: On the Incomprehensible Nature of God* (Washington: Catholic University of America Press, 1984) 33, 271.

49.John alludes to the situation in In Col 11.

50.This is discussed by Robert T. Meyer in "Palladius as Biographer and Autobiographer." *Studia Patristica* 17 (1982): 66-71.

51.Sozomen. *Ecclesiastical History*. 8,17,6, Palladius, *Dialogue*. 105, Derwas J. Chitty, *The Desert A City: An Introduction to the Study of Egyptian and*

Palestinian Monasticism under the Christian Empire (Oxford: Basil Blackwell, 1966) 59, Norman H. Baynes, "Alexandria and Constantinople: A Study in Ecclesiastical Diplomacy." *Journal of Egyptian Archaeology* 72 (1926): 148-156.

52.T.M. Parker, *Christianity and the State in the Light of History* (London: Adam and Charles Black, 1955) 61, John Francis Baldovin, "The Urban Character of Christian Worship in Jerusalem, Rome, and Constantinople from the Fourth to the Tenth Century." (Ph. D. diss. Yale University, 1982) 310, P.R. Coleman-Norton, "The Correspondence of St. John Chrysostom with Special Reference to His Epistle to Pope Innocent I." *Classical Philology* 24 (1929): 279-284, J.F. D'Alton, "Saint John Chrysostom in Exile." *Irish Ecclesiastical Record* 46 (1935): 225-238, Florent Van Ommeslaeghe, "Jean Chrysostome en Conflit avec l'Imperatice Eudoxie: Le Dossier et les Origines d'une Legende." *Analecta Bollandiana* 97 (1979): 131-159, Antoine Wenger, "Homelie de Saint Jean Chrysostome à Son Asia d'Asia." *Revue de Étude Byzantines* 19(1961): 110-123, G. Bardy, "La Chronologie de Lettres de Saint Jean Chrysostome à Olympias." *Melanges de Science Religieuse* 2 (l945): 271-284,

CHAPTER 3

THE DESERT FATHER

John saw Christ as an example of one who was in the world but not of it. He saw this exemplified in Christ's not having a place to lay His head.[1] Jesus sought to nurture His relationship with the Father by lessened commitment to the choking cares and attachments of this world. As John preached about Christ's retreat to the mountain to pray, he declared the necessity of quiet retreat.

> For what purpose did He go up into the mountain? To teach us that loneliness and retirement is good when we are to pray to God. With this in view, you see, He is continually withdrawing into the wilderness, and there often spends the whole night in prayer, teaching us earnestly to seek such quietness in our prayers, as the time and place may confer. For the wilderness is the mother of quiet; it is a calm and a harbor, delivering us from all turmoils.[2]

When John recalled the early days of his friendship with Basil and their decision to enter a monastic community, he described it as a blessed life where true philosophy can be practiced.[3] There was some time between John's decision to enter the monastic life and his retreat to the quiet; most probably he waited until the death of his mother whose pleading with him to remain with her until her death was so graphically recorded in his treatise on the priesthood.[4] When he preached at Antioch some years later he gave a rather romantic rendering of his life in the desert where he studied with Theodore, later Bishop of Mopsuestia, under Diodore of Tarsus.[5]

> To go to the monastery of a holy man is to pass, as it were, from earth to heaven. You don't see there what is seen in a private house. That company is free from all impurity. There is silence and profound quiet. The words "mine" and "yours" are not in use among them. And if you remain there a whole day or even two the more pleasure you will enjoy. There, as soon as it is day, or rather before day, the cock crows, and you see it not as you may

see it in a house, the servants snoring, the doors shut, all sleeping like the dead, while the mule driver without is ringing his bells. There is nothing of all of this. All, immediately shaking off sleep, reverently rise when the president calls them, and forming themselves into a holy choir, they stand, and lifting up their hands all at once sing the sacred hymns. For they are not like us who require many hours to shake off sleep from our heavy heads. We indeed, as soon as we are waked sit some time stretching our limbs, go as nature calls, then proceed to wash our face and our hands; afterwards we take our shoes and clothes and a deal of time is spent.

It is not so there. No one calls for his servant, for each waits upon himself. Neither does he require many clothes, nor need to shake off sleep. For as soon as he opens his eyes, he is like one who has been long awake in collectedness. For when his heart is not stifled within by excess of food, it soon recovers itself, and is immediately wakeful. The hands are always pure for his sleep is composed and regular. No one among them is found snoring or breathing hard or tossing about in sleep or with his body exposed, but they lie in sleep as decently as those who are awake, and all this is the effect of the orderly state of their souls. These are truly saints and angels among men. And marvel not when you hear these things. For their great fear of God suffers them not to go down into the depths of sleep and to drown their minds, but it falls lightly upon them, merely affording them rest. And as their sleep is, such are their dreams, not full of wild fancies and monstrous visions.

But, as I said, at the crowing of the cock their president comes, and gently touching the sleeper with his foot, rouses them all. For there are none sleeping naked, for as they have arisen they stand up, and sing the prophetic hymns with much harmony and well composed tunes.[6]

He further described the day of the monks focussed on spiritual things and compared it to the day of the typical member of his audience with all of its cares. He described the monks reading the Scriptures, some copying out books, gathering at intervals during the day for prayer and singing. He compared the immoderate consumption of food in the city to the spiritual focus and clarity of mind moderation brought in the monks.[7]

The picture of the desert John painted was one of rigor and moderation.[8] John's advice to his friend, Stagirius, who seemed to break under the weight of monastic rigor, was one of comfort and encouragement.[9]

John realized that the monks did not fight the battles that are fought by those who live for Christ in the cities. Monks have rest from the battle.[10] He even considered monks as separating themselves from the body of believers.

> But mark how great is the present disorder. They, who were living virtuously, and who under any circumstances might have confidence, have taken possession of the tops of the mountains, and have escaped out of the world, separating themselves as from an enemy and an alien and not from a body to which they belonged.[11]

Also, in his work on the priesthood, John stated that the monastic vocation was not good preparation for the work of a priest ministering to the Church.[12]

However, life in the desert was relevant to those in his audience. When he preached on the portion of the gospel of Matthew on the descent of Mary and Joseph and the infant Jesus into Egypt he pointed out the biography of the great Egyptian monk, Anthony, by Athanasius. He suggested that reading and emulating the life of this saint would greatly benefit his congregation.[13] John also exhorted the people of Antioch that hard work is a sort of asceticism.

> Let none there of those who have trades be ashamed, but those who are brought up to nothing and are idle, who enjoy many attendants, and are served by an immense retinue. For to be supported by continual hard work is a sort of asceticism. The souls of such men are clearer and their minds better strung.[14]

The image of the desert was one with rich application in John's preaching, even for those who lived their Christian life far from the solitude and quiet of the wilderness. The Christian living in the city could practice the moderation and spiritual focus of the monks in their daily life and learn from the lives of the desert fathers.

1.In Rom 24.

2.In Mat. 50,1. (NPNF 10, 310).

3.De sac 1,3.

4.De sac 1,5.

5.John speaks of the rigors and his difficulty in living the ascetic life in Ad Dem de comp 1,6. The significance of this period in John's life is discussed by Galusha Anderson, "The Elements of Chrysostom's Power as a Preacher," *Decennial Publications of the University of Chicago* 3:54-55. His enthusiastic portrayal to Theodore must be balanced with his more cautious comments in his letter to Stragirius (Ad Stagirium a daemone vexatum libre 1-3). This balanced enthusiasm is discussed by David G. Hunter in *A Comparison Between a King and a Monk/ Against the Opponents of the Monastic Life.* (Lewiston, NY: Edwin Mellen, 1988) 15-17.

6.In 1 Tim 14. (NPNF 13, 456).

7.In 1 Tim 13; 14;

8.This balance is discussed in Herbert A. Musurillo, "The Problem of Ascetical Fasting in the Greek Patristic Writers," *Traditio* 12 (1956) passim; Galusha Anderson, "The Elements of Chrysostom's Power as a Preacher," *Decennial Publications of the University of Chicago* 3:5; Donald Attwater, *Saint John Chrysostom: The Voice of Gold* (Milwaukee: Bruce, 1939), 31; and Palladius, *The Lausiac History of Palladius* (New York: Macmillan, 1918), 10.

9.Ad Stag a dae 1-3.

10.De Laz 3; De b Phil 19.

11.In Eph 6. (NPNF 13,78).

12.De sac 6, 5-7. These paragraphs are discussed in M. Hyatt, The Active and the Contemplative Life in Saint John Chrysostom's Treatise on the Priesthood," *Diakonia* 15 (1980): 192.

13.In Mat 8,7.

14.In 1 Cor 5,11. (NPNF 12, 28).

CHAPTER 4
THE MARTYR

The development of the cult of martyrs in the Church was tied to the rise of the white martyrdom of ascetic denial. Monks often were leaders in the veneration of the relics found during the first century after Constantine. They seemed to consciously tie their renunciation of society and search for spiritual purity with the confessions that culminated in death in the years preceding the Christianization of the imperial purple.[1]

Even though the age of martyrdom was past when John ministered at Antioch and Constantinople, the notion of martyrdom played an important part in his preaching. Martyrdom was the greatest example of Christian love and holiness.[2] It was also a manifestation of the Christian struggle in which the sexes were equal. He compared Christians facing martyrdom as athletes victorious in combat.

> Lately, for instance, a maiden quite young and unmarried, the blessed martyr Pelagia, entertained us, with much joy. Today again, this blessed and noble martyr Ignatius has succeeded to her feast. The persons are different; the table is one. The wrestlings are varied; the crown is one. The contests are manifold; the prize is the same. For in the case of the heathen contests, since the tasks are bodily, men alone are, with reason, admitted. But here, since the contest is wholly concerning the soul, the lists are open to each sex, for each kind the theater is arranged.... But on this side and on that many are proclaimed conquerors, and are crowned, in order that you may learn by means of the exploits themselves that in Christ Jesus neither male or female,[3] neither sex nor weakness of body or age nor any such thing could be a hindrance to those who run in the course of religion if there be a noble readiness and an eager mind and a fear of God, fervent and kindling, be established in our souls.[4]

John noted in his introduction to his series of homilies on Paul's epistle to the Romans that the writings of that Apostle were read on the feasts of the martyrs to John's great pleasure. He mentioned that these feasts took place three or four times per week.[5]

The martyrs fought for orthodoxy with their lives and wounds.[6] They were also great teachers in the church even after their death.   John commented to those before him for baptismal instruction that "just as the word falls short of the deed, so my instruction falls short of what these holy ones have taught us by their deeds."[7]   In addition to their instructive lives, the martyrs provided "spiritual fountains" in their tombs.[8] As John continued to describe the power of the relics of the martyrs in this catechetical homily, he saw benefits realized when the Christian came to the tombs in a proper attitude of "zeal and eagerness to contribute his fair share."[9] The Christian who came properly left with a heightened focus on the things of God.

> He who comes with these dispositions straightway carries away blessings beyond number, since the grace of God, working invisibly, lightens the burden of his conscience, brings him abundant assurance, and prepares him henceforth to put off from the shore of the earth and to weigh anchor for heaven. For it is possible for a man who is still in the embrace of his body to have nothing in common with the earth, but to set before his eyes all the joys of heaven and to contemplate them unceasingly.[10]

A significant part of the heritage of the Antiochene church was the spiritual power of the relics of the Bishop-martyr Babylas. Their presence stopped the prophetic powers of the oracle of Apollo.[11] Julian sought the advice of this pagan guide and was forced to move the casket of the bishop to restore its voice. John also saw physical manifestations of the power of the martyred Babylas when "famine swept the earth," and springs in the region of Antioch which usually overflowed dried up during the reign of the apostate emperor.[12]

In his homily on Saint Babylas and against the emperor Julian, John cited Christ's prophecy that his followers would do greater works than He did as pointing to the powerful works of the martyrs both before and after their confession in death.[13] For John, Christ lives in the souls of the martyrs. This is a facet of the mystical union that ties the members of Christ's Body, the Church, to their Lord. The martyrs, because of their particular dedication to the cause of Christ, manifest Him uniquely.[14] The miracles performed by the relics of the martyrs were also proof of their life after death. In this manner they served as proof of the Christian doctrine of a physical resurrection.[15] In sum, John saw their miracles in death as a natural result of major Christian doctrinal distinctives, the mystical union within the Body of Christ, the resurrection from the dead, and the resurrection of the body.

John's day was not a time of bonds and execution as it had been in the recent past, but there were greater challenges to the Christian.[16] The Christian was to live in the midst of demonic persecution and the temptations of the world as a "living sacrifice." As John compared the life of the Apostle Paul with those of Abel, Noah, and other heroes of the Old Testament, he saw Paul as the example of a "living sacrifice."

> But if you examine the sacrifice of Paul it will be seen to surpass Abel's as much as the heavens surpass the earth. You ask what I mean? Simply this, that Paul made a complete sacrifice of himself every day, and his oblation was twofold: first, he died daily,[17] and secondly, he was always bearing about in his body the death of Jesus.[18]

In emulating the virtues of the martyrs, Christians could live for Christ with greater strength and dedication.

1.J.N. Hillgarth, *Christianity and Paganism, 350-750* (Philadelphia: University of Pennsylvania Press, 1986) 18-20.

2.In s Igna 1.

3.This phrase probably alludes to Gal. 3:28.

4.In s Igna 1. (NPNF 9, 135).

5.In Rom arg,1.

6.Adv Jud 3,3,4f.

7.Cat ill 7,2. The following paragraphs of the homily continue the development of this thought.

8.Cat ill 7,10.

9.Cat ill 7,10.

10.Cat ill 7,11. (Harkins. *Saint John Chrysostom: Baptismal Instructions.* 108).

11.De s Bab c Jul 73-75.

12.De laud s Paul 4; De s Bab c Jul 67f; 80f; De s h Bab 1f; This is discussed in Margaret A. Schatkin and Paul W. Harkins. *Saint John Chrysostom Apologist.* (Washington, DC: Catholic University of America Press, 1985), 32.

13.John 14:12. John discusses this power of the martyrs in De s Bab c Jul, prologue and In Princ Acts 4.

14.De. s Bab c Jul 36; De s Dros (cited from Schatkin and Harkins *Saint John Chrysostom Apologist.* 43).

15.De s Bab c Jul 93. Augustine also argued that the miracles of the relics proved the resurrection of Christ and the resurrection of the flesh De Civ 22, 8-9.

16.In Acta 24,3; In Jn 74,3; In Eph 9.

17.Cf. 1 Cor. 15:31.

18.De laud s Paul 1. (Halton. *In Praise of Saint Paul.* 16); cf. 2 Cor. 4:10. The martyrs chapels also served as an exhortation to act as a living sacrifice because the poor and the sick sat in the martyrs' chapels to receive alms from the faithful. In 1 Thess 11. (NPNF 13, 374).

CHAPTER 5
THE BISHOP AS THE FATHER OF THE PEOPLE

The Bishop and the City

During the first century and a quarter of imperial patronage, the era from Nicea to Chalcedon, the bishops of the large cities were a dominant force in Christianity. As the hierarchies both of church and of state became instruments of the imperial direction of the divine will for the empire, ecclesiastical power became more concentrated in the hands of the archbishops of the large cities of the Mediterranean world. The power wielded by an Archbishop such as Chrysostom in this era was a result of the place of his audience in society, the material and military resources of his imperial patron, and the place of the city in the social order of the empire.

This era was marked by a rapidly accelerating trend toward centralization of power in the hands of the emperor. In contrast, Julian promoted the power of the cities as part of his plan for a restoration of a purer Hellenism. This was fueled both by his loyalty to the past ideal and his need to neutralize the decidedly Christian capital in the east, Constantinople.[1] Chrysostom's study under Libanius was in the context of this Julianic countertrend. He felt the impact of this movement because much of Julian's effort was centered in Antioch, and a high view of the Hellenistic city was a significant element in Libanius' thought. Julian died on the Persian frontier before his dreams did anything but alienate him both from the Christians who viewed him as the Apostate and from the greater populace who saw his moralism as no more liberating than that of the bishops. Libanius might continue to praise and promote an idealization of the past but the trend toward more centralized imperial power continued after Julian's death.

John would surely oppose the civic cults, theater, and games but he was a product of the urban culture of Antioch and used urban life as a source of illustrations in his sermons. He saw a model for the ministry of the Christian in the urban context. He exhorted the congregation in Antioch that "good works which are confined to ourselves" are good but the Christian should move on to those which benefit others, "almsgiving, teaching, charity."[2] He continued his message with the implication that Christians are to seek their neighbors' edification above all else.

> For the blessed Paul is at hand, giving his judgment and saying, "To depart and to be with Christ is better, nevertheless to abide in the flesh is more needful for you,"[3] even to his removal to Christ did he prefer his neighbor's edification. For this is in the highest sense to be with Christ, even to be doing His will, but nothing is so much His will, as that which is for one's neighbor's good....
>
> For, if in worldly matters no man lives for himself but artisan and soldier and farmer and merchant, all of them contribute to the common good, and to their neighbor's advantage; much more ought we to do this in things spiritual. For this is most properly to live: since he at least who is living for himself only, and overlooking all others is useless, and is not so much as a human being, nor of our race.[4]

Paul the Model for Ministry

John preached through the entire Pauline corpus, which he believed included the letter to the Hebrews. He consistently held forth the apostle as a model for ministry as well as piety for his congregation. Part of the impetus for this is seen in John's observation that Paul and the Christians in Antioch in the fourth century were of the same culture.

> Paul's nature was no different from ours. His soul was no different. He was an inhabitant of no different world. In the same world, the same country, with the same laws and customs, he surpassed in virtue all men, present and past. Where now are those who protest that virtue is difficult and vice all too easy?[5]

John's fixation on Paul as the example for the Christian was so strong that even in his Old Testament homilies he brought forth the apostle as an example for his congregation.

Was not blessed Paul of the same nature as ourselves? I mean, for this man I have an intense regard, and hence I do not cease bringing him constantly to mind; fixing my eyes on his soul as though on some exemplary model, I marvel at his control of passion, the eminence of his manly spirit, the ardor of his love for God; and the realization comes to me that one man set his mind on achieving in his person all that multitude of virtues, whereas each of us perhaps hasn't even the inclination, let alone the achievement.[6]

John, addressing candidates for baptism, saw Paul as one who went everywhere and did everything for the cause of the salvation of men.[7] Paul won people to the Church by his life, not by the great miracles that he performed.[8] When John brought forth examples from the life of Paul to the people he often accompanied them with hyperbolic praise.[9] Paul was a towering genius[10] and "the loftiest of souls."[11] Truly, for John, "there is indeed no one like Paul,"[12] and "nothing can be more blessed than the spirit of Paul."[13] And finally, because the apostle did not fear death, John exclaimed, "Oh that spirit of Paul! nothing was ever like it, nor ever will be!"[14]

Paul was a great example in ministry because he mastered many spiritual treatments for the people whom he shepherded.

A doctor's treatment varies: he cauterizes, prescribes diet, operates, administers drugs, forbids foods and drinks, leaves some wounds uncovered, covers others, prescribes a phial full of cool waters for fevers. He is not censured for not employing uniformity of treatment, or for constant change. Rather, you praise his art when you see the confidence with which he administers apparently conflicting and injurious remedies and guarantees that they are safe. This is a man proficient in his craft.

If we accept a doctor who varies his treatment, we should be even more ready to proclaim Paul's psychology as he ministers to those who are ill. For the sick in soul need variety of treatment no less than the sick in body. To treat them in a uniform and stereotyped manner would jeopardize their salvation.[15]

It is no wonder that John enjoyed the hearing of Paul's works when they were read in church, sometimes three or four times per week at the feasts of the martyrs.[16] He saw in the writings of the apostle the example of a great teacher, mixing the language of hell and the awesome eternal consequences of sin and rebellion with a soothing message of commendation and acknowledgement of the zeal of his hearers.[17] Paul's experiences in ministry made him an example both to Timothy in his day and to all who follow in the service of the Church.[18]

Chrysostom's Ministry in the Aftermath of the Tax Revolt of 388

John saw in Paul a varied approach in dealing with the spiritual ills of God's people. He admired this skill and cultivated it in his own ministry. His development in this area was shaped by what was probably the most significant event of the early years of his ministry in Antioch, the tax riot and destruction of the images of the emperor and empress in the early spring of 388. John had been a priest for two years and this series of twenty-one homilies preached, with two exceptions, in March and April that year endeared him to the populace of the city and spread his fame broadly. Before his elevation to the see in Constantinople ten years later he was prominent enough to be noted by Jerome in his *Virs Illustris*, a compendium of short references to famous Christians.[19]

In late February the news of the proclamation of a new tax reached Antioch. The emperor Theodosius was approaching the celebration of the tenth anniversary of his rise to the purple as well as the fifth year of the coregency of his son Arcadius. These celebrations as well as the Gothic threat on the frontier near the Danube necessitated a levy on the eastern provinces of the Empire. This tax was also resisted by the populace of Alexandria but unrest was put down quickly by the Prefect Cynegius.

The riot happened quickly, and in a few hours the baths were ransacked and the mob turned on the governor's palace. Not finding him there, they overturned the statues of the emperor and his recently deceased wife and dragged them through the street.   Soon the people realized the seriousness of their challenge to the sovereign and sought the supplication of the aged Archbishop Flavian on behalf of the city before the emperor.   The 800-mile journey could be made in six days under good circumstances and the bishop soon left for the capital city.   John preached to the people of the city six days in the week following the riot and on Sunday, March 3, 388 he addressed a congregation that feared for the status of its city and the punishments of a raging emperor.   John's first words that day focussed the people on the Archbishop who had already left.

> When I look on that throne, deserted and bereft of our teacher, I rejoice and weep at the same time. I weep, because I do not see our father with us! but I rejoice that he has set out on a journey for our preservation; that he is gone to snatch so great a multitude from the wrath of the Emperor! Here is both an ornament to you and a crown to him! An ornament to you, that such a father has been allotted to you; a crown to him, because he is so affectionate towards his children and has confirmed by actual deeds what Christ said. For having learned that "the good shepherd lays down his life for the sheep"[20] he took his departure; venturing his own life for us all, not withstanding there were many things to hinder his absence, and enforce his stay. And first, his time of life, extended as it is to the utmost limits of old age; next, the bodily infirmity and the season of the year, as well as the necessity for his presence at the holy festival;[21] and besides these reasons, his only sister even now at her last breath! He has disregarded, however, the ties of kindred, of old age, of infirmity, and the severity of the season, and the toils of the journey; and preferring you and your safety above all things, he has broken through all these restraints. And, even as a youth, the aged man in now hastening along, borne upon the wings of zeal![22]

The news of the riot travelled quickly to Constantinople and on Tuesday, March 16, Hellebichus and Caesarius arrived from the emperor to deal with the rebellious city.   Antioch was deprived of its metropolitan rank, which was transferred to Laodicea, and the public baths were closed.[23]   The municipal senate was imprisoned and trials began the next day. People fled the city and monks came to intercede before the imperial investigators.[24] Caesarius stated that the sentence would be left to the Emperor, and he returned to the capital city after a stay of two days on Thursday the 18th. By the time half of the lenten fast had passed on Sunday April 4th word had come that the city would be spared, but the senate was still in prison.

The anger of Theodosius was certainly to be feared. Three years later 7,000 men, women, and children were killed in Thessolonica after an official was killed in a riot. John may have alluded to the volatile nature of the emperor in his fourth homily preached in the week after the riot.

> At the present time then, a man is angry with us, a man of like passions, and of like soul, and we are afraid.... a man who is at one time angry, at another time is reconciled; and we are never-theless dead with fear.[25]

The Archbishop was successful in his mission to the emperor, and he returned to the city as a hero greeted by a vast welcoming throng with torches aloft as he entered the city. Libanius delivered an oration in honor of the forgiving emperor and the city rejoiced in its reconfirmed status. John was not part of the welcoming celebration. He was ill. He had preached at least twenty-five times in the nine weeks of the controversy and was kept away by exhaustion.

For John the significance of this event was twofold. His powerful and fearless preaching endeared him to the people, and he became established as a significant force in the city two years after entering the ministry. He also saw the power of the office of Archbishop in defense of the endangered. This example served him well when he was translated to the Archbishopric of the capital city ten years later. John's ministry was marked by a significant social and political presence that he learned from his mentor, Flavian.

Leading the Church in Its Relationship to the State

When John preached on the role of the state in society his words were set in the context of his basic view that God's way is the way of monarchy, not of democracy.

> For since equality of honor does many times lead to fightings, He has made many governments and forms of subjection; as that for instance, of man and wife, that of son and father, that of old men and young, that of bond and free, that of ruler and ruled, and of master and disciple. And why are you surprised in the case of mankind, when even in the body He has made the same thing? For even here He has not made all parts of equal honor, but He has made one less and another greater, and some of the limbs He has made to rule and some to be ruled. And among the unreasoning creatures one may notice this same principle, as among the bees, among cranes, among herds of wild cattle. And even the sea itself is not without this goodly subordination; for there too many of the clans are ranged under one among the fishes, and are thus led like an army, and make long expeditions from home. For anarchy, be where it may, is an evil, and a cause of confusion.[26]

John even defended civil government when he spoke about the role of Pilate in the death of Christ.[27]

John often used the visible majesty of the emperor as an illustration of the loftier position of God in His church. John used the sight of a royal procession with military units and banners held aloft and extravagant pomp as illustrations in his sermons. On one occasion he praised the loftiness of the apostles and their lives as greater from an eternal perspective than the imperial processions of his day.[28]

His view of the state was not so romantic as to be untempered by the realities of the politics of his day. As he preached to the people from the fourth chapter of Paul's letter to the Philippians on the need to cast their cares on God he reminded the people that no one is free from cares, not even the Emperor. He told them to "not look to his purple robe, but to his soul, which is darker than purple. His crown does not so closely bind his brow as care does his soul."[29] He then continued by recounting the burdens of the imperial life with graphic examples.

> For it is not possible to find a private house laden with so many cares as the king's palace. Violent deaths are each day expected, and the vision of blood is seen as they sit down to eat and drink. Nor can we say how often he is disturbed in the night season and leaps up haunted with visions. And all this in peace, but if war should overtake him, what could be more piteous than such a life as this.... No, and of a truth the pavement of a king's house is always full of blood, the blood of his own relatives. And if you will I will also relate some instances and you will readily see; chiefly old occurrences, but also some things that have happened in our own times. One, it is said, having suspected his wife of adultery bound her naked upon mules and exposed her to wild beasts, though she had already been the mother to him of many princes. What sort of life do you think that man lived?[30]

John ended the homily with descriptions of poisonings, murders, and torture from the lives of the emperors of the fourth century and then gave examples of grievous personal lives from the kings of the Old Testament. John's view of the imperial state was also tempered by the untrustworthy character of those who held the office. Julian's impious rule during John's adolescence brought judgment from God who always reigns above all powers on earth.[31]

Ideally there was cooperation between the church and the government. Christians were to participate in the affairs of state that were within their abilities as far as their class and means would allow and as far as could be done without sin.[32] John noted the new era in the relationship between the church and the government in his day. As he preached on the imprisonment of Paul, the imprisonment and beheading of John the Baptist, and the bonds and martyrdom of Babylas, third-century bishop of Antioch, he could tell his audience that he did not wish for them to go to prison for Christ because the time for bonds was past.[33] However, he acknowledged that there were martyrs during his day in Persia.[34]

The new era of cooperation was not without its problems. The church grew sluggish with the weight of nominalism as it received imperial favor.

When a Christian ascends the imperial throne, far from being shored up by human honors, Christianity deteriorates. On the other hand, when rule is held by an impious man, who persecutes us in every way and subjects us to countless evils, then our cause acquires renown and becomes more brilliant, then is the time of valor and of trophies, then is the opportunity to attain crowns, praises, and every distinction.[35]

In John's mind there was a sensitive balance between the power of the state and the power of the church in a land ruled by a Christian. The state could not ask the bishop to abandon his ministry. At the end of his ministry in Constantinople John was deposed and removed from the city by the emperor. If the secular forces removed a bishop from office, the bishop would not be responsible for forsaking his ministry. The end of his ministry was an outworking of principles he expounded in the capital city a few years earlier. John was ordered to leave the church and the city by the Emperor Arcadius. John's response revealed his understanding of the balance between secular and religious power.

I have received this church from God our Savior for the care of the salvation of my people and I cannot abandon her. But if you desire this (for the city belongs to you) then expel me by force so that I may defend myself on the grounds that I went by your command rather than that I abandoned my charge.[36]

In his eighth homily on Acts he threatened to discipline all who continued swearing in the marketplace and made the following conclusion to his threat.

Behold again: I give warning, and proclaim with a loud voice, let no one think it a laughing matter. I will exclude and prohibit the disobedient; and as long as I sit on this throne, I will give up not one of its rights. If any one depose me from it, then I am no longer responsible; as long as I am responsible, I cannot disregard them; on account not of my own punishment, but of your salvation. For I do exceedingly long for your salvation.[37]

John clearly realized that he could be deposed by the emperor but while he was on the episcopal throne no one could ask him to neglect the responsibilities of his ministry in the city.

John was also unwilling to give the state the prerogative of setting morality by its legal decrees. The sanction of adultery by men in his era was not God's will and he was careful to differentiate between God's standards and those of Roman law in his fifth homily on 1 Thessalonians.

> For as we punish women, when, being married to us, they give themselves to others, so also are we punished, though not by Roman laws but by God. For this also is adultery. For not only is adultery committed in doing so by her who is married to another but by him also, who is yoked to a wife. For although what is said is offensive to many, it is necessary to be said, to set the matter right for the future. Not only is this adultery, when we defile a woman who is married to a man; but if we ourselves being married to a woman defile one who is free and disengaged, the matter is adultery.[38]

The Christian should not use the arm of the state to forcibly convert those outside the church. Unlike pagan emperors who attacked the Church, the Christian must use moral suasion. John could issue the following apologetic challenge to those outside the Faith.

> Such is the character of our doctrine; what about yours? No one ever persecuted it, nor is it right for Christians to eradicate error by constraint and force, but to save humanity by persuasion and reason and gentleness.[39]

The Church was superior to the state because it watched over the souls of humanity and prepared people for eternity.[40] However the Church could lower itself to the level of the secular rulers if she did not maintain her high spiritual calling and lowered herself to use the methods of secular rulers to build an empire on earth.[41]

1.G. W. Bowersock, *Julian the Apostate*. (Cambridge: Harvard University Press, 1978), 73-75.

2.In Mat 77,5.

3.Phil. 1:23-24.

4.In Mat 77,6. (NPNF 10, 468-469).

5.De laud s Paul 2. (Halton. *In Praise of Saint Paul*. 29)

6.In Gen 11, 12. (Hill. *Homilies on Genesis 1-17*. 150-151). The praise of Paul continues through the end of the homily.

7.Cat ill 4,22.

8.In Eph 6.

9.John preached a series of seven panegyrics in praise of the Apostle in Antioch (English translation by Thomas Halton, *In Praise of Saint Paul*). Boston: Daughters of Saint Paul, 1964.). The entire series is replete with hyperbole. In the first homily Paul is declared to be greater than the biblical heroes of the faith including Abel, Noah, Abraham, Isaac, Jacob, Joseph, Job, Moses, David, Elijah, John the Baptist, and the angels as well. The stylistic rhetorical reasoning noted that Noah merely saved his family on the ark while Paul saved people throughout the world; Abraham left his fatherland but Paul abandoned the world for Christ's sake. The language of the other homilies is similar. In the opening of the first homily John sees Paul as great example of synergistic co-working with God in his salvation. Paul was a "vessel of election" but also "purified himself."

10.In Gen 3, 19.

11.Cat ill 1,4.

12.In Phil 1. (NPNF 13, 187).

13.In Phil 4. (NPNF 13, 198); cf. De laud s Paul 1.

14.In Phil 4. (NPNF 13, 198). In In Gal 2:18 John, like Jerome, sought to preserve the reputation of both Peter and Paul in their interpretation of the incident of confrontation recorded in Galatians, chapter 2. John saw it as a staged teaching incident for those present.

15.De laud s Paul 5. (Halton. *In Praise of Saint Paul.* 80). Other examples where John noted Paul's reaching out to his audience where they were spiritually and using adaptive teaching methods are In 1 Cor 3,5 and 28,1.

16.In Rom arg,1.

17.In Heb 21,1.

18.In 2 Tim 4.

19.*Virs Illustris* 129.

20.John 10:11

21.John is referring to the approach of Easter. The Sunday after he preached this message began Lent.

22.Ad pop Anti 3,1. (NPNF 9, 354). The roles of Flavian and John in the controversy are discussed in Robert Browning, "The Riot of A.D. 387 in Antioch: The Role of the Theatrical Claques in the Later Empire." *Journal of Roman Studies* 42 (1952): 13-20.

23.Ad pop Anti 14,15; 17,10.

24.Ad pop Anti 13,2

25.Ad pop Anti 4,5. (NPNF 9, 366).

26.In Rom 23,1. (NPNF 11, 511-512). In In 1 Cor 24,6 he applies the principles more fully to the family.

> Further, in order that one might be subject and the other rule, for equality is oftentimes prone to bring strife, he suffered it not to be a democracy, but a monarchy; as in an army, this order is seen in every family. In the rank of monarch, for instance, there is the husband; but in the rank of lieutenant and general, the wife; and the children too are allotted a third station in command. Then after these a fourth order, that of the servants.

A discussion of John's views on the role of power and authority in maintaining order in a fallen world is contained in Elaine Pagels, *Adam, Eve, and the Serpent* (New York: Random House, 1988) 101-103.

27.In Jn 84,1.

28.De laud s Paul 7.

29.In Phil 15. (NPNF 13, 253).

30.In Phil 15. (NPNF 13, 253-254).

31.De laud s Paul 4; De s Bab c Jul 118f.

32.De inani gloria 89.

33.In Eph 9.

34.Con Jud et gen 1,9.

35.De s Bab c Jul 42 (Schatkin and Harkins. *Saint John Chrysostom: Apologist*, 99). In In Acta 29 John also discussed the fact that the Church's fortune does not depend on imperial favor. However he does point out in In Mat 33,6 that Christians in his days will have less excuse for their shortcomings because of the fact that they do not live under persecution.

36.Palladius 9. (Meyer. *Palladius*. 61).

37.In Acta 8,3. (NPNF 11,54).

38.In 1 Thess 5. (NPNF 13, 345).

39.De s Bab c Jul 13. (Schatkin and Harkins. *Saint John Chrysostom: Apologist*. 83). Cf. also De s Dros 2. In De Sac 2,3 the priest is not permitted to "forcibly correct the failings of those who sin" and the conclusion is that "it is not possible for any one to cure a man by compulsion against his will."

40.In 2 Cor 15,5 and De sac 3,1 are examples of this theme in John's works.

41.De sac 3,15.

CHAPTER 6
THE BISHOP AS A TEACHER TO GOD'S PEOPLE

Preaching- An Act of Love and Responsibility

John loved to mount the pulpit. When he rose to speak to the congregation gathered before him, he viewed it as both spiritually invigorating to him and spiritually nourishing to his flock. He began his homilies on Genesis with typical enthusiasm.

> I am pleased and delighted to see the church of God adorned today with the throng of her children, and to see you all coming together with great joy. I mean, whenever I look upon your beaming faces, I take it as an infallible sign of the satisfaction you feel at heart. As the wise man said "The face betrays the joy of the heart."[1] So naturally I myself arose this morning with more than the usual enthusiasm since I was to share with you this spiritual happiness and I wanted to become a herald for you of the approach of Lent - the medicine, I might say, for your souls.[2]

John therefore saw preaching as an activity that benefitted both the preacher and the congregation. As he exercised his office and gift in this area his own spiritual and even physical health was improved.

> Preaching improves me. When I begin weariness disappears; when I begin to teach fatigue too disappears. Thus neither sickness itself nor indeed any other obstacle is able to separate me from your love.[3]

At times he spoke in almost romantic terms about the relationship between the preacher and his congregation as he proclaimed his own focus on his audience and their own desire to see him return to the pulpit after a time of illness. He acknowledged that he dreamed of his relationship with the congregation in the terms used to describe that of lovers in Song of Solomon.

> Did you even think of me as long as I was away from you? For my part, I have never been able to forget you. Rather your image was always before my eyes... With me it was as it was with

Solomon, for I too slept but my heart kept watch. The power of sleep closed my eyes but the power of love opened the eyes of my soul. Oftentimes in my dreams I see myself in the pulpit speaking to you... And even though I could not see you with the eyes of my body, nevertheless I plainly saw you with the eyes of my heart... You kept crying to me begging me to come to you and indeed urging me to break off my rest before the proper time. In fact because of you I now see health, rest and all that concerns myself in relation to you.[4]

A passage that further reveals the complexities of this relationship is found in his homilies on Hebrews.

I could have wished to know for certain whether any hear with fitting earnestness the things that are said, whether we are not casting the seeds by the wayside. For in that case I should have made my instructions with more cheerfulness. For we speak, though no one hear, for the fear which is laid on us by our Savior. For, he said testify to this people, even if they hear not, you yourself shall be guiltless.[5] If however I had been persuaded of your earnestness, I should have spoken not for fear only, but should have done it with pleasure also. For now indeed, even if no man hear, even if my work, so long as I fulfill my own part, brings no danger still the labor is not altogether pleasant. For what profit is it, when though I am not blamed, yet no one is benefitted? But if any would give heed we shall receive advantage not so much from avoiding punishment ourselves as from your progress.

How then shall I know this? Having taken notice of some of you, who are not very attentive, I shall question them privately when I meet them. And if I find that they retain any of the things that have been spoken (I say not all, for this would not be very easy for you.) but even if a few things out of many, it is plain I should have no further doubts about the rest.... For that I shall question you, I have forewarned you; but when I shall question you I do not as yet make evident. For perhaps it may be today; perhaps tomorrow, perhaps after twenty or thirty days, perhaps after fewer, perhaps after more. Thus has God also made uncertain the day of our death.... Thus too I have said that I shall question you, but I have not added when, wishing you always to be thoughtful.[6]

John believed that the preacher, like a doctor, should vary his treatments. He praised the Apostle Paul for this strategy and also saw it in the ministry of Christ.[7] He used suspense and would continue preaching the same message even if it were not totally grasped and applied.[8] He also promised that he would answer their questions if they showed enthusiasm.[9]

When John began his sixth homily against the Judaizing tendencies of some of his flock in Antioch and the influence of the Jewish community in the city, he lamented that he was hoarse from a long sermon the previous day. John's power as a weaver of illustrations is seen in this passage.

> You see that my voice has grown weaker and cannot again last for so long a time. I think that what has happened to me is much the same as what happens to a soldier in battle. He cuts to pieces a number of his foes, courageously throws himself against enemy lines, strews the ground with corpses, but then breaks his sword; disheartened by this mishap he must retreat to his own ranks. Indeed what has happened to me is worse. The soldier who has broken his sword can snatch another from some bystander, prove his courage, and show how eager he is for victory. But when the voice becomes weak and exhausted, you cannot borrow another from somebody else.[10]

John preached often. He preached twice per week through the Gospel of John. He remarked that this was not a difficult schedule for him or his audience as children went about the business of their lessons every day of the week.[11] He even preached daily during Lent but said he was not up to the task.[12]

John wrestled with the issue of the responsibility of the preacher for the results of his message. Was he liable for judgment if the lives in his congregation were not changed as a result of his words? Once he concluded in despair that his work was wasted because of the spiritual lethargy of his congregation.

> But all is in vain; all is to no purpose. For your zeal is spent on
> things of this life, and of things spiritual no account is made.[13]

In his eighth and ninth homilies on the book of Hebrews he concluded that
the preacher must continue even if the message is ignored. But later in the
series, preached under increasingly difficult circumstance in Constantinople,
his frustration was expressed in even more somber terms.

> But I cannot be a father if I do not weep. I am a father full of
> affection. Hear how Paul exclaims, "My little children, of whom
> I travail in birth again."[14] What mother in childbirth cries so
> bitter as he! Would it were possible for you to see the very fire
> that is in my heart, and you would know that I burn with grief
> more intense than any woman or girl that suffers untimely
> widowhood. She does not so mourn over her husband as I do
> over this multitude that is here with us.
>
> I see no progress. Everything turns to calumnies and accusations.
> No man makes it his business to please God; but he says "let us
> speak evil of so and so or so and so," "So and so is unfit to be
> among the clergy," "So and so does not lead a respectable life."[15]

At other times, John expressed the view that the preacher would receive his
reward even if his congregation did not respond to his message.[16] However,
the dominant theme on this issue in his sermons was the awesome responsibility of the preacher for his flock.

He considered the calling to shepherd the flock of God to require the
same sense of selflessness that is seen in Christ as the Shepherd who lays
down His life.

> A great matter, beloved, a great matter it is to preside over a
> church: a matter needing wisdom and courage as great as that of
> which Christ speaks, that a man should lay down his life for the
> sheep, and never leave them deserted or naked; that he should
> stand against the wolf nobly. For in this the shepherd differs
> from the hireling, the one always looks to his own safety, caring
> not for the sheep; the other always seeks that of the sheep,
> neglecting his own.[17]

In addition to the great call of Christ to the priesthood this care is rooted in the Apostle Paul's concept of the Body of Christ taught in Romans and 1 Corinthians. John noted, as he justified regularly repeating points from the previous sermon in his series on Genesis, that although it may seem like a "nuisance" he did it both for those who were absent and for those whose memories need refreshing.

> Thus the instruction may be adequate also for those not present on the first occasion, and they may not suffer any handicap from their absence. The reason is that a loving father keeps the leftovers from the table for his absent children so that when they come they may find the leftovers kept for them as a consolation for their absence. According, we too have as much care for everyone of you coming along here as for our own limbs, and we make your progress our own pride and glory, wanting you all to be shown to be perfect and mature for the glory of God, the credit of the Church and our boast.[18]

The Bishop as Orator

When he preached to the people, the bishop was viewed in the context of the art and science of oratory in John's world. John entered into this role while he was a priest in Antioch before he was raised to the episcopal throne in Constantinople. The great age of Flavian, the Archbishop of Antioch during John's priesthood, probably contributed as much to this advancement as did John's discernable aptitude, talents, and training.[19] John's power in the ministry was no doubt enhanced by this earlier expansion of his priestly role in a major center of the Christian Church.

There was the danger of the bishop's sermons being grouped with the other uses of oratory as he preached. He would be judged by standards of entertainment and the content of his proclamation would be lost in the expectations of form. Sophistic orators were an important part of the local administration and served as a force in civic pride during this period.[20] They spoke to justify past actions of the body politic or to simply narrate the past as much or more than to influence action.[21] Clearly any association of

Christian preaching with this sophistic manipulation of truth to justify the present perception of reality would undermine the very nature of the prophetic discourse. The Christian preacher should speak to motivate the congregation to more godly living, not to justify perceptions of reality.

John noted that the audience was "accustomed to listen not for profit, but for pleasure, sitting like critics of tragedies and of musical entertainments."[22] He found it difficult to articulate a balance in a climate where oratory was highly prized. The preacher was to be skilled in argument like the Apostle Paul but must avoid giving place to the desire of the "Greeks" for "acuteness of sophistry."[23]

Libanius, the Antiochene rhetor under whom John studied, undoubtedly influenced his student. John referred to Libanius' praise of his mother's vocation of widowhood and quoted Libanius as a foil in his homily in praise of Saint Babylas and against the apostate emperor Julian.[24] Julian studied under Libanius when the rhetor taught at Nicomedia before Libanius came to Antioch. John was well aware of the rhetor's hope for the restoration of the traditional religions under Julian.[25] Another member of the Antiochene community of philosophers who did not embrace the Christian faith was Ammianus Marcellinus, the historian. He was with Julian during his last military campaign against the Persians when the emperor was killed in battle in 362. Ammianus remained active in the Antiochene community until about 378.[26] John's years of study as a part of the literary community influenced his preaching. Demosthenes was the chief object of study and emulation for Libanius and John developed a pleasing and powerful oratorical style under this influence.[27]

John may have depreciated style on occasion but his practice betrayed a more pragmatic stance. In addition to the desire for oratory by the people, good oratory was an ally in helping people listen to truth.[28] As he preached to the people of Antioch just before the desecration of the imperial statues, he stressed the need for a style that made the instruction from the Scriptures clear to the audience.[29]   On another occasion he began his series on the Gospel of John by preaching the first four sermons on the first verse. As he began the fourth homily on the words from John 1:1, "In the beginning was the Word and the Word was with God" he gave the reason for this strategy.

> When children are just brought to their learning, their teachers do not give them many tasks in succession, nor do they set them once for all, but they often repeat to them the same short ones, so that what is said may be easily implanted in their minds, and they may not be vexed at the first onset with the quantity, and with finding it hard to remember, and become less active in picking up what is given them, a kind of sluggishness arising from the difficulty. And I, who wish to effect the same with you, and to render your labor easy, take by little and little the food which lies on this Divine table and instill it into your souls. On this account I shall handle again the same words, not so as to say again the same things, but to set before you only what yet remains. Come then, let us apply our discourse to the introduction.[30]

John and Non-Christian Writings

John, as would be expected from the student of Libanius, had a broad familiarity with non-Christian writings.[31] The allusions to them in his sermons were extensive considering a basic preconception that would prejudice him against seeing them as a source of edification for his congregation. John believed that God used things counted foolish by this world to confound the wise. The fisherman has conquered the philosopher.[32] Plato had been cast out by the Apostles; he had faded, but the words of the Apostles live on.[33] He saw some value in the writings of those outside the Church in that their writings contain examples of the fleeting nature of this world's treasures.

> Think of those who are very rich who perish anyhow in war; look round on the houses, that belonged to the great and illustrious, and are now leveled to the ground. Consider how mighty they were, and now not even a memorial of them is left. For, if you will, every day you may find examples of these things- the successions of rulers- the confiscations of rich men's goods. "Many tyrants have sat on the ground and he who was never thought on,

has worn the diadem."[34] Do not these things happen every day? Do not our affairs resemble a kind of wheel? Read, if you will, both our own and those outside, for they also abound in such examples. If you despise ours and this from pride, if you admire the works of philosophers, go even to them. They will instruct you, relating ancient calamities, as will poets and orators and sophists and all historians. From every side, if you will, you may find examples.[35]

When John introduced his series of sermons on First Corinthians, he pointed to the accounts of the pagan writers who describe the city as "the rich" and as a place abounding in orators and philosophers.[36] In his introduction to the letter to the Ephesians, he noted that Pythagorus, Zeno, and Democritus were philosophers who came from this region of Asia Minor.[37] He agreed with Socrates that "we do not live in order to eat and drink; but we eat in order to live."[38]

Even though John's view on the soul greatly resembled that of Plato, some of his strongest criticism was reserved for this sage of the Academy.[39] The *Republic* was labelled as ridiculous, and its sexuality caused John to term the philosopher a "foe to modesty and an enemy to good order."[40] Plato ignored God's revelation in nature and became an atheist.[41] However, he then played the hypocrite because he worshipped the gods whose existence he doubted.[42] He was sold into slavery and could not convert any to his view of the gods or government.[43]

Another reference to a non-biblical source is a reference to Josephus attributing the war between the Jews and the Romans to the death of John the Baptist.[44]

John's Style

The Scriptures were the key to the knowledge that the preacher of God must bring to his task. John freely quotes and alludes to the Scriptures in his sermons and does so with surprising accuracy.[45] The wisdom of the non-Christian was to be used with great caution and usually as an example of folly. He valued precision and considered this an important element of good style.[46] His sermons were usually part of a series and most often through books of Scripture. However there were also sermons on topics such as one entitled "Excessive Grief at the Death of Friends", founded on 1 Thess 4:13.[47].

His sermons were taken down by stenographers, and he apparently edited them before they were copied for circulation. Some of his homilies, such as those on Acts that were preached during the turbulent times in Constantinople near the end of his ministry, do not appear to have been revised and have come down in a rough, and at times, disorganized form. At times during his ministry he assumed the availability of his works. In his homilies on Hebrews, delivered in Constantinople, he referred to his sermons on First Corinthians preached some years earlier in Antioch.[48] In these homilies on First Corinthians he referred to an earlier work on virginity. He used the existence of this work to excuse his passing over lightly some of the issues in the seventh chapter of First Corinthians and referred his hearers to his other work for further explanation.[49]

John and His Audience

John's relationship with his audience was one marked with a combination of candor, affection, and, as noted earlier, a curious form of intimacy. He sought their spiritual good, and his ministry depended on their response to his message.

John also put a burden of preparation on his congregation and expected them to come ready to hear his sermon.[50] In a series delivered in the mornings to what may have been a more motivated audience, he told them that if they were prepared they would get more out of the sermons.[51] He suggested that his congregation read the passage carefully beforehand.[52] He likened the preparation of the mind for the sermon to the preparing of the bridal chamber.[53] Not only did he want his audience to come prepared, but he expected that they would ruminate on his sermon after they left the assembly.[54]

Even though John used the fruit of his training as a rhetor when he preached, he still acknowledged that there were those in his audience who were unconvinced. At one point he stated that even if he argued his point more strongly, the unconvinced would not be brought to their senses by greater evidence.[55] He was often aware that his sermons were wearing on his audience and testing their ability to listen.[56] At one point he even acknowledged that he was getting carried away.[57] He was aware that his congregation did not like to follow long arguments.[58] However, one almost humorous point reveals that even with these qualifications, he was a captivating preacher. As a consequence of their attention, he felt the need to warn them about the presence of pickpockets who preyed on those in the congregation who were too attentive to his sermon.[59]

He summarized his messages and paced his instruction, seeing the process of teaching like that of moving a child to solid food.[60] He believed that instruction must be in an orderly progression for the best results.[61] When he preached his second sermon on the parable on the rich man and poor Lazarus, he congratulated his audience because they had responded properly to his previous message. He noted that their response was not as complete as he expected, but they were on a path toward maturity, and he was thankful for their initial growth.[62] This opening paragraph, noting the audience's reaction from the previous message, is typical of the linkages that John established between his sermons. He would give a promise of further teaching in a message and make good on the promise later. Some sermons appear to be continuations of a previous message.[63] John sought to divide the books he preached through into small units for the ease of his congregation.[64] Upon coming to a difficult passage on the divinity of Christ, he announced that he would wait till the next day to proceed with his teaching.[65]

A cursory glance at John's homilies might give the impression that he was unseemingly dogmatic and viewed himself solely in a prophetic and authoritarian role before his congregation. However, before his audience he wrestled as to how dogmatic he should be in proposed applications and even gave the option of different interpretations for the passage before him.[66] He was aware of his sharp language and apologized for it, excusing it as a tone he used because of his love for the people. He believed that a preacher must use forceful or mild language as necessary as he sought the best for his congregation.[67]

The Reaction of the Crowd

John drew energy from the reaction of his audience. He was happy at his third sermon in Constantinople when the crowd increased from his previous message, after he had exhorted the people to enlarge the congregation by inviting those who were not present.[68]

John preached in such a way that the crowds were often visibly moved as he spoke. At emotional points in his message there was crying among the people.[69] His audience often responded in applause to his words.[70]

He reminded his audience that the apostles, Christ, and even the pagan philosophers spoke and their audiences were quiet. He halfheartedly proposed a rule that the people must listen in silence to his messages but quickly abandoned the idea.[71] John did, however, make it clear to his audience that his desire was not applause but changed lives.

> Did you utter applause here? No, here is not the time for applause; but in what follows: for applauding, I say, and for imitating also.[72]

The positive reactions to his messages moved him. He responded to the eagerness of the crowd when it surged and pushed to get a better place for hearing his message.[73] He enjoyed the acclaim, and his desire was that he not go unheard.[74]

Not all of the reactions to John's preaching were positive. He knew that his exhortations brought him enemies as well as admirers.

> I know that many hate us because of these words; but I feel no hatred towards them; rather I pity and bewail those who are so

disposed.   Even should they choose to strike, I would gladly endure it.[75]

After his strong criticism of excesses at marriage celebrations, he speculated on the feeling of his audience for him and his message.

Now I know that I am a troublesome sort of person and disagreeable and morose as though I were curtailing life of some of its pleasure.[76]

At another time he said he would continue even if his message was unpopular.

And now I know that I am giving disgust to my hearers. But what must I do? For this I am set, and I shall not cease to say these things, whether anything come of them or not.[77]

He also knew that he was greeted with unbelief and expected it because it also happened to the prophets before him.[78]   He looked out over his congregation and noticed yawning, scratching and dozing.[79]   There was talking during his sermons as well as during the prayer time and even the benediction.[80]   He complained that some in his audience could not give up the affairs of business for even one day per week and discussed business during the worship.[81]   He even drew upon the lustful glances of the men in his audience at the women present as an illustration for his message.[82]

John called to the attention of the congregation the poor attendance often caused by people leaving the church for the horse races at the circus. People also left after the sermon and missed the prayers and the Eucharist.[83] Negative responses manifested themselves in a number of ways but the greatest blow to the preacher was when there was no change in the lives of those who gathered before him to hear his words.[84]

1.Proverbs 15:13

2.In Gen 1,1. (Hill, R. *Saint John Chrysostom: Homilies on Genesis 1-17*. 20).

3.De ter motu. (Carroll, *Preaching the Word*. 107).

4.De san pent 1,1. (Carroll, *Preaching the Word*. 107).

5.Ez 3:19.

6.In Heb 4,1. (NPNF 14, 382).

7.De laud s Paul 5; In Mat 38,1; 41,1; and 41,5.

8.In Heb 8,fin-9,1.

9.In Mat 1,15.

10.Adv Jud 6,1,3. (Harkins. *Discourses Against Judaizing Christians*. 148).

11.In Jn 25,1; In In Mat 52,5 he noted that it had been three days between sermons. He also preached in the middle of the week in his series against Judaizing tendencies in his congregation as noted in Adv Jud 1,1,1.

12.In Gen 11,8; 13,1

13.In Heb 8, fin. (NPNF 14, 408).

14.Galatians 4:19

15.In Heb 23,9 (NPNF 14, 473).

16.In Jn 13,1; Cat ill 6,3; and De s Bab c Jul 52.

17.In Jn 60,1. (NPNF 14, 216).

18.In Gen 9,5. (Hill. *Homilies on Genesis 1-17*. 119). He continued to speak of being perceived as a nuisance in In Gen 9,6.

19.This point is noted by Paul Harkins (*Saint John Chrysostom: Discourses*

Against Judaizing Christians. Washington: Catholic University of America Press, 1979. xxiii.) and discussed by C. Baur (*John Chrysostom and His Time.* Westminster, Maryland: Newman, 1960. I, 390-395).

20.G.W. Bowersock, *Greek Sophists in the Roman Empire.* Oxford: Clarendon, 1969. 43.

21.Jerome Carcopino, *Daily Life in Ancient Rome: the People and the City at the Height of the Empire* (New Haven: Yale University Press, 1940) 114. This was a reverse of Aristotle's priorities in *Rhetoric.* I.3.

22.De sac 5,1. In In Jn 1,1 he contended that the preacher is in competition with the games, the sophists and the musicians.

23.De sac 4,5; In 1 Cor 4,5. Gregory of Nazianzus notes the same problem in Oration 42,24. This is discussed by Harry M. Hubbel in "Chrysostom and Rhetoric." *Classical Philology*, 19 (1924): 263.

24.De s Bab c Jul 98. The relationship between John and Libanius has been discussed in A.F. Norman. *Libanius. Selected Works: The Julianic Orations* (Cambridge: Harvard University Press, 1969); Thomas Ameringer, *The Stylistic Influence of the Second Sophistic on the Panegyrical Sermons of Saint John Chrysostom: A Study in Greek Rhetoric* (Washington: Catholic University of America Press, 1921); Anton Naegele, "Chrysostomus und Libanios." *Chrysostomika* (Rome: Sacra Congregazione de Propaganda Fide, 1908); G.F. Hollinghurst, "The Ministry of Teaching in the Christian Church to the Death of Saint Augustine." (D. Phil. diss. Oxford University, 1954); and Hilary Feldman, "Some Aspects of the Christian Reaction to the Tradition of Classical Munificence with Particular Reference to the Works of John Chrysostom and Libanius." (M. Litt. thesis. Oxford University, 1980).

25.Libanius. Or. 18,13; Socrates. *Ecclesiastical History*, 3,1,45; Polymia Athanassiadi-Fowden, "An Emperor and Hellenism: Studies in the thought and action of the Emperor Julian." (D. Phil. diss. Oxford University, 1976) and *Julian and Hellenism* (Oxford: Clarendon Press, 1981); and H. Muller, "The Spiritual Campaign between Christians and Pagans from Lactantius to Augustine." (B. Litt. thesis. Oxford University, 1945).

26.M.L.W. Laistner. *The Greater Roman Historians*. (Berkeley: University of California Press, 1963) 143.

27.Charles Darwin Adams, *Demosthenes and His Influence*. (New York: Longmans, Green and Company, 1927), 127. and Thomas K. Carroll, *Preaching the Word*. (Wilmington, Del.: Michael Glazier, 1984), 99.

28.De sac 5,7; Ex in Ps 41; De proph obscur (MG 56,165); Thomas K. Carroll, *Preaching the Word*. (Wilmington, Del.: Michael Glazier, 1984), 98-99; George Kennedy, *Classical Rhetoric and Its Christian and Secular Tradition From Ancient to Modern Times*. (Chapel Hill: University of North Carolina Press, 1980), 145; For more specific studies of John's rhetorical style see R.J. Murray, "The Use of Conditional Sentences in Saint John Chrysostom's Homilies on the Gospel on St. John." Ph. D. diss. Ohio State University, 1960; John Alexander Sawhill, *The Use of Athletic Metaphors in the Biblical Homilies of Saint John Chrysostom*. (Princeton: The University Press, 1928); William A. Maat, *A Rhetorical Study of Saint John Chrysostom's De Sacerdotio*. Washington: The Catholic University of America Press, 1944; Julia Alissandratos, "The Structure of the Funeral Oration in John Chrysostom's Eulogy of Meletius." *Byzantine Studies* 7 (1980): 182-198; and, Mary Albania Burns, *Saint John Chrysostom's Homilies on the Statues: A Study of the Rhetorical Qualities and Form* (Washington: Catholic University of America Press, 1930).

29.Ad pop Ant 1,3.

30.In Jn 4,1. (NPNF 14, 16).

31.He refers to Plato and Pythagoras in In Jn 2,3; 2,5; Epimenides in In Tit 3; Zeno In Mat 1,10; the Stoics In Mat 33,5; Demosthenes In Mat 17,6; Ad pop Anti 7,9; Zoroaster and Zamolxis De s Bab c Jul 10; Celsus In 1 Cor 6,6; and Plotinus In 1 Cor 6,6. Studies of John's use of non-Christian literature include P.R. Coleman-Norton, P.R. "St. Chrysostom and the Greek Philosophers." *Classical Philology* 25 (1930): 305-317; "St. Chrysostom's Use of Josephus." *Classical Philology* 26 (1931): 85-89; "St Chrysostom's Use of the Greek Poets." *Classical Philology* 27 (1932): 213-221; Stephanus Bezdeki, "Joannes Chrysostomus et Plato." *Ephemeris Dacoroma-*

nia 1 (1923): 291-337; "La Theorie des Peines Futures chez Platon et Jean Chrysostome." *Annuarul Instituti de Studii Classice* 2 (1935): 1-33; Jean Dumortier, "Platon et Saint Jean Chrysostome." *Association G. Bude* (1953): 186-189. Stoic influence can be easily seen in his writings. This is discussed by P.J. Ryan in "Chrysostom: A Derived Stylist." *Vigiliae Christianae* 36 (1982): 13.); and M. Soffray, "Saint Jean Chrysostome et la Litterature Paienne." *Phoenix* 2 (1948): 82-85.

32.In 1 Cor 4,8-9. Adv Jud 5,3,1-2.

33.In Acta 4,3-4. In 1 Cor 4,4, In Jn 68,3.

34.Ecclus 11:15.

35.In 1 Thess 1. (NPNF 13, 379).

36.In 1 Cor Arg, 1.

37.In Eph Arg.

38.De Laz 1. He also referred to Socrates In In 1 Cor 26,8 and Adv Jud 5,3,1-2.

39.De inani gloria 65. Thomas Halton, "Saint John Chrysostom on Education." *The Catholic Educational Review* 61 (1963): 163,175; M.L.W. Laistner, *Christianity and Pagan Culture in the Later Roman Empire, with John Chrysostom's Address on Vainglory and the Right Way for Parents to Bring Up Their Children.* (Ithica: Cornell University Press, 1967) 78.

40.In Mat 1,10.

41.In Rom 3; 4; and 5.

42.In 1 Cor 7,15.

43.In Mat 33,5.

44.In Jn 13,1.

45.John rarely made mistakes in quotation. In In 1 Thess 8 he cited Carmi as the Israelite who stole the devoted goods at the Fall of Jericho. In reality it was Carmi's son Achan. In In Jn 64,4 he cited a verse as being from Nahum which is most probably from Jeremiah. Considering the thousands of citations and allusions in his sermons these few examples are testimony to his knowledge of the Scriptures. Also, because of his fondness for scriptural allusions and examples in his works he also serves as a good witness to the textual tradition of his era. For an example of research in this area see Frederick C. Conybeare, "On the Western Text of Acts as Evidenced by Chrysostom." *American Journal of Philology* 17 (1896): 135-171.

46.In 2 Tim 5, 493. For discussions of this characteristic of John's preaching se M.W. Clow, "The Preaching of Chrysostom." Expositor 23 (1922): 359-368 and Robbie James Harris, "John Chrysostom's Use of the Homily." (M.A. Thesis. Southern Baptist Seminary, 1957).

47.Galusha Anderson, "The Elements of Chrysostom's Power as a Preacher." *Decennial Publications of the University of Chicago* 3:51-66.

48.In Heb 3,11.

49.In 1 Cor 19, 7 fin.

50.In Jn 1,6; 51,1; Cat ill 5,12; In Gen 1,3; 8,1; In Mat 2,1.

51.In Jn 9,1.

52.In Jn 11,1, In Mat 1,13.

53.In Gen 1,4.

54.In Gen 14,22.

55.In Eph 3.

56.In Eph 6; In Jn 2,10; Cat ill 4,30; In Gen 6,7; In Mat 7,8.

57.In 1 Cor 15,15.

58.Con Jud et gen 1,1-2.

59.De incomp die 4,46.

60.De Laz 2; 3; 7; De incomp die 5,1.

61.De incomp die 5,4.

62.De Laz 2.

63.De Laz 4 and In Gen 14,1 are examples of such linkage.

64.In Jn 25,1.

65.In Col 2 and 3. Other examples of John on difficult passages In 1 Cor 29f; and 36,2.

66.In Jn 65,3 and In Gen 19.

67.In Jn 12,1 and In Jn 44,1.

68.De Chris divin 1-3.

69.In 2 Cor 3,7.

70.Passages where John alludes to applause include: De incomp die 3,32; In 1 Cor 4,6; 4,11; 26,8 In il Si esur 1; Ad pop Anti 2,4; 2,12; 7,10; De Consub 2; Con Anom 4,7; and, In Mat 17,7.

71.In Acta 30,4. Two passages where John said that he preferred silence to applause are De Laz 2 and In Acta 30,4. John also noted that it was difficult to get the proper reaction to a sermon De sac 5,2.

72.In 1 Cor 13,5. John told his audience that he wanted changed lives not applause in De incomp die 3,43; 4,32; In 1 Cor 13,5. He referred to this problem in De sac 5,5. Also, at the close of his fourth homily on 1 Corinthians he made instant use of the applause of his congregation. "You have given," he exclaimed, "vehement applause and acclamation: but with all your applause have a care lest you be among those of whom these things are said."

73.In Jn 3,1; In Mat 17,7; In Gen 31,1, (cited in Carroll. *Preaching the Word*. 108)

74.In Mat 32,9.

75.In 1 Cor 9,10. Other examples of negative responses are seen in In Mat 32,9; In 1 Cor 9,10; 12,11; 40,6; and Q nemo 1.

76.In 1 Cor 12,11.

77. In 1 Cor 40,6.

78. In Col 2.

79. In Col 2.

80. In 1 Cor 36,9 and In Acta 24,4.

81. In Mat 88, fin.

82. In Mat 73,3.

83. In 1 Cor 3,6; 4,4-5 and In il Si esur 1.

84. In il Si esur 1 fin.

CHAPTER 7

THE SCRIPTURES

John's view of the Scriptures may be summed up in two concepts. He viewed them as an example of divine condescension, and he viewed them as truthful or precise. As a result of these two factors there was power from God in the words.[1]

Divine Condescension or Considerateness

John's concept of condescension or accommodation has led some to assume that he saw flaws and imperfections in the text of Scripture.[2] However, this understanding is not rooted in John's use of the term, which might be better translated "considerateness," as proposed by Robert Hill.[3] Either this translation or that of "graciousness" best explains John's notion. He used this term to refer to divine activity toward humanity, reaching men and women at their point of need. He saw such graciousness as necessary because of man's spiritual condition. It was the crowning mark of God's love. John's concept of considerateness was broad enough to include a notion of progress in revelation. During his homilies on Genesis, he often commented on the fact that this was the beginning of biblical revelation and later Scriptures built upon its words. Commenting on the creation account in Genesis, chapter one, he noted that Moses spoke in simple terms and that the New Testament built more developed thought on this base.[4]

John also saw God's considerateness in many of the divine acts revealed in Scripture. He saw it in God's explaining our creation to us by revealing what is recorded in the first chapter of Genesis to Moses.[5] His considerateness was also revealed when He sought out Adam and Eve in the garden after their sin.[6] God also graciously sought out Cain and sought to prevent his sin.[7] The transfiguration was another example of this considerateness as was the appearance of God to Isaiah.[8] A further example was the miraculous light in the sky that appeared at the birth of Christ.[9] Christ also acted

graciously when He used the visible form of praying to the Father in the
garden when he could have communicated without the external postures that
served as   examples for us.[10]   Special terms in the Scriptures are used
graciously to aid our understanding of divine truth. An example of this is the
use of the term 'only-begotten' in John, chapter three.[11] The force of this
concept in John's thought as revealed in his understanding of all of these examples was God's action toward man. It was His gracious seeking of man
in his condition to bring him to Himself.

<u>The Truthfulness of Scripture</u>

John demonstrated his belief in the truthfulness of Scripture as he
applied its precision in his sermons. When the Scriptures prophesy that the
Messiah will "come out" of Bethlehem,[12] John notes the precise way in Christ
fulfilled this prediction by the circumstances of His birth.

> But mark the exactness of the prophecy. For it does not say, "He
> will abide in Bethlehem," but "He will come out thence." So that
> this too was a subject of prophecy, His simply being born there.

> Some of them, however, being past shame, say that these things
> were spoken of Zorobabel. But how can they be right? For
> surely "his goings forth" were not "from of old, from everlasting."
> And how can that suit him which is said at the beginning, "Out
> of thee shall He come forth:" Zorobabel not having been born in
> Judea, but in Babylon, this is why he was called Zorobabel,
> because he had his origin there? And as many as know the
> Syrians' language know what I say.[13]

John's explanation of many of the details of the birth narrative of Matthew
was rooted in a belief in the precision of the text and a confidence in the
truthfulness of the prophecies pertaining to the birth of Christ.   Other
applications of this notion of precision were the comments by John that the
text as written was precisely what God wished to communicate to man.[14]

John also manifested his belief in the veracity of the Gospels when he
consistently harmonized any difficulties in the texts and rationalized the need

for four Gospels.[15]   He noted that the Marcionites were wrong when they read the phrase "which is not another Gospel" as limiting the number of gospel records.   He said that they are "as diseased people [who] are injured even by healthy food."   He was convinced that "it is clear that the four Gospels are one Gospel" and "Paul is not speaking of the number but of the discrepancy of the things spoken."[16]   There were, for John, no discrepancies in the Gospel accounts.

In his explanations of difficulties or apparently contradictory texts, John consistently assumed their truthfulness.   He faced a potential problem in the creation narrative when he saw that man is given dominion over the beasts and reptiles of the earth as well as the fish of the sea and the birds of the air.

> The fact that now we have fear and dread of wild animals and have lost control of them, I personally don't dispute: but this doesn't betray a false promise on God's part.   From the beginning, you see, things weren't like this; instead, the wild beasts were in fear and trembling, and responded to direction.   But when through disobedience human beings forfeited their position of trust, their control was also lost.   As evidence, after all, that everything was placed under the human being's control, listen to Scripture saying, "He brought the wild animals and all the brute beasts to Adam to see what he would call them."   And seeing the animals near him, he didn't shrink back, but like a master giving names to slaves in his service, he gave them all names: the text says, "They each bore the name Adam gave them," this being a symbol of his dominion.   Hence God was wanting to teach him through this the dignity of his authority so he entrusted to him the giving of names.[17]

Throughout this explanation John assumed the truth of the text.   He used the text to resolve difficulties and speculated that a consequence of the Fall accounted for the lack of dominion in his day.

His harmonistic tendency was also seen in his series of homilies on Matthew.   He consistently used Mark and Luke to explain the text and addressed difficulties in these gospels as he preached on the first gospel.[18] He saw the need to harmonize any apparent difficulties in the genealogies of Christ found in the gospels.[19] He also recognized a potential problem in the reference to Abiathar in Mark 2:24.[20] He even attempted the difficult reference to a double sabbath in Luke 6:1 as he commented on the parallel passages in Matthew.[21] He also pointed to the accuracy of the text in matters of geography as a testimony to the truthfulness of Scripture.[22]

John's Canon

John devoted little energy to discussions of canonicity. He recognized the differences between canonical and chronological order and saw the date of composition as significant in understanding the message of an inspired writer. He made a curious statement in explaining Matthew's claim that a prophecy fulfilled in the birth of Christ was that "He shall be called a Nazarene."[23] He warned his congregation not to be "curious nor overbusy" and noted that many of the prophetic writings have been lost because of the negligence and ungodliness of the Jews who lost some and destroyed others. He cited the finding of the lost book of the law in the temple and the destruction of Jeremiah's writings as evidence of Jewish indifference to the sacred texts.[24]

He believed that different teachings on similar issues in the various epistles of Paul were a form a divine graciousness or considerateness to the readers. As he explained the differences in attitude toward food taboos in Romans and Colossians, he did not see these as compromising the truth of the Scriptures.

> [The epistle] to the Galatians seems to me to be before that to the Romans. But if they have a different order in the Bible, that is nothing wonderful, since the twelve Prophets, though not exceeding one another in order of time, but standing at great intervals from one another, are in succession. Thus Haggai and Zechariah and the Messenger [Malachi] prophesied after Ezekiel and Daniel, and long after Jonah and Zephaniah and all the rest. Yet they are nevertheless joined with all those from whom they

stand so far off in time.

But let no one consider this an undertaking beside the purpose, nor a search of this kind a piece of superfluous curiosity; for the date of the Epistles contributes no little to what we are looking after. For when I see him writing to the Romans and to the Colossians about the same subjects; but to the former with much condescension, as when he says, "Him that is weak in the faith receive but not to doubtful disputations; for one believes that he may eat all things, another who is weak eats herbs."[25] But to the Colossians he writes in this way, though about the same things, but with greater boldness of speech. "Wherefore if you are dead with Christ," he says, "why, as though living in the world, are you subject to ordinances, touch not, taste not, handle not, which are all to perish with the using, not in any honor to the satisfying of the flesh."[26] I find no other reason for this difference than the time of transaction. For at the first it was needful to be condescending, but afterward it became no more so.[27]

John then continued by giving his often-used illustration of the physician who varies the treatment to suit the patient, combining this with the illustration of the teacher who varies instruction.

John used the Septuagint as his Old Testament and accepted its translation under "King Ptolemy" as a "work of divine providence."[28] He used the canon of the Greek Old Testament, labelling books not in the Hebrew text as Scripture.[29] However, he did criticize the text of the Septuagint and was aware of other translations of the Old Testament into Greek.[30] He was ignorant of Hebrew and referred his audience to an understanding of Syriac to explain Hebrew terms.[31]

It has been assumed traditionally that his canon is that of the Syriac Peshitta translation.[32] This must be tempered with the denigrating remarks made by Chrysostom on Syriac culture. He refers to the language as a "barbarous tongue[33]" and notes that the Syriac-speaking inhabitants of the countryside are "separated from us in language."[34] The Syriac Peshitta may have had influence in the countryside, but John was a child of the city and his Scriptures were written in the Greek language. He describes Greek as "so admirable and beautiful" in a context where he is describing the disdain of the Latins for Hebrew and notes that if the Italians despised Greek, they would have a much lower opinion of Hebrew. In this context he also said that Syriac has "affinity with the Hebrew."[35]

<u>Interpreting the Scriptures</u>

The Scriptures must be interpreted with care and skill. Before John began his exposition of difficult words of Christ in John, chapter five, he warned about the dangers of careless interpretation.

> If I bear witness of Myself, My witness is not true; there is another that bears witness of Me, and I know that the witness which he witnesses of Me is true.[36]

> If any one unpracticed in the art undertakes to work in a mine, he will get no gold, but confounding all aimlessly and together, will undergo a labor unprofitable and pernicious: so also they who understand not the method of Holy Scripture, nor search out its peculiarities and laws, but go over all its points carelessly and in one manner, will mix the gold with earth, and never discover the treasure which is laid up in it. I say this now because the passage before us contains much gold, not indeed manifest to view, but covered over with much obscurity, and therefore by digging and purifying we must arrive at the legitimate sense.[37]

John saw the method of interpretation as arising from the text itself and he favored a literal as opposed to a multilayered understanding of the text. He believed that the literal meaning and not the various possible allegorical senses was the key to both interpreting and applying the text. When the term allegory was used by Paul in Galatians 4:24, John explained away any opening this use might give to multilayered interpretation.

> Contrary to usage, he calls a type an allegory; his meaning is as follows: this history not only declares that which appears on the face of it, but announces somewhat farther, whence it is called an allegory. And what has it announced? No less that all the things now present.[38]

For John, part of the interpretive method of Scripture was the interpretation of the text by itself and other texts.[39]   John also noted other "laws" of interpretation.   He saw a "law of Prophecy" that "in many cases much that is spoken of one set of persons is fulfilled in another."[40]   This led to an extensive use of typology by John as he sought the sense of a text.   He maintains that this was Paul's sense of the word "allegory" in Galatians 4:24.[41] John also used the term similarly in this limited sense.[42]   John saw typology as a vehicle for divine prophecy when the reality of the type and antitype were maintained and the relationship between them was given by the inspiration of the Spirit in Scripture.[43]   He seemed to find types often and even saw any use of water in the Old Testament as a type of baptism.

> It was necessary too that many things should prepare the way for baptism; yes, thousands of things; those, for instance, in the Old Testament, those of the Pool, the cleansing of him that was not sound in health, the deluge itself, and all the things that have been done in water, the Baptism of John....
>
> Types, then of all these things, if we are so inclined, we shall find by searching in the Scriptures.[44]

As John interpreted texts, he noted those features that addressed issues in their cultural context.   In applying the admonition against men wearing long hair in First Corinthians, chapter 11, he noted that long hair was worn by the those who devoted their time to schools of Grecian philosophy.[45]   This point was easily made before his congregation in Antioch where the Emperor Julian had appeared in philosophical garb a quarter of a century earlier. He also recognized that there was not always unanimity in the Christian community in interpreting various passages on Scripture and allowed his congregation to pick between different views on difficult passages.[46]

1.In In Gen 6,22 John refers to the Scriptures as "... a divine book in our hands... refresh our minds and theirs with the divine words." In In Gen 4,5 John taught that "after all, it is not by his own power he speaks; instead, whatever the grace of the Spirit inspires in him, this he utters with his own tongue for the instruction of mankind."

2.F. Fabbi, "La Condiscendenza Divina nell' ispirazione Biblica secondo S. Giovanni Crisostomo." *Biblica* 14 (1933): 330-347; Yves Congar. *Lay People in the Church* (Westminster, MD: Christian Classics, 1985), 55. Robert Hill, "On Looking Again at *Sunkatabasis*." *Prudentia* 13 (1981): 3-11 and *Saint John Chrysostom: Homilies on Genesis 1-17.* (Washington, DC: Catholic University of America Press, 1986), 17; and Frederic Henry Chase, *Chrysostom: A Study in the History of Biblical Interpretation* (Cambridge: Deighton, Bell and Company, 1887), 42.

3.Robert Hill, *Saint John Chrysostom: Homilies on Genesis 1-17* (Washington, DC: Catholic University of America Press, 1986), 17-19. Hill has also summarized the use of terms of intimate discourse in John's homilies for the process of God's communication through the Scriptures further linking condescension or considerateness with a gracious movement of God toward man rather than the content of the communication ("Saint John Chrysostom's Teaching on Inspiration in 'Sixth Homily on Isaiah'." *Vigiliae Christianae* 22 (1968): 26-27).

4.In Gen 2, passim. In Ex in Ps 44 John gives a more general principle that the the writers of the New Testament tell "everything in order" building upon the accounts of the Old Testament prophets. See also the discussion in Robert Hill "St. John Chrysostom's Teaching on Inspiration in His Old Testament Homilies." (Ph. D. diss. Pontificiam Universitatem S. Thomas de Urbe, Sidney, 1981.) 5-9.

5.In Gen 3,6 and In Gen 12,12.

6.In Gen 17,3; In quat Laz A 5.

7.In quat Laz A 6.

8.De incomp die 3,17. This is discussed in John A. McGuckin, "The Patristic Exegesis of the Transfiguration." *Studia Patristica* 18 (1985) I, 336.

9.In Mat 6,2; 6,3.

10.In quat Laz A 1-2; De Chris prec 17.

11.In Jn 3,4.

12.Micah 5:2

13.In Mat 7,2. (NPNF 10, 44).

14.In Gen 5,14; 6,18; 7, 10-12; 8,10; 10, 12-14; 12,15; 13,6; and 15,3. This concept is discussed by Robert Hill in "*Akribeia*: a Principle of Chrysostom's Exegesis." *Colloquium* 14 (1981): 32-36 and *Saint John Chrysostom: Homilies on Genesis 1-17* (Washington, DC: Catholic University of America Press, 1986) 18.

15.Examples include In Mat 1,6f and In Mat 76,2; In Mat 26,3; 28,1; In para 3; and In Jn 23,2. See also the discussion in Jerome D. Quin, "Saint John Chrysostom on History in the Synoptics," *The Catholic Biblical Quarterly* 24 (1962): 140-147.

16.In Gal 1:7.

17.In Gen 9,8. (Hill. *Homilies on Genesis 1-17*. 121-122).

18.In Mat 3,8; 13,2; 25,2; 27,1; 29,1; 30,1; 68,1, etc.

19.In Gen 9,8.

20.In Mat 39,1.

21.In Mat 39,1.

22.In 1 Thess 8.

23.Mat. 2:23.

24.In Mat 9,6.

25.Rom. 16:1-2.

26.Col. 2:20-23.

27.In Rom Arg, 1. (NPNF 11, 336-337).

28.In Gen 4,9.

29.For John's citations of the apocryphal Old Testament books see R.A. Krupp, *Saint John Chrysostom: A Scripture Index* (Lanham, MD: University Press of America, 1984) 94-101.

30.In Gen 15, 13 and In Gen 18.

31.In Gen 4,10 and In Mat 7,2.

32.David G. Dunbar, "The Biblical Canon," In *Hermeneutics, Authority and Canon* (Grand Rapids: Zondervan, 1986) 317. Dunbar cites B.F. Westcott, *A General Survey of the History of the Canon of the New Testament*, 6th ed. (New York: Macmillan, 1889. reprint Grand Rapids: Baker, 1980) 441-442 and Edgar J. Goodspeed, *The Formation of the New Testament* (Chicago: University of Chicago Press, 1926) 128-130. in support of his assertion. See also the discussion of John's canon in C. Baur, "Der Kanon des Johannes Chrysostomus," *Theologische Quartalschrift* 105 (1924): 258-271; J. Geerlings and N. Silva, "Chrysostom's Text of the Gospel of Saint Mark," *Harvard Theological Review* 24 (1931): 121-142; F.T. Gignac, "The Text of Acts in Chrysostom's Homilies," *Traditio* 26 (1970): 308-315; and G.D. Fee, "The Text of John and Mark in the Writings of Chrysostom," *New Testament Studies* 26 (1980): 525-547.

33.In 2 Tim 4 (NPNF 13, 490); Cat ill 8,2.

34.Ad pop Anti 19, 2; In Cat ill 8, 1-4 he points out the rural origin of the Syriac speaking visitors in the congregation. He reminds his audience to overlook both the "barbarous tongue" (8,2) and appearance (8,4) of the visitors.

35.In 2 Tim 4, 490. In this context Chrysostom's prejudices seem to cloud his argument as he makes the point that Paul was "a tent-maker, a poor man, unskilled in the wisdom of those without, knowing only the Hebrew tongue, a language despised by all, especially the Italians." In De laud s Paul 2 he correctly noted that Paul was from Tarsus in the region of Antioch and chided his congregation to imitate the apostle by noting that he "was an inhabitant of no different world; in the same world, the same country, with the same laws and customs."

36.Jn 5:31-32.

37.In Jn 40,1. (NPNF 14, 143).

38.In Gal 4:24. (NPNF 13,34).   Many reviewers of the history of herme-neutics and John's interpretive method correctly see him as a member of the Antiochene school of thought with its avoidance of allegory and its search for the singular sense of the text. These include the following. Frederic Henry Chase, *Chrysostom: A Study in the History of Biblical Interpretation* (Cambridge: Deighton, Bell and Company, 1887); Leon Dieu, "Le Commentaire de Saint Jean Chrysostome sur Job." (*Revue d'Histoire Ecclesiastique* 13 (1912): 640-658.); Robert M. Grant, and David Tracy. *A Short History of the Interpretation of the Bible* (Philadelphia: Fortress, 1984); Robert Hill, "*Akribeia*: a Principle of Chrysostom's Exegesis." (*Colloquium* 14 (1981): 32-36.); Thomas R. McKibbens, "The Exegesis of John Chrysos-tom: Homilies on the Gospels." (*Expository Times* 93 (1982): 264.); I. Moisescu, "Holy Scripture and Its Interpretation in the Works of Saint John Chrysostom." (*Candela* 50-51 (1939-1941): 116-238.); Henry S. Nash, "The Exegesis of the School of Antioch." (*Journal of Biblical Literature* 11 (1892): 22-37.); E. Nestle, "Chrysostom on the Life of John the Apostle."-(*American Journal of Theology* 9 (1905): 519-520.); Elaine Pagels, "The Politics of Paradise: Augustine's Exegesis of Genesis 1-3 Versus that of John Chrysostom." (*Harvard Theological Review* 79 (1985): 67-99.); Beryl Smalley, *The Study of the Bible in the Middle Ages* (Notre Dame, IN: University of Notre Dame Press, 1964) 15; R.G. Tanner, "Chrysostom's Exegesis of Romans." (*Studia Patristica* 17 (1982): 1185.); G.H. Whiteker, "Chrysostom on 1 Corinthians 1:13."(*Journal of Theological Studies*, 15 (1914): 254-257.); Frances M. Young, "John Chrysostom on First and Second Corinthians." (*Studia Patristica*. 18 (1985) vol. 1. 349-352.); and Joseph Rickaby, "Saint John Chrysostom on Faith and Reason." *The Month* 62 (1888):250-256.

39.In Gen 13,8.

40.In Mat 8,5.

41.In Gal 4:24.   This is discussed in H.A. Wolfson, *The Philosophy of the Church Fathers* (Cambridge: Harvard University Press, 1956) 64.

42.In Mat 52,1; In Jn 85,1. H.A. Wolfson, *The Philosophy of the Church Fathers* (Cambridge: Harvard University Press, 1956) 65.

43.In Mat 52,1; In Jn 85,1; and In Gal 4:24. See also discussion in John Breck, *The Power of the Word in the Worshipping Church* (Crestwood, NY: St. Vladimir's Seminary Press, 1986) 87-88, on this point.

44.In Col 5. (NPNF 13, 283). John's typology becomes difficult to distinguish from allegory. Other examples of this practice in his corpus include In Phil 10; In Jn 14,4; De Laz 6; and In Heb 12,3. In his interpretation of parables he often sees many doctrines as taught in a given parable. An example of this occurs in In Mat 68,1. See also a discussion of this phenomenon in Robert M. Grant and David Tracy, *A Short History of the Interpretation of the Bible.* (Philadelphia: Fortress, 1984) 66 (citing In Is 5), and 68; Thomas K. Carroll, *Preaching the Word.* (Wilmington, Del.: Michael Glazier, 1984) 117; and Robert L. Wilken, *Judaism and the Early Christian Mind* (New Haven: Yale University Press, 1970) 437.

45.In 1 Cor 26,1.

46.An example would be in In Gen 19 on Gen 4:8 as cited in Robert Hill *Saint John Chrysostom: Homilies on Genesis 1-17.* (Washington, DC: Catholic University of America Press, 1986) 14.

CHAPTER 8
THE BISHOP AND THE SPIRITUAL LIFE OF THE PEOPLE

When the bishop addressed the people, he was a representative of God in their midst. He preached to them about God and preached to bring them to God. Two emphases of John's preaching that were basic to his messages of personal repentance and social reform were the knowability of God and His kingship in His creation.

The Knowability of God

God can be known in this life and fellowship with Him will continue in heaven. The knowledge of Him may be incomplete, but we have glimpses of a fuller and clearer knowledge of Him in Scripture. This should motivate us to pursue Him to our fullest on this earth so that we may participate in the fellowship of the eternal kingdom.

When he exhorted Theodore, who was considering the abandonment of his ascetic vows for marriage, John pointed to the vision of the transfigured Christ and his coming kingdom that should have motivated Theodore to keep his promise to God.[1] In another work John contrasted the knowability of the true God which was different than the seemingly trivial ways in which the pagan gods were appeased and addressed.[2]

God's Lordship in His Creation

John emphasized the Kingship of God but often expressed it in the context of God's love and care for people. He used the doctrine of divine providence in his counsel of the young widow after the death of her husband.[3] He did not flinch from saying that the death of her husband, a high ranking government official, was "a severe blow, and that the weapon directed from above was planted in a vital part all will readily admit, and none even of the rigid moralists will deny it."[4] John distanced himself from those who would say with Job's counselors that all calamity comes as a result of sin. He saw even this untimely death as a part of God's lordship in His creation. However, God's lordship did not end with the untimely death but continued with His provision of the Church as a haven for the widow after her loss. By becoming a widow in service of the Church she could free herself from the cares of managing the affairs of the estate and the oppressed position she would probably occupy in society. God was Providential Lord both in her loss and this provision. John told the widow that "since God took him [her husband] to Himself He has supplied his place to you."[5] He then quoted the Psalmist's praise of God's support for the fatherless and the widow.[6] Even the tragedy of early widowhood could be used by God for a double blessing. The husband was now in His presence and the widow could live a life of close dependence on God in His service.

God uses many methods to bring people to Himself and after more pleasing means are rejected He uses punishment. Even this is a manifestation of His care for those who err.[7] Even events such as earthquakes are used by God as part of His caring. John saw these events occurring because of the spiritual laxity of the people.[8] God's love is such that even before the creation of the universe He was planning how to love those who would follow Him.

> The reason, you see, that he produced all created things and formed us was not that we should perish nor to consign us to punishment, but to save us, to free us from error and reward us with the enjoyment of the kingdom. This, after all, is what he prepared for us, not at this late stage after our coming into existence but before the foundation of the world, as he himself says: "Come you blessed of my Father, take possession of the kingdom prepared for you before the foundation of the world." See the lovingkindness of the Lord, how even before creation, even before he produced human beings, he had prepared for them countless good things, revealing the extent of his care for our race and his wish for everyone to be saved.[9]

In short, God has prepared the eternal kingdom for those who would follow Him. He now works providentially to move all toward repentance. Those who die in rebellion do so because they have rejected numerous divine efforts to reach them.

Another aspect of the divine kingship over creation is God's working through different "economies" toward his creatures. John saw different economies when God's kingship was expressed differently over all humanity in general and the faithful in particular.[10]   A second economic aspect of kingship was seen in the progressive way in which God works in his creation. The time of Moses was referred to the "Old Dispensation."[11]   The race run by the faithful is different in each dispensation.[12]   The faithful must live in accordance with God's demands for them in their economy or dispensation.

Spiritual Birth and Synergism

The bishop and the priest have an awesome responsibility as the primary stewards of the means of spiritual birth in the life of the church. As John reflected on the privilege that the Christian has of calling God "Our Father" in the prayer that Christ gave to His Church, he reminded his audience of the many graces contained in this relationship.

> For he who calls God Father, by him both remission of sins, and taking away of punishment, and righteousness, and sanctification, and redemption, and adoption, and inheritance, and brotherhood with the Only-Begotten, and the supply of the Spirit are acknowledged in the single title. For one cannot call God Father, without having attained to all those blessings.[13]

John's understanding of the spiritual birth of the Christian was based on the principle of synergism, God and the one coming to Him working together mysteriously in this singularly significant event. As he taught from the first chapter of Paul's letter to the Ephesians on the role of God's elective grace in the salvation of His people, he began his moral exhortations with a warning against spiritual slothfulness based on a misunderstanding of these words, "Let not the hearing, however, make us too much at ease; for although He did it for His own sake, yet not withstanding He requires a duty on our part."[14]

He told the catechumens that God's many favors toward us "move us to look to our own salvation."[15]   Paul was an example of the process of salvation. He was a "vessel of election" but also "purified himself."[16]

God gives the gift of faith to His people, but they must do their part. Their part is to live a godly life building on what God has provided.[17] Faith is from God and surpasses human sight and reasoning. It is a supernatural trust that God enables the Christian to exert toward Him.[18] God initiates salvation, but faith is not enough. John, accepting Pauline authorship of the letter to the Hebrews, saw the Apostle exhorting his readers to build upon the divine foundation of faith as he comments on the exhortation, "Let us labor to enter into that rest."[19]

> Faith is indeed great and brings salvation, and without it, it is not
> possible to be saved. It suffices not however of itself to ac-
> complish this, but there is need of a right life as well. So on this
> account Paul also exhorts those who had been already counted
> worthy of the mysteries; saying, "Let us labor," faith not sufficing,
> the life also ought to be added thereto, and our earnestness to
> be great; for truly there is need of much earnestness too, in order
> to go up to Heaven.[20]

Synergism is a mystery and John did not attempt to express the relationship between the activity of God and the role of the Christian in salvation with logical precision. He saw both roles clearly taught in Scripture and proclaimed them to his congregation.

The Nature and Work of Christ.

The cross of Christ is central in the Christian's experience. This is not only an abstract theological truth but an intimate reality. This reality is seen in the prominence of the sign of the cross in the Christian's experience.

> Everything is done by the cross. Baptism is given by the cross-
> we must receive the sphragis [seal]- the laying on of hands is
> done by the cross. Wherever we are, travelling or at home, the
> cross is a great good, a saving protection, an impregnable barrier
> against the Devil.[21]

Underneath the practical reality of the sign of the cross is the mysterious supernatural faith. Part of the supernatural faith that God gives is the ability to believe in Christ. Christ cannot be comprehended unaided by God. His generation is not comprehensible to man.[22] He is fully divine and consubstantial with the Father.[23] As he explained the kenosis passage in Philippians, chapter two, John emphasized Paul's statement that Christ did not seize equality with God; it was in His nature. Seizure or any other act of Christ did not bring Him into the Trinity. He has been eternally God and John contrasted this view with that of various heretical groups.[24] As John reflected on the passage "the Word became flesh and dwelt among us,"[25] he saw the incarnation not as lowering Christ but raising humanity.

> Having declared that they who received Him were "born of God" and had become "sons of God" he adds the cause and reason of this unspeakable honor. It is that "the Word became flesh," that the Master took on Him the form of a servant. For He became Son of Man, who was God's own Son in order that He might make the sons of men to be children of God. For the high when it associates with the low touches not at all its own honor, while it raises up the other from its excessive lowness; and even thus it was with the Lord. He in nothing diminished His own Nature by this condescension, but raised us, who had always sat in disgrace and darkness, to glory unspeakable.[26]

Christ was a leaven in the world because of His purity and thus became a force leading people toward righteousness.[27]

John believed that Satan was deceived by the divine plan for the atonement of humanity and that the Deceiver was outwitted by God.[28] Once Satan saw the course of Christ's life moving toward Calvary, he tried to thwart the death of Christ in order to frustrate God's plan of atonement through His sacrifice.[29]

Christ died for all, even those who reject Him. "Truly the Sacrifice was offered for all mankind, and was sufficient to save all, but those who enjoy the blessing are the believing only."[30] Those who believe in Christ are united with Him and receive the Spirit who forms the basis for life in the Christian community.[31]

<u>The Working of the Faithful in their Salvation</u>

Man must add to the faith that God gives. John expressed his concern that he would work the necessary part of his salvation in his apology to Basil for avoiding the priesthood.[32] Even though God loves us, we must do our part. God was benevolently disposed toward mankind, but everyone must still work their part of the synergistic salvation. John saw this attitude in Christ's words, "If any man will come after me, let him renounce himself, and take up his cross and follow Me."[33]

> "If any man will come after me." "I force not, I compel not, but each one I make lord of his own choice; wherefore also I say, "If any man will...."
>
> For so, if one were a judge at the games and had a friend in the lists, he would not wish to crown him by favor only, but also for his own toils; and for this reason especially, because he loves him. Even so Christ also; whom He loves most, those He most of all will have to approve themselves by their own means also, and not from His help alone.
>
> But see how at the same time He makes His saying not a grievous one. For He does by no means compass them only with His terror but He puts forth the doctrine generally to the world, saying, "If any one will," be it women or man, ruler or subject, let him come this way.[34]

John saw synergism as a mystery of joint action, and at times his comments seem inconsistent if pressed for a strict chronology or other logical relationship between divine and human action in spiritual birth. He usually only affirmed synergism, the divine and human coworking.

He told the catechumens that we must bring "a generous faith and a strong reason," although he usually affirmed that faith is from God.[35] He also maintained the priority of divine action but acknowledged that God's gift does not have any effect if we do not first make the choice.[36]   He saw election as equal to foreknowledge.[37]   God's love toward a person depends on their response to God's provision of salvation.[38]   The remedies for sin given by God to His people call the Christian to participate in the synergistic process.

Now to this end God has opened to us many ways.

For "Tell first" says He, "your sins, that you may be justified."[39] And again, "I said, I have declared mine iniquity to You, and You have taken away the unrighteousness of my heart."[40]   Since a continual accusation and remembrance of sins contributes not a little to lessen their magnitude.

But there is another more prevailing way than this; to bear malice against none of those who have offended against us, to forgive their trespasses to all those who have trespassed against us.

Will you learn a third? Hear Daniel saying, "Redeem thy sins by almsdeeds, and thine iniquities by showing mercy to the poor."[41]

And there is another way besides this; constancy in prayer and persevering attendance on the intercessions made to God.

In like manner fasting brings to us some, and that not small comfort and release from sins committed, provided it be attended with kindness to others and quenches the vehemence of the wrath of God. For "water will quench a blazing fire, and by almsgiving sins are purged away."[42]

Let us then travel along all these ways; for if we give ourselves wholly to these employments, if on them we spend our time, not only shall we wash off our bygone transgressions, but shall gain very great profit for the future. For we shall not allow the Devil to assault us with leisure either for slothful living or for pernicious curiosity, since by these among other means, and in consequence of these, he leads us to foolish questions and hurtful disputations, from seeing us at leisure and idle, and taking no forethought for excellency of living.[43]

The synergism in our salvation was more than our working and God's working. Others also worked in our salvation. John included those God used to bring the message of repentance to us as part of the synergistic effort on the behalf of our salvation.[44]

Human Nature

Human nature is that part of us which is immutable and common to all of our race. John asserted this against those who would say that character traits such as cowardice and bravery or certain sins are natural.[45]   In exhorting those who were soon to be baptized, he embraced a creationist understanding of the soul's origin. He saw it as coming from the creative hand of God. He prodded them by saying, "What could be more ugly than the soul which has abandoned its proper dignity, forgotten its noble birth from on high."[46] When he applied Christ's words, "Is not the soul more than meat and the body more than the raiment?"[47] from the Sermon on the Mount, he saw Christ's thrust as playing on the divine origin of the soul. "He therefore has given the greater, how shall He not give the less?"[48]   The human soul is a gift of great value from God and John exhorted his hearers to watch their souls as they would a virgin daughter. He saw folly in those who protected the daughter and allow their souls to fall victim to so many spiritual adulteries.[49]

God created people so that they would not be complete in themselves, but that they would be social beings. Our social nature is used by God for our advantage as our needs are met by one another.[50] The image of God in man also included the display of sovereignty in human affairs. This sovereignty is creative as men and women used the resources of God's creation to create in art and material culture. It also involves the exercise of authority in human government.[51]

The Fall

Before the first sin, Adam and Eve had unmarred communication with

God and enjoyed a life full of great blessing.[52] This changed with the first act of disobedience and the results of the first sin of Adam and Eve are upon all of us. However, we can not use our fallen nature as an excuse to multiply evil. Our rational capacity is not fallen.[53] Individual sins are not part of our nature. When John preached on Christ's words, "For if you, being evil, know how to give good gifts to your children, how much more your heavenly Father,"[54] he did not see the reference to evil in humanity as being absolute but comparative.

> Now this He said, not to bring an evil name on man's nature, nor to condemn our race as bad; but in contrast to His own goodness He calls paternal tenderness evil, so great is the excess of His love to man.[55]

The result of the Fall for the human race was physical death. John contrasted this condition as natural as opposed to the spiritual death that is by choice.

> There is, we know, a corporal, and there is a also a spiritual dying. On the first it is no crime to partake, nor is there any peril in it, inasmuch as there is no blame attached to it, for it is a matter of nature, not of deliberate choice. It has its origin in the transgression of the first--created man, and thence forward in its issue it passed into a nature, and, at all events, will quickly be brought to a termination; whereas this spiritual dying, being a matter a deliberate choice has criminality, and has no termination.[56]

Free Will

A key factor in John's understanding of synergism in salvation and his concept of human nature was his dogmatic stance against any form of fatalism.[57] The wrongful exercise of the individual will is the source of evil.

> "Whence then are evils?" one may say. From willing and not willing. "But the very thing of our willing and not willing, whence is it?" From ourselves. But you do the same in asking, as if when you have asked, whence is seeing and not seeing? then when I said from closing the eyes or not closing the eyes, you were to ask again; the very closing of the eyes or not, whence is it? Then

having heard that it was of ourselves, and our will, you were to look again for another cause.

For evil is nothing else than disobedience to God. ....

It is quite plain, and there is no one who would not say this. Wherefore I entreat you to be in earnest, and to cleave to virtue, and you will have no need of these questions. For our evils are mere names, if we be willing. Inquire not then whence are evils, neither perplex yourself; but having found that they are from remissness only, flee evil deeds. ....

But if evils were by nature, superfluous were all this admonition and advice, superfluous the precaution by the means that have been mentioned. But if it be not superfluous, as surely it is not superfluous, it is quite clear that wickedness is of the will.[58]

John had a difficult time articulating the cause of evil except by indicting the will and cautioning his congregation that they should not perplex themselves by tracing series of evils back to an ultimate source. However, he was confident that the key to living a godly life was in the will. The changing of the attitudes of the soul is not a matter of nature but a result of acts of the will.[59] Election is foreknowledge and the passages that speak of God's choice are interpreted by John in a way that does not contradict the assumed free will.[60] Even the crucifixion of Christ, which came according to the plan of God, did not violate the wills of all of the participants in His death. He acknowledges that the involvement was "mystical," but the Jews and Pilate were responsible for their actions.[61] Even when we fall victim to the wiles of the Devil, it is by our choice.[62] Even though we have mortal bodies as a result of the Fall, we are not compelled to sin. Sins are not sourced in our physical flesh but in our will.[63]

Neither are our good works done under compulsion. Even though the Apostle Paul might say that he was set apart from his mother's womb, his ministry was not one of compulsion.[64] Even though Christ might say to the

Twelve that they had not chosen Him but He had chosen them, their ministry was not without the free acts of their wills.[65]   After John cited these ministries in his fourth sermon in praise of the ministry of Paul, he reminded his audience "not [to] conclude from hearing this that the call was mandatory. God does not compel. He leaves men masters of their own will even after He calls them."[66]

The circumstances of life, whether riches or poverty, married or virgin do not limit our coming to God nor do they make one prone to sin.

> You have seen men approved in wealth, you have seen them in poverty also, you have seem them in marriage, you have seen them in virginity too; on the contrary behold some lost in marriage and virginity, in wealth and poverty. For example many men have perished in marriage as Samson, yet not from marriage, but from his own deliberate choice. Likewise in virginity, as the five virgins. In wealth, as the rich man, who disregarded Lazarus. in poverty, innumerable poor men even now are lost.   In a kingdom, I can point to many who have perished, and in ruling the people. Would you like to see men saved in the rank of soldier? There is Cornelius, and in the government of a household? There is the eunuch of the Ethiopian Queen. Thus is it universally. If we use our wealth as is fit, nothing will destroy us; but if not, all things will destroy us, whether a kingdom, or poverty, or wealth. But nothing will have power to hurt the man who keeps well awake.[67]

John then continued to cite examples of differing circumstances that did not limit people coming to God and acting in a godly manner. He cites Joseph, the three men in the fiery furnace, Daniel, Job, Lazarus, and Timothy.[68]

The Faith

Faith is not only the capacity to believe, but it also is the term used for the object of the Christian's belief. When John preached on the words from Hebrews, "hold firmly to the faith,"[69] he used the passage as a vehicle to enunciate the creedal content of his understanding of faith.

> What sort of profession does he mean? That there is a resurrection, that there is a retribution, there there are good things

innumerable, that Christ is God, that the Faith is right. These
things let us profess, these things let us hold fast.[70]

Belief in these truths served as a base for the Christian's relationship
with others as well as further growth in holiness. The fellowship that
Christians enjoy in the Body of Christ is built on the common faith that they
share.[71] It serves as the foundation for their further spiritual growth because
true belief is not overly curious but responds in obedience.[72] John regularly
used faith to describe both belief and the creedal content of the Christian's
profession.

Conversion

A changed life is a natural outgrowth of faith. Faith without this
change will not bring about salvation.

> Faith is indeed great and bringeth salvation and without it, it is
> not possible ever to be saved. It suffices not however of itself to
> accomplish this, but there is need of a right conversation also.
> So that on this account Paul also exhorts those who have already
> been counted worthy of the mysteries; saying "Let us labor." Faith
> not sufficing. The life also ought to be added, and our earnest-
> ness to be great; for truly there is need of much earnestness too,
> in order to go up into Heaven.[73]

Faith alone does not save. There will be many in Hell who had faith but did
not live a holy life.

> For though we have all faith and all knowledge of the Scriptures,
> yet if we be naked and destitute of the protection derived from
> holy living, there is nothing to hinder us from being hurried into
> the fire of hell and burning forever in the unquenchable flame.
> For as they who have done good shall rise to life everlasting, so
> they who have dared the contrary shall rise to everlasting
> punishment, which never has an end.[74]

Repentance and conversion are always possible. In his sixty-seventh homily
on Matthew, John instructed his audience that no one should ever despair
of the ability to change their life, "for it is an easy thing to rise up out of the
very abysses of wickedness."[75] He then cited with great detail the conversion

of a former prostitute from Phoenicia who would have been known to his congregation in Antioch. She had risen to fame on the stage and was known throughout Asia Minor. She destroyed many homes, stole fortunes, and "won even the brother of the empress."[76] But then she renounced her former life. John attributed this change to an act of her will. Her life of debauchery did not render her unable to repent and follow God.

> But all at once, I know not how, or rather I do know well, for it was being so minded, and converting, and bringing down upon herself God's grace, she despised all those things, and having cast away the arts of the devils, mounted up to heaven.[77]

John concluded her story by noting that she continued after baptism with "much self restraint" and did not allow herself to see her former lovers. She ended her days living among the dedicated virgins of the church.[78]

John's emphasis on the necessity of the works that reveal faith did not lead him to conclude that works alone mark the life of the true child of God. Faith and works together mark God's children.[79] There was also the need to be watchful of one's spirituality until death. John tied the account of the converted prostitute to Christ's words that the "last shall be first and the first shall be last" and reminded his audience that the will has the power to change lives for good or ill, and that they must live the Christian life until death.[80] John saw no place for one living a worldly life to be called a Christian. Those labelled "fleshly" by Paul in 1 Corinthians 3:1-3 were not "carnal believers" but unsaved. They were the same false followers Christ addressed in the words contained in Matthew's gospel, "Depart from Me, I never knew you."[81] He concluded with a solemn warning, "and yet they both cast out devils, and raised the dead, and uttered prophecies. So it is possible even for one who wrought miracles to be carnal."[82] For John, to be carnal was to be unsaved, and he cited as examples of carnal people Balaam, Pharaoh (the ruler in the time of the Patriarch Joseph who received dreams revealing the future), Nebuchadnezzar, and Caiaphas.[83]

John tempered the more absolute stand he usually took on the
necessity of good works for the salvation of the child of God when he
commented on the words of Hebrews 7:25-26 concerning the complete ability
of Christ to save those who come to Him as the great High Priest. He
allowed that it might be possible for a Christian to enter heaven without
good works, but this Christian will receive no rewards and his despondency
will be unbearable when he sees others rewarded.

> But let us suppose, if you will, that a man dies, after having done
> innumerable evil things, (which however I think does not really
> happen), tell me, how will he depart from here? Not indeed
> called to account for the deeds he had done but yet without
> confidence; as is reasonable. For when after living a hundred
> years, he has no good work to show, but only that he has not
> sinned, or rather not even this, but that he was saved by grace
> only, and when he sees others crowned in splendor, and highly
> approved: even if he fall not into hell, tell me, will he endure his
> despondency?[84]

Baptism

Baptism is necessary for salvation and is the event when the Holy Spirit
comes into the convert. Christ's baptism by John the Baptist foreshadowed
the Christian rite with the coming of the Spirit from heaven in the form of
a dove.[85] However, this was the only ministry of baptism by John that bears
this quality. The other baptisms he performed were devoid of the Spirit.[86]
Baptism was a solemn rite that began one's life in the Church, and the
Christian emerges from its waters as a new creature. When John explained
the rituals associated with the ceremony to those who were about to be baptized he reflected with emotion on his own baptism.

> Sacred custom bids you to remain on your knees, so as to
> acknowledge His absolute rule even by your posture, for to bend
> the knee is a mark of those who acknowledge their servitude.
> Hear what St. Paul says, "To Him every knee shall bend of those
> in heaven, on earth, and under the earth."[87] And after you have
> bent your knees, those who are initiating you bid you to speak

those words, "I renounce you, Satan."

Just now tears welled up in my eyes; my mind was confounded
and bitterly did I groan. Why did I mention that holy night on
which I was brought to the dreadful and holy initiation? I
remember my purity at that time and the sins I have piled up
from that day to this.[88]

The rite of baptism was a great responsibility of the priesthood.[89]
Those in this ministry were present at the moment of spiritual birth. John
realized that many in the priesthood were not worthy of this honor but the
unworthiness of the priest did not frustrate the working of God's grace in the
rite.[90]

Preparation for this initiatory rite was very important for John. Fasting
was a significant element of this preparation as well as the instruction given
to the catechumens before their initiation.[91] The liturgy of baptism was
another important aspect of the sacrament. The new children of God were
brought into the Body of Christ in a manner that was theologically significant
and instructive.[92] In John's mind, they shared the same ritual of entrance
that was used in the life of each generation of God's people as a sign of the
mystical unity in His Body, the Church.[93] The union of the new Christian
with the Spirit of God in baptism made this rite inseparable from faith and
conversion in the process of coming to Christ.[94] As a result of baptism, the
child of God was united with Christ.[95] Sins were removed by baptism.[96] It
was impossible to be saved without baptism and its spiritual benefits.[97] John
clearly made the point that the intention to be baptized is not enough. The
catechumen is unsaved; even just before the ceremony the uninitiated remains
an outsider to the Body of Christ.[98]

John was opposed to the practice of putting off baptism until near
death as was done to prevent losing its benefits through sins committed after
initiation.[99] Baptism under these circumstances was perverted. It should be
the beginning of a life in the Church in service of God. It should be a happy

event, but for those who put it off it was a sign of impending death.

> I not only count you blessed but I praise your good will, because, unlike men of laxity, you do not approach baptism at your final gasp....

> Even if the grace is the same for you and for those who are initiated on their deathbeds, neither the choice nor the preparations are the same. They receive baptism in their beds, but you receive it in the bosom of the common mother of us all, the Church; they receive baptism amidst laments and tears, but you are baptized with rejoicing and gladness; they are groaning, while you are giving thanks; their high fever leaves them in a stupor, while you are filled with an abundance of spiritual pleasure.[100]

John continued the discussion by comparing for his audience the scene in the Church with the initiates contemplating their future with that of the man on his deathbed looking at his children as orphans and his wife as a widow and his villa soon to be deserted. The entire scene was perverted- it was not one of joy but of despondency.[101] Baptism began a life of Spirit-empowered service for God and was not a final cleansing of the uninitiated for death.

1.Ad Theo 1,11.

2.In Rom 3,2. See also the discussion in Ludwig Ott, *Fundamentals of Catholic Dogma* (Rockford,Ill: Tan, 1960) 14; Pericles G. Vallianos, "The Attitude of the Three Hierarchs Towards Knowledge and Learning," *Greek Orthodox Theological Review* 24 (1979): 43f; Paul Harkins, *Saint John Chrysostom: On the Incomprehensible Nature of God* (Washington: Catholic University of America Press, 1984) 22f.

3.Ad vid jun 1f.

4.Ad vid jun 1.

5.Ad vid jun 1.

6.Ad vid jun 1 quoting Ps 136:9.

7.In Jn 10,1.

8.De Laz 6. Another example of God using evil events is seen in Adv Jud 5. John's views in this area is discussed in Yves Congar, *Lay People in the Church*. (Westminster, MD: Christian Classics, 1985) 439.

9.In Gen 3,15. (Hill. *Homilies on Genesis 1-17.* 46). When discussing the passage for Matthew's gospel in In Mat 79,2 it is clear that he equates any notion of divine election in this passages with divine foreknowledge. This is consistent with his understanding of other passages on the same subject in the New Testament.

10.In 1 Cor 39,11.

11.De laud s Paul 4.

12.In Rom 12.

13.In Mat 19,6. (NPNF 10, 134).

14.In Eph 2. (NPNF 13, 57).

15.Cat ill 2,2. The principles of synergism is also seen in In 2 Cor 6,3; In 1 Cor 3,6; 23,2; 42,5; In Acta 11,1; 36,3; In Mat 24,1; 33,3f; 41,6; 55,1; 78,3; 82,4; In Jn 10; In Rom 14,7; 19,1; and In Heb 12,3..

16.De laud s Paul 1. An excellent discussion of the balance between divine and human activity in John's understanding of salvation is contained in Ephrem Boularand, "La Venue de l'Homme à la Foi d'après Saint Jean Chrysostome." *Analecta Gregoriana* 18 (1939): 1-189.

17.In Eph 4; In Jn 6,fin; and In Acta 30,3.

18.John defined faith as needing to surpass reason in In Heb 21,4 and 22,1. Se also In Mat 8,1; and In Rom 2.

19.Heb. 4:11.

20.In Heb 7,1. (NPNF 14, 398).

21.In Phil 13,1. (Erickson. *Participating in Worship*. 173).

22.In Jn 7,1.

23.In Jn 14,1; 39,1; 52,4; 54,2; and In 1 Cor 29,4. For an overview of John's Christology see Frances M. Young, "Christological Ideas in the Greek Commentaries on the Epistle to the Hebrews." *Journal of Theological Studies* New Series 20 (1969): 150-63.

24.In Phil 7.

25.John 1:14.

26.In John 11,1. (NPNF 14, 38). See also John's comments in In Heb 16, 29, and 25. John's unwillingness to probe the mystery of the incarnation is discussed in C. Hay, "Antiochene Exegesis and Christology." *Australian Biblical Review* 12 (1964): 10-23. Robert Hill correctly notes that John saw the incarnation as a consummate expression of divine condescension or considerateness ("St. John Chrysostom and the Incarnation of the Word in Scripture." *Compass Theology Review* 14 (1980): 34-38).

27.In 1 Cor 24,4.

28.Passages which show John embracing a form of the Ransom from Satan theory include: In Jn 62,2; In Rom 13,5; and In Mat 54,7. Other passages on the atonement In Gal 2,8; In Heb 15,2; 17,2; In 2 Cor 11,3-4; In Eph 17,1; In Rom 10, 1-3; and In Jn 67, 2-3.

29.In Mat 54,6.

30.In Gal 2:20. John also taught that Christ died for the heathen in In 1 Tim 7. The power of the blood was taught to those about to be baptized in Cat ill 3,12f.

31.In Gal 3,5; In Mat 82,5 and In 1 Cor 24,2.

32.De sac 3,10.

33.Mat 16:24.

34.In Mat 55,1. (NPNF 10, 339).

35.Cat ill 2,9.

36.In Jn 10,2.

37.In Mat 65,2.

38."For even His love to man has a kind of proportion; depending on the faith of them that are healed." In Mat 32,1.

39.Is 43:26 LXX.

40.Ps 32:5 LXX.

41.Dan 4:27 LXX. In In Mat 78,1 John stated that the parable of Christ in Matthew, chapter twenty-five, "in different ways admonishing us about the same things. I mean about diligence in almsgiving, and about helping our neighbor by all means which we are able to use, since it is not possible to be saved in another way."

42.Ecclesiasticus 3:30 LXX.

43.In Jn 7,2. (NPNF 14, 29).

44.In 1 Cor 2,1.

45.In Jn 78,1. Other passages dealing with human nature in general include Ad pop Anti 11,2; In Gen 16,5; and 17,2.

46.Cat ill 1,5.

47.Matthew 6:25.

48.In Mat 21,3.

49.In Mat 42,4.

50.In John 19,1.

51.In Gen 3,9; 9,3-4; 16,5; 16, 5f; 8,4; Ad pop Anti 7,2; 11,12 In Rom 16; and In Heb 12.

52.In Mat 68,3.

53.In Jn 3,2; In 1 Cor 11,6.

54.Matthew 7:11.

55.In Mat 23,5. (NPNF 10, 161). He also uses this line of reasoning in In Eph 2. and In Mat 45,2.

56.In Eph 4,1. (NPNF 13, 65). John sees each human being as participating in Adam's sin in In Jn 36,2 and In Mat 31,4.

57.De diab tent 3,2 and In 1 Cor 22,7.

58.In Mat 59, 3-4. (NPNF 10, 366-367). Other passages where John speaks of the will as free include In Jn 5; 10; 45; 46; and In 1 Cor 2.

59.Cat ill 8. This is also taught in In Mat 45,2 when John seeks to show that Christ's teaching in parables did not nullify the free will of His hearers. In Cat ill 1,10 he taught new converts that the soul can be changed by choice. In Cat ill 1,15 he taught that Christians must bring "good will" into our relationship with Christ. Se also Cat ill 1,25; In 1 Cor 2,11; and 8,3. The willfulness of action in John's view of ethics is discussed in E.F. Bruck, "Ethics vs Law: Saint Paul, the Fathers of the Church, and the Cheerful Giver in Roman Law." *Traditio* 2 (1944): 97-98.

60.In Eph 2,1; In Col 4; In Phil 8; In 2 Cor 7,3; and In Rom 16.

61.In Jn 84,2.

62.De Laz 2.

63.In 1 Cor 17,5; Other passages where John concluded that we never act under compulsion include In Jn 10,3.

64.In Gal 1:15-16.

65.John 15:16.

66.De laud s Paul 4. (Halton. *In Praise of Saint Paul.* 55).

67.In Phil 12. (NPNF 13, 241).

68.In Phil 12.

69.Heb. 4:14.

70.In Heb 7,5. (NPNF 14, 399-400). Other passages where John taught the need for faith include In Jn 55,3; Cat ill 1,20; 11,15; and In Rom 8.

71.In Tit 1.

72.In Col 4; In Mat 9,6 and In 2 Tim 8. In In 1 Tim 1 John states, "for where faith is, there is no need of questions."

73.In Heb 7,1. (NPNF 14, 398). Another passage where John teaches the necessity of a changed life is In 2 Thess 4,2.

74.In Jn 6, fin. (NPNF 14, 27). Other passages where John teaches that faith alone does not save In Mat 47,3; 69,2; 81,5; and In 1 Cor 23,1.

75.In Mat 67,3.

76.In Mat 67,3.

77.In Mat 67,3. (NPNF 10, 412).

78.In Mat 67,3-4.

79.In Rom 8.

80.In Mat 67,4. He also spoke of the need to continue in the converted life in conjunction with faith in In Eph 4 and In Mat 46,3.

81.Mat 7:23.

82.In 1 Cor 8,2.

83.In 1 Cor 8,2.

84.In Heb 13,9. (NPNF 14, 431).

85.In Mat 2,3.

86.In Mat 12,4.

87.Phil. 2:10.

88.Cat ill 11,22-23. (Harkins. Baptismal Instructions. 167).

89.De Sac 3,5.

90.In Mat 8,2.

91.In Acta 1,6. The fasting lasted for 30 days and ended on Holy Thursday Cat ill 9,27; 11,1; 11,19.

92.The state of the baptismal liturgy in John's day and its treatment in his writings is discussed in Thomas Finn, *The Liturgy of Baptism in the Baptismal Instructions of Saint John Chrysostom* (Washington: Catholic University of America Press, 1967) 89f; H. Benedict Green, "The Significance of the Pre-Baptismal Seal in Saint John Chrysostom." *Studia Patristica* 6 (1962): 84-90; Paul Harkins, "Pre-Baptismal Rites in Chrysostom's Baptismal Catecheses." *Studia Patristica* 8 (1966): 219-238; Leonel A. Mitchell, "The Baptismal Rite in Chrysostom." *Anglican Theological Review* 43 (1961): 397-403; and Hugh Riley, *Christian Initiation* (Washington: Catholic University of America Press, 1974).

93.Cat ill 2,12f.

94.In Acta 1,5; 15.

95.In 2 Cor 3,7; 6,2; In Gal 3:5; Cat ill 1,1f; 3,5f; In Acta 1,8; and In 1 Cor 7,20.

96.In Eph 4; In Jn 27,1; 53,1; 73,3; Cat ill 3,17; 9,12; 9.21; 1,25; In Acta 1,6; 7,45; and In 1 Cor 40,2.

97.In 1 Cor 3,6.

98.In Jn 25,3; In 1 Cor 29,3; Cat ill 9,1; In Gen 12,1; In Heb 13,10; and In 2 Cor 2,6.

99.Most of Chrysostom's teaching about baptism presupposes adult converts receiving this sacrament. However, he did recognize infant and clinical baptism as well. Infant baptism was a growing phenomena but did not receive much attention in his preaching. Clinical baptism, often consciously put off until the candidate was near death, was condemned by John. Thomas Finn, *The Liturgy of Baptism in the Baptismal Instructions of Saint John Chrysostom* (Washington: Catholic University of America Press, 1967) 25.

100.Cat ill 9,4-5. (Harkins. *Baptismal Instructions*. 132-133). John also addresses this issue in In Heb 13,10; and In Acta 1,7.

101.Cat ill 9, 4-11 and 9,9 fin. John even questions if a person who is unconscious ("differing in no way from a corpse") derives any benefit from the rite.

CHAPTER 9
SINS IN THE LIFE OF THE CHRISTIAN

Spiritual Combat

After the initiatory rite of baptism, the Christian lives a life of spiritual combat. The new child of God is the target of the temptations and seductions of Satan and his allies, the demons and the fallen world system. When John taught the catechumens who were soon to enter this spiritual warfare, he used an extended athletic metaphor.[1] He likened the life of the catechumen to a training school for wrestling, but soon, after baptism, they would go forth to the arena of competition. Christ would be the judge, and heavenly rewards were the prizes in the combat.

> Up to now you have been in a school for training and exercise; the falls were forgiven. But from today on, the arena stands open, the contest is at hand, the spectators have taken their seats. Not only are men watching the combats but the hosts of angels as well, as St. Paul cries out in his letter to the Corinthians, "We have been made a spectacle to the world and to angels and to men".[2] And whereas the angels are spectators, the Lord of angels presides over the contest as judge. This is not only an honor for us, but assures our safety. Is it not an honor and assurance for us when He who is judge of the contest is the one who laid down His life for us?

> In the Olympic combats the judge stands impartially aloof for the combatants, favoring neither the one nor the other, but awaiting the outcome. He stands in the middle because his judgment is impartial. But in our combat with the Devil, Christ does not stand aloof but is wholly on our side.[3]

John continued the illustration, noting that Christ has bound the Devil but has anointed us for the contest. He has passed sentence on the Devil but has clothed us with the armor mentioned in the sixth chapter of Ephesians for spiritual warfare. The contest was further structured in our favor because if the Devil gains a victory he is further punished, while if Christians win they receive crowns from the Judge who is their Savior.[4]

Sins are acts of willful disobedience against God's standards. If people disobeyed because of ignorance, then God would not punish them.[5] Christians should be able to avoid sin after the graces of baptism, but, in fact, they do not.[6] When John reflected on his baptism he told the catechumens, "I remember my purity at that time and the sins which I have piled up from that day to this".[7] Post-baptismal sins were difficult for John to explain. As a result of the initiatory rite Christians are indwelt by God's Spirit but yet they sin and exercise their wills against the God who indwells them.[8] These sins must be confessed, and if they are not abandoned will become the source of consequences here on earth as well as when we meet God as our Judge.[9]

Sin blinds the mind and leads to magnified and multiple evils. People blinded by sin accelerate the evil in their lives. As John preached against prostitution he saw a link between sins from drunkenness to abortion.

> Wherefore I beseech you flee fornication, and the mother of it, drunkenness. Why sow where reaping is impossible, or rather even if you do reap, the fruit brings you great shame? For even if a child be born, it at once brings you disgrace and injustice is done to the child because it is born illegitimate and base.... Why then bring disgrace upon all these? Why sow where the ground makes it its care to destroy the fruit? Where there are so many efforts at abortion? Where there is murder before birth? For even the harlot you do not let continue a mere harlot but make her a murderer also. You see how drunkenness leads to whoredom, whoredom to adultery, adultery to murder; or rather to something even worse than murder. For I have no name to give it, since it does not take off the thing born but prevents its being born. Why then do you abuse the gift of God, and fight His laws, and follow after what is a curse as if a blessing, and make the chamber of procreation a chamber for murder, and arm the woman that was given for childbirth to slaughter.[10]

Dealing with sin in the Christian community is a grave responsibility of those in the priesthood. Pastoral discipline must be skillfully exercised.[11] The shepherd must aid God's people as they recover from their failings. This ministry is critical because God has provided means for recovery from sins. John exhorted the catechumens preparing for their baptism that if willing, they would be able to recover the purity experienced upon entering the Church when later in the Christian life they had sinned.[12] When John wrote to Theodore, later bishop of Mopsuestia, after he had set a course to abandon his vow of celibacy to God, John argued the possibility of repentance even from entangling sin. John wrote to Theodore after he had abandoned the ascetic brotherhood they shared, lived a worldly life for a season, and planned to marry Hermione. John cited the example of Urbanus the Phoenician who abandoned a life of monastic study and reassumed reckless luxury. Urbanus later repented and returned to his pious ways.[13]

Repentance

Repentance is the answer to sins in the life of the Christian. Repentance is turning away from a sinful act and not repeating it.[14] However, one can repent wrongly and not in submission to God, as did Judas when he took his life.[15] Repentance is the remedy for post-baptismal sins, because there is no second baptism for those who have already been initiated.[16] True repentance can wash away the stains of sin.[17] When John preached on the first three verses of the sixth chapter of Hebrews which exhorts readers to move on to maturity after laying a base in the elementary doctrines of Christ, he expounded his doctrine of repentance. In this exposition he spoke of the "medicine" of repentance. He taught his audience disciplines of piety that could bring them to the point where they would truly repent and abandon their sins.[18] The first medicine is the condemnation of our own sin. His homily is ambiguous whether this condemnation should be public.

> What then is the medicine of repentance? And how is it made up? First, of the condemnation of our own sins. "For mine iniquity I have not hid,"[19] and again, "I will confess against myself my lawlessness unto the Lord, and You forgave the iniquity of my heart." And "declare when you first sin that you may be just-

ified."[20]   And, "the righteous man is an accuser of himself at the first speaking."[21]

A second medicine of repentance is the maintenance of a humble spirit. The third is intense prayer. The fourth is almsgiving. John saw scriptural support for the role of charity in the gospels, "give alms and all shall be clean,"[22] and Proverbs, "by almsgiving and acts of faithfulness sins are purged away."[23]   He also saw support for this in Ecclesiasticus, "water will quench a flaming fire and alms will do away with great sins."[24]   The fifth vehicle of repentance is not being angry with anyone and forgiving those who wrong us. As John preached on the teaching of Christ in the Lord's Prayer, "forgive us our trespasses as we forgive those who trespass against us," he concluded that the Christian must forgive others in order to be forgiven.[25]   A sixth way in which true repentance is demonstrated is by being an agent of redemption seeking the conversion of others from their sins.[26]

John saw an essential unity in the process of purifying repentance. These six disciplines were vehicles toward true repentance, which was the changing of sinful behavior. They were also the marks of one who has truly repented, and they were acts of penance to earn forgiveness of post-baptismal sins. Passages where he supports this third aspect are seen in his homilies on Paul's epistle to the Ephesians. He told thieves to restore their thefts fourfold because this "pleads our cause to God."[27]   He was more explicit later in the series.

> Let us make our acts of mercy counterbalance them [burdens of sins]... far exceed them that not only the sins may be quenched but that the acts of righteousness may be accounted unto us for righteousness.[28]

For John, these three understandings of spiritual disciplines fused to undergird the primary point of application in most of these homilies. Christians must avoid acts of sin and lead a life of discipline and moderation that is pleasing to God. John's broad offer of forgiveness may have provoked some of the clergy against him in Constantinople, but he believed that Christians could recover from sin if they renounced their failing and bring themselves to a true change of their will.

1.Athletic metaphors and illustrations are numerous in John's writings. Athletic competition was the focus of civic pride and entertainment in Antioch and Constantinople. For a detailed treatment of this imagery in John's works see John Alexander Sawhill, *The Use of Athletic Metaphors in the Biblical Homilies of Saint John Chrysostom* (Princeton: The University Press, 1928) passim.

2.1 Cor. 4:9.

3.Cat ill 3,8-9. (Harkins. *Baptismal Instructions*. 58).

4.Cat ill 3,8-11.

5.In Rom 13,1; In Acta 10,1.

6.Cat ill 6,21.

7.Cat ill 11,23.

8.Their reality was acknowledged in passages such as In Jn 28,2 and their seriousness was taught to those about to be baptized in Cat ill 12,21.

9.De incomp die 5,56 and In Mat 14,5 are examples of this emphasis.

10.In Rom 24. (NPNF 11, 520).

11.De sac 2,4.

12.Cat ill 5,24f; 6,23.

13.Ad Theo 1,17.

14.The key element in John's understanding of repentance is not doing the sin again. This alone is true repentance. In Jn 34,3; In Mat 10,7; and In 1 Cor 23,6 fin.

15.In Heb 31,4.

16.In Eph 5; Cat Ill 3,23; In Heb 9,8; 10,1.

17.In Heb 9,8; In Acta 1,7.

18.In Heb 9,8. He gives a similar list of "remedies" which can effect salvation in In Mat 41,6 fin. The list in In Mat includes "alms, prayer, compuncture, repentance, humility, a contrite heart, and contempt of possessions."

19.Ps 32:5.

20.Is 43:26.

21.Prov 18:17. In Heb 9,8. (NPNF 14, 411-412). John also discusses this vehicle to repentance in In Mat 14,5; 41,6; In 1 Cor 23,6; 28,2; and Ad Theo 1,19; 2,1.

22.Luke 11:41.

23.Prov 16:6.

24.Ecclus 3:30. John also advocated almsgiving in this light in In Mat 50,5; 78,1; In Acts 25, 2-3; and In 1 Cor 23,6. In Acts 22,3 he cited the bringing of Peter to Cornelius' household by God as evidence of the power of almsgiving. In In Jn 73,2 he taught that almsgiving wipes away the filthiness caused by sins.

25.In Mat 19,9; 23,2; and In 1 Cor 23,6.

26.In Heb 30,6; In Mat 59,6.

27.In Eph 18. (NPNF 13, 136). Another possible mention of penance is In Eph 4. Keane is most probably correct when he concluded the public confession of sin before the congregation was not envisioned by Chrysostom when he taught on the subject ("The Sacrament of Penance in Saint John Chrysostom." *The Irish Theological Quarterly* 14 (1919): 313-314). The issue is also discussed in P. Martain, "Saint Jean Chrysostome et la Confession." *Revue Augustinenne* 6 (1907): 460-462. An excellent summary of John's theology of repentance and the various means of repentance and the necessity of a reformed will turning away from sin is contained in James L. Travis, "Confession and the Penitential System in John Chrysostom." M.A. thesis. Southern Baptist Seminary, 1964. An overview is given in Oscar D. Watkins *A History of Penance* (New York: Burt Franklin, 2 vols. 1961) I, 330-361.

28.In Eph 24. (NPNF 13, 172).

CHAPTER 10
THE CHURCH

Images of the Church

In one of his homilies to those new in the faith, perhaps even the same day as their baptism, John painted an intimate picture of the relationship of the atoning work of Christ to the Church. He directed his audience to the scene of Christ on the cross when the soldier pierced his side and water and blood flowed forth. He saw the water as a symbol of baptism and the blood as a symbol of the Eucharist.[1] John also saw further symbolism in this event.

> There came out from His side water and blood. Beloved, do not pass this mystery by without a thought. For I have still another mystical explanation to give. I said that there was a symbol of Baptism and the mysteries in that blood and water. It is from both of these that the Church is sprung through the bath of regeneration and renewed by the Holy Spirit, through baptism and the mysteries. But the symbols of baptism and mysteries come from the side of Christ. It is from His side, that Christ formed His church, just as He formed Eve from the side of Adam.[2]

In addition to being the Body of Christ in this vivid way, the Church is represented by many other images in John's works.[3] It was the pharmacy of the spirit where those who are ill can come for remedy.[4] The Church was also Christ's army, and those who were about to be baptized were recruits for this spiritual force. Unlike the armies of the empire, the soldier did not need to be a free man because Christ called slaves as well as the free and those who are old and sick serve as well.[5] When Eutropius the fallen leader sought sanctuary in the church, John used this vivid illustration of the church as a place of sanctuary when he rose to preach.

> "Vanity of vanities, all is vanity." It is always seasonable to utter this but more especially at the present time. Where are now the brilliant surroundings of the consulship? Where are the gleaming torches? Where is the dancing, and the noise of dancer's feet,

and the banquets and the festivals? Where are the garlands and
the curtains of the theatre? Where is the applause which greeted
you in the city? Where the acclamation in the hippodrome and
the flatteries of spectators? They are gone, all gone.... Where
are your feigned friends? Where is the swarm of parasites, and
the wine which used to be poured forth all day long and the
manifold dainties invented by your cooks? Where are they who
courted your power and did and said everything to win your
favor?

And the Church which you treated as an enemy has opened her
bosom and received you into it; whereas the theatres which you
courted and about which you were often times indignant with me
have betrayed and ruined you.... But the Church which experienced your untimely wrath is hurrying in every direction in
her desire to pluck you out of the net.[6]

John later related how the emperor told the soldiers who wanted to kill
the fallen consul that he had fled to the church and sought its sanctuary. In
this way the emperor appeased their anger and ended the search for him.[7]
Eutropius later left the sanctuary and was beheaded, but the church he
bullied while in power fought to preserve his life when the politics of the
capital city turned against him.

The Church was also the spiritual mother of the faithful, bringing them
to birth in Christ and nurturing them in their faith.[8] The catechumens were
exhorted to pray for her at their baptism. John saw himself and the Church
as having been stained by the impurity of post-baptismal sins. These
catechumens who were about to enter the bath of regeneration should pray
in their baptismal purity for those who had compromised their spirituality
with acts of rebellion against God.[9] The Church was the mother of all of the
faithful and contained the saints of the Old and New Covenants.[10]

The Laity

Three emphases are found in the Chrysostom corpus concerning the
laity. He exalted virginity and the monastic calling but often remarked that

the monks lived away from the temptations of daily life and might not excel as bishops and priests.   They were away from the primary life of the Church.[11] The Christians living out their lives in the cites and towns, raising families, working in society were the front line of spiritual warfare.

The laity also played important roles in the Body of Christ. An obvious point was that the eternally significant ministries of the teacher and priest would be impossible without the laity. This was part of a general theme in John that those who were ministered to were essential to those who ministered, because they were God's vehicle to provide the opportunity to give eternal service.[12]

Finally, the laity served as advisors to bishops.[13] An important aspect of this function was seen in *On the Priesthood* in the events surrounding John's fleeing the priesthood and Basil's ordination when a council of the laity was the selector for clerical office.[14]

The Bishop

The bishop was the leader of the church, and as he maintained the unity and discipline of the flock he was a figure of Christ the Shepherd. During John's years as priest in Antioch he made note of the absence of Bishop Flavian when travel in the service of the Church prevented him from attending the divine service.

> What is this I see? The shepherd is not here and still his sheep
> show a well disciplined attitude. And this marks the pastoral
> success and virtue of the shepherd when, whether he is present
> or away, his flocks display complete earnestness and attention.[15]

Preserving the Unity of the Flock. Part of the mission of the bishop was to preserve the unity of the flock. The church in Antioch was not united in the years of John's priesthood there. The party of Paulinus was at odds with Bishop Flavian who succeeded Meletius in 381. Meletius was exiled by the Arian Emperor Constantius in 360 soon after he preached an inaugural sermon demonstrating Trinitarian orthodoxy. When he returned to his see under the amnesty of the Emperor Julian the response of the other leading sees was mixed. Athanasius of Alexandria was opposed to him, but he had the support of Basil, bishop of Caesarea. Some of the supporters of Bishop Eustantius of Antioch (c.324-330) suspected the orthodoxy of Meletius and elected Paulinus as a rival bishop in 362. This rival party had the support of the bishop of Rome and it was to this party that Jerome allied himself when he was in Antioch. It may be that their allegiance to difference parties in Antioch at formative stages in their careers led, in part, to Jerome's role as a supporter of the later efforts by Bishop Theophilus of Alexandria to depose John and discredit him among the Western churches.[16]

In John's exposition of Paul's admonition on factionalism to the Corinthian church in the first century, he recognized the differences between factions within the church and heretics, seeing the latter as differing from the true church in areas of doctrine.[17] In this homily and the fifty-ninth on Matthew, he exhorted from Christ's teaching that there would be great punishment to those through whom division entered the community. John lamented the offense to the cause of Christ that divisions within the community of Christians brought.[18] In *On the Priesthood*, he also lamented the scandalous scenes at the election of bishops, which also tore at the church's unity.[19]

John saw the schism in the church at Antioch as being caused by the secession of the party of Paulinus. In the eleventh homily on Ephesians, he pointed out that being orthodox is not enough.

> Tell me, do you think that this is enough, to say that they are orthodox? Is then the ordination of clergy past and done away? And what is the advantage of other things, if this be not strictly observed? For as we need to contend for the faith, so must we for this also. For if it is lawful for anyone, according to the phrase of them of old, "to fill his hands,"[20] and to become a priest, let all approach to minister.[21]

As he continued in the homily, John asked the rhetorical question, "If they have the same doctrines, if the same mysteries, wherefore does a ruler of one church invade another?" He answered that the root cause is pride.[22] After condemning their rival clergy, he noted that the complaint of the sect of Paulinus against Meletius and his followers was that forgiveness for sin and restoration was more easily granted in the Meletian church.[23] It was the charge of being too ready to grant forgiveness that was raised against John at the Synod of the Oak later in Constantinople. As noted earlier, Jerome gave support to Theophilus in his machinations against John. It may very well be that either the charge followed John to Constantinople through the agency of Jerome who was associated with Paulinus during this period or that John's association with Meletius left him open to this charge later in his ministry.

Another challenge to the bishop as he maintained the unity of the church was the false doctrines of the heretics. John saw heresy as a perversion that followed revealed truth. It was the tares sown in among the wheat in Christ's parable of Matthew, chapter 13.[24] The true Christian should avoid contact with heretics and pray for them to be delivered from the deceit of the Devil.[25] John organized parades against the Arians, seeking to use a means the Arians used among their supporters, to rally the orthodox community.[26]

Leading the Ministry of the Church. In addition to the role of preserving the unity of the church, John also saw the bishop as leading the church in its ministry. A primary aspect of this role was the unity and leadership seen in the divine liturgy.

The liturgy during John's ministry had two focuses, the ministry of the Word and the sacrament of the Eucharist. Neither was celebrated at the expense of the other. The participation of the Christian in the body of Christ in the Eucharist was a moment of solemn dread and awesome wonder for John. His words to Basil are characteristic of his thought.

For when you see the Lord sacrificed, and laid on the altar, and the priest standing and praying over the victim, and all the worshipers empurpled with the precious blood, can you then think that you are still among men and standing on the earth? Are you not, on the contrary immediately translated to heaven, and casting out every carnal thought from the soul, do you not with disembodied spirit and pure reason contemplate the things that are in Heaven? Oh! what a marvel! what love of God to man! He that sits on high with the Father is at that hour held in the hands of all, and gives Himself to those who are willing to embrace and grasp.[27]

John's realistic understanding of the sacrament was a consistent theme in his preaching about this Christian mystery.[28] The presence of Christ in the elements was so real for John that he did not shrink from saying that Christ drank His own blood at the initiation of the sacrament.[29] Although he used sacrificial language to refer to the mystery, he proclaimed the historic sacrifice of Christ on Calvary and saw the sacrament as the Christian sharing in that sacrifice.[30] The sharing was both a proclamation and a participation.[31] He mentioned on one occasion that it was a daily sacrifice.[32] On another he said that it was celebrated three times per week.[33] When the believer participated in the sacrament, he attained a mystical unity with Christ who was present in the elements.[34] This mystical unity formed the basis for the unity that was to take place in the church. Sacramental unity was the basis for organizational unity. John even saw unity as part of the purpose for this mystery.

For indeed there are many things to bind us together. One table is set before all, one Father begat us, we are the issue of the same birthpains, the same drink has been given to all; or rather not only the same drink but also the same cup. For our Father desiring to lead us to a kindly affection, has devised this also, that we should drink out of one cup; a thing which belongs to intense love.[35]

An event so central to the life of the Christian as this sacrament of proclamation, participation, and unity must not be approached unworthily. Both the celebrant and the communicant must be pure in heart at its celebration.

> These things I say to you that receive and to you that minister. For it is necessary to address myself to you, also, that you may, with much care, distribute the gifts there. There is no small punishment for you, if being conscious of any wickedness in any man, you allow him to partake of this table. "His blood shall be required at your hands."[36] ....

> Let no one communicate who is not of his disciples. Let no Judas receive, lest he suffer the fate of Judas. This multitude also is Christ's body. Take heed, therefore, you that minister at the mysteries, lest you provoke the Lord, by purging his body. Give not a sword instead of meat.[37]

Before the Christian approached the table of the mysteries he should have prepared himself and cleansed his heart by fasting, praying, alms, and repenting of his sin.[38]

There were some who left the service after the preaching of the word and before the sacrament. They were criticized for abandoning the sacrament and John admonished them from the pulpit not to leave before it was celebrated.[39]

The church calendar was in a significant phase of its development during John's ministry. When he preached in Antioch on Pentecost in 386 he mentioned only three Christian holidays: Epiphany, Easter, and Pentecost.[40] In another homily he noted the celebration of the Ascension.[41] He referred to Epiphany as the celebration of the appearance of God on earth and this celebration focussed on the incarnation generally and the central event was the baptism of Christ and the commencement of his ministry.[42] Easter was referred to as "the feast of salvation on the Day of Resurrection."[43] The season of Lent was a time of fasting and preparation for the celebration of the Christian "Pasch," including the final preparation of the catechumens for baptism.

> You did not need exhortation and advice during the holy season of Lent as much as you need it now. During that season the

practice of fasting made you be temperate, even in spite of yourselves; but now I am afraid and I fear the freedom from this obligation and the relaxation which it produces. Human nature is inclined to nothing so harmful as ease.[44]

A key development in the church calendar during John's ministry was the spread of the celebration of Christmas as a separate festival from Epiphany. When Chrysostom preached on Christmas at Antioch in 386 he began by noting that the holiday had been celebrated by the congregation at Antioch for less than ten years.[45] He stated that the date of the census mentioned in the Gospels was known from the archives in Rome, and the church in Rome was the first to institute the celebration of the birth of Christ. From there it spread rapidly throughout the churches. He cited three evidences for the correctness of the date: its rapid acceptance, the availability of the proof of the date in the Roman archives, and thirdly the fact that Zacharias was in the "Holy of Holies," which would have only have been allowed in September on the Day of Atonement. So the appearance to Mary six months later was in March and the birth of Christ nine months later would have been in December.[46] Although the third line of reasoning is spurious, as Zacharias was not the High Priest who would serve uniquely on the Day of Atonement, the appeal to Roman archives indicated both the surety of John on the issue and may have justified, for him, the spread of the observance.[47]

There were numerous feasts dedicated to the memory of the martyrs on the church calendar in John's day, as he acknowledged in his introduction to his series of homilies of Romans. The epistles of Paul are read on these "memorials of the holy martyrs ... twice every week, and often three or four times."[48]

The Church Offices

In addition to presiding over the worship of the Church, the bishop presided over its hierarchy. As John pointed out when he preached on the ministry of Stephen in Acts 6, ordination gave the officer greater access to the Spirit.

> See how even among the seven one was preeminent and won the prize. For though ordination was common to him and them, yet he drew upon himself greater grace. And observe how he wrought no signs and wonders before this time, but only when he became publicly known; to show that grace alone is not sufficient, but there must be ordination also; so that there was a further access of the Spirit.[49]

Because ordination conveyed such awesome responsibility there was great weight put upon the those who selected and ordained clergy.[50] John complained about simony in the obtaining of clerical offices, and it was an investigation into these practices in the region of Ephesus during his tenure in Constantinople that alienated many of the clergy against him.

The responsibility of the bishop in the supervision of the hierarchy of the church was complicated by the size of those supported by the church in addition to actual officers. During John's tenure at Antioch there were 3,000 widows on the church roles.[51]

As John interpreted the New Testament passages on polity he integrated their teaching with the situation in his day. He assumes a distinction between bishops (overseers) and presbyters (elders) that does not seem to arise in the text.[52] He saw James as having already received, evidently from Christ, the "Bishopric of Jerusalem" and marked his modesty at not speaking at Pentecost.[53] John's words on the responsibilities and accountability of a bishop in his third homily on Acts, preached while he occupied the bishopric in the capital city, are among the most sobering in his sermons.

> Don't you know that the Bishop is bound to belong to all, to bear the burden of all; that others, if they are angry are pardoned, but he never, that others, if they sin, have excuses made for them, he has none....

He is harassed with cares every day and night. He has many to hate him, many to envy him...

The paupers and beggars abuse him openly in the marketplace.

Either, perhaps, I am a poor, wretched, incompetent creature, or else, the case is as I say.

I speak not otherwise than it is, but as I find it in my own actual experience. I do not think there are many among bishops that will be saved, but many more that perish...

And then, others do wrong, and he bears all of the blame. To pass over everything else, if one soul departs unbaptized, does not this subvert all his own prospect of salvation? The loss of one soul carries with it a penalty which no language can represent. For if the salvation was of such value, that the Son of God became a man and suffered so much, think how sore a punishment must be the losing of it bring! And if in this present life he who is the cause of another's destruction is worthy of death, much more in the next world. Do not tell me that the presbyter is at fault or the deacon. The guilt of all these comes upon the head of those who ordained them....

I mean, that even if you have sinned, but in your own person merely, you will have no such great punishment, nothing like it: but if you sin as a bishop, you are lost. Remember what Moses endured, what wisdom he displayed, what good deeds he exhibited, but for committing one sin only, he was bitterly punished and with good reason; for this fault was attended with injury to the rest. Not in regard that the sin was public, but because it was the sin of the spiritual ruler...

But the bishop cannot sin unobserved.

However, if it happen to any of you to fall into sin, just stand by my bedside, when I am laid down to rest and should be asleep; see whether I am not like a palsied man, like one beside himself, and, in the language of the prophet, "the light of mine eyes, it also is gone from me."[54] For where is our hope, if you do not make progress? Where our despondency, if you do excellently? I seem to have wings, when I hear any good of you. "Fulfill my joy."[55] This one thing is the burden of my prayers, that I long for your advancement. But that in which I strive with all is this, that I love, that I am wrapped up in you, that you are my all, father, mother, brothers, children. Think not then that any thing that has been said was said in a hostile spirit, no, it is for your amendment.[56]

This great responsibility was not given by God without great power. The throne on which John sat as Archbishop of Constantinople had greater power than that of Moses for it was the throne of Christ.[57] From this throne he threatened to withhold the Eucharist from the city if swearing was not eliminated from the marketplace.[58]

Closely tied to his view of the bishop was his view of the priest. The bishop's role significantly diverged from the role of the priest only where the church's hierarchy had grown to accommodate the large numbers of Christians or the complexity of ministry in the urban setting. The priests of the Old Testament were seen as models for the priests of the church.[59] In this light the exclusion of women seemed natural.[60] The divine call of the priest must never be forgotten and in the selection of those for the office men must view themselves as coworkers with God in the selection process. Even though his day lacked some of the vehicles for supernatural revelation seen in the Scriptures, God's Spirit was still at work in the selection process.[61] As with the bishop, the awesome responsibility of the office loomed significantly in John's teaching. The priest must minister at the Eucharist; he was also privileged to be at the spiritual birth of members of his flock at baptism; and his ministry brought the forgiveness of sins to his people.[62]

In addition to his sacramental duties, the priest was also responsible for the spiritual health of his flock, and he must visit them regularly to inspect the fruit of his ministry.[63] Because of the intimate knowledge of the spiritual condition of his charges and his status as leader in the Christian community, the priest was also called upon to decide disputes among the people. John viewed this as among the most hazardous duties of the office.[64]

The offices of deacon and deaconess were significant elements of the Church's hierarchy in John's era, in part because the Church was greatly involved in social programs in both Antioch and Constantinople. These offices were also a stepping stone for men in the clerical hierarchy. For women, the office of deaconess was an important path of liberation from the roles reserved for them in the family structure of that era. John was inconsistent as to whether the deaconate began with the appointments of Stephen and the others as recorded in the sixth chapter of Acts.[65] He also viewed deacons as inferior to the apostles and prophets and evangelists.[66]

The office of deaconess was part of a significant social phenomena in the late fourth and early fifth centuries. Female celibacy was a liberating force in John's era. It freed women from early forced marriages and gave them some equality with men in the service of the Church. In female monastic communities there was also a chance for some autonomy.[67] John held a view of marriage that gave a subservient role to the wife.[68] However, among the celibate and as deaconess women found equality to men in ministry.[69] The deaconess Olympias was one of the key figures in the hierarchy of the church at Constantinople.[70] Olympias was a wealthy woman widowed at twenty years old. Her grandfather rose from obscurity to be military governor of the capital city and consul in 331. Her father and husband were also high-ranking officials. After the premature death of her husband she resisted the wishes of the Emperor Theodosius to procure her as a wife for a relative and vowed celibacy. She was ordained a deaconess a few years before John came to Constantinople as Archbishop in 398.[71] When John came to the city he found in her a soulmate and supporter. They both were raised in the upper class and sought to combine a commitment to the ascetic life with ministry in the city. Olympias founded a community of celibate women in the capital city, which numbered about 250.

An indicator of her status in society was that fifty of the sisters were her former servants.[72] She also opened a place for visiting clergy to stay while in the capital city and provided for their needs at her own expense.[73] We can get a picture of her relationship with John from the seventeen extant letters that he wrote to her during the three-year exile that preceded his death. He said that her good deeds for the faithful were as numerous as the waves of the sea and that she bore suffering-much of it caused by her loyalty to the deposed John- with a beautiful crown of patience.[74] The relationship revealed by the correspondence was closer than John had with any of the clergy, and her loyalty to him when he fell from favor showed a closeness that transcended any fidelity to him as Archbishop. These letters reveal a similarity of purpose and understanding of the Christian life that belied the great difference that John preached separated the sexes.[75]

John's view of women in the service of the church in his day was also seen in his laudatory exhortations to his congregation based on the Pauline praises for women in ministry in the last chapter of his letter to the Christians at Rome.[76] The ministry of deaconesses in John's era can also be seen in the declarations of the *Apostolic Constitutions*. Deaconesses assisted the clergy in the baptism of women in order to preserve modesty. They also taught women and were sent to serve women in households when the service of a deacon would have been a source for temptation and rumor.[77] John's use of deaconesses may be tied to the same sentiments that caused him to reject strongly the practice of the cohabitation of male and female celibates.[78] There was a great need in the Church to preserve modesty in relations between the sexes. Christians must remain above reproach. Their conduct must both not produce temptations for themselves and scandal among the pagans, discrediting the cause of Christ.

Another indicator of the status of deaconesses in the eastern churches was that their ordination was traced to the authority of the Apostle Bartholomew who took the Gospel to India.[79] Following the apostolic injunction to the bishops to ordain deaconesses is a prayer prescribed for the rite.

> O eternal God, the Father of our Lord Jesus Christ, the Creator of man and of woman, who did fill with the Spirit Miriam, and Deborah, and Anna, and Huldah, who did not deem unworthy that you only-begotten Son should be born of a woman, who also in the tent of witness and in the Temple ordained women as keepers of your holy gates: now look upon this your servant who is being ordained as a deaconess, and give her the Holy Spirit, and purify her from any defilement of the flesh and spirit, so that she may worthily accomplish the work entrusted to her and to your glory and the praise of your Christ, with whom to you and to the Holy Spirit be glory and adoration forever. Amen.[80]

The Primacy of Peter

The view of Peter that emerges from John's sermons was one of respect and certainly forms part of the base for his view of Roman primacy. Peter was seen as the leader of the apostles.[81] He also justified Peter's observance of the law and saw Paul's dispute with him recorded in Galatians, chapter two, as a staged event for the teaching of those present.[82]

After his exile in correspondence with Innocent I, bishop of Rome, Chrysostom recognized the unique position of the bishop of Rome. However, the letter was also addressed to the bishops of Milan and Aquileia, and the request in the letter was to convene a synod that would vindicate him of the charges he believed were falsely levelled against him.[83] Also, during his reign in Constantinople John achieved the reconciliation of Flavian, Bishop of Antioch, to the see of Rome ending the schism in Antioch that had lasted for about four decades.[84]

1.Cat ill 3,16. For a discussion of the dating of this sermon as an Easter homily see Harkins. *Baptismal Instructions*. 11-12. An overview of John's views concerning the Church is contained in P. Rancillac, *L'Église Manifestation de l'Esprit chez Saint Jean Chrysostome* (Beyrouth: Dar al-Kalima, 1970).

2.Cat ill 3,17. (Harkins. *Baptismal Instructions*. 62).

3.Other passages where the Church is seen as the Body of Christ include: In Eph 11,5; In 1 Cor Arg; In Mat 54,2; In Il Vidi dom 4,2; and In 1 Tim 11,1. The church is seen as a pure body in In 2 Tim 6. For more complete discussions of this usage of the Body of Christ concept by Chrysostom see Delores Greeley, "The Church as 'Body of Christ' According to the Teaching of Saint John Chrysostom." (Ph. D. diss. The University of Notre Dame, 1971) and Thomas Halton, "Some Images of the Church in Saint John Chrysostom." *American Ecclesiastical Review* 153 (1965): 96-106.

4.In Gen 1,3.

5.Cat ill 12,30.

6.In Eut 1,1. (NPNF 9, 249).

7.In Eut 1,4.

8.Cat ill 4,1; Adv Jud 3,6,1.

9.Cat ill 11,30.

10.In Eph 10 and In 1 Thess 4. In In Eph 10,1 John indicated that he believed that the saints before Christ knew Him as Messiah citing as evidence Christ's comment contained in John 8:56 that Abraham saw His day and His words recorded in John 5:46 that Moses wrote of Him. (NPNF 13, 99).

11.In Heb 7,4; In Gen 21,6; In Mat 7,7 ; De sac 6,5; In 2 Cor 18,3. Yves Congar, *Lay People in the Church*. (Westminster, MD: Christian Classics, 1985), 227.

12.In Acta 37,3 John applied this principle to the laity - clergy relationship.

13.In 2 Cor 18,3. Yves Congar, *Lay People in the Church*. (Westminster, MD: Christian Classics, 1985), 250.

14.De sac 1,6.

15.De incomp die 1,1. (Harkins. *On the Incomprehensible Nature of God.* 51). There is also a similar notice of Flavian's absence in In Kal 1.

16.It should be noted that Jerome mentioned John as a presbyter in Antioch before his elevation to the see of Constantinople in his *De Viris Illustribus*, chapter 129. He noted that John was the author of many books but that he has only read *De Sacerdotio* (On the Priesthood). Baur concludes that Jerome and Cl rysostom probably knew each other during this period of their lives. (C. Baur, "Saint Jerome et Saint Jean Chrysostome." *Revue Benedictine* 23 (1906): 430)

17.In 1 Cor 27,3. John displayed a similar attitude toward the protopaschites, those who dated Easter on the basis of the Jewish calendar as opposed to the system of reckoning adopted by the rest of the Christian community (Adv Jud 3,1f). The thrust of this homily is particular and of the series in general is not against the Jewish community but rather Christians with Judaizing tendencies. Paul Harkins notes this in his translation of the series (*Saint John Chrysostom: Discourses Against Judaizing Christians*. Washington: Catholic University of America Press, 1979. Introduction I,14f p. xxvii) See also Margaret A. Schatkin's comments on the homily in the introduction to her translation of this particular homily. ("Saint John Chrysostom's Homily on the Protopaschites: Introduction and Translation." *Orientalia Christiana Analecta*. 195 (1973): 167-172.).

18.In Mat 59,1.

19.De sac 3,15. Most of the third book is devoted to the issue of pride and the temptations of the political aspects of church office.

20.Probably an allusion to Ex. 29:9.

21.In Eph 11. (NPNF 13, 107).

22.In Eph 11.

23.In Eph 11.

24.In Mat 46,1. The historian Socrates mentioned that John deprived various heretical groups of the use of churches during his episcopal reign in Constantinople (*Ecclesiastical History* 6,19).

25.De incomp die 2,55.

26.Sozomen. *Ecclesiastical History* 8,8. See also the discussion in Thomas Cuming Hall, *History of Ethics Within Organized Christianity* (New York: Charles Scribner's Sons, 1910) 232.

27.De sac 3,4. (NPNF 9, 46).

28.Examples of this theme are numerous in the Chrysostom corpus and include De prod Jud 1,6; In Mat 82,5 In Eph 3,4; In Jn 46,3; In Rom 8,8; De b Phil 28; De sac 3,4; In 1 Cor 24,1; and Adv Jud 3,4,3.

29.In Mat 82,1.

30.In Heb 17,3.

31.Adv Jud 3,4,3-4.

32.In Eph 3.

33.Adv Jud 3,4,3. In In Eph 3,4 and De incomp die 3,32 Chrysostom complained that no communicant was present and the church was empty when the daily sacrifice was offered. But perhaps this was for rhetorical emphasis because in In Mat 50,3 he said that the Eucharist was "so to say" celebrated each day. In In 1 Tim 5,3 and Adv Jud 3,4 he stated that the mysteries were celebrated on Friday, Saturday, and Sunday. See also the discussion in Hans Lietzmann, *From Constantine to Julian* (New York: Charles Scribner's Sons, 1950) 298.

34.In 1 Cor 24,2; In 1 Tim 15,4; and In Mat 82,5.

35.In Mat 32,10. (NPNF 10, 217-218).

36.Ez 33:8.

37.In Mat 82,6. (NPNF 10, 496). Other passages where he warns against taking the Eucharist lightly include In 1 Cor 27,4; 28,4; and In Eph 3.

38.De b Phil 36.

39.In Eph 3,4; De incomp die 3,6.

40.De san pent 1, 1-2. The pouring out of the Spirit at Pentecost was an indication of the power that the Spirit could have in God's people in any age. Chrysostom wrestled with the lack of spiritual power both in charismatic manifestations and powerful dedicated lives. (Boris Bobrinskoy, "L'ésprit du Christ dans les sacraments chez Jean Chrysostome et Augustine."In *Jean Chrysostome et Augustine* (Paris: éditions Beauchesne, 1975), 256-257.

41.De b Phil 24.

42.De san pent 1, 1-2. He also refers to Epiphany in this light in In Eph 3 and De b Phil 24. Hans Lietzmann. *From Constantine to Julian* (NY: Charles Scribner's Sons, 1950) 315.

43.Cat ill 6,1. See also discussion in Michel Aubineau, "Les Homelies Pascales de Saint Jean Chrysostome" In *Symposium*, 112-119. (Thessaloniki: Patriarchal Institute for Patristic Studies, 1973.) passim.

44.Cat ill 5,15. (Harkins. *Baptismal Instructions*. 86). The season of Lent receives similar mention in In Eph 3; Cat Ill 6,1; and Adv Jud 3,4,3.

45.In diem nat 1.

46.In diem nat, passim.

47.See also the discussions in R.V. Schoder, "Saint Chrysostom and the Date of Christ's Nativity." *Theological Studies* 3 (1942): 140-144. and J.E. Bickersteth, "Hyopante: Studies in the Festival of the Purification of Saint Mary the Virgin in the early Byzantine Church." (D. Phil. diss. Oxford University, 1952).

48.In Rom arg,1.

49.In Acta 15,1. (NPNF 11, 94).

50.De sac 4,1.

51.In Mat 66,2.

52.In 1 Tim 11 and 13 are examples of this tendency. He deals with the plural in Phil 1:1 by equating presbyter to bishops but reads his own view of the hierarchy into the passage (In Phil 1).

53.In Acta 3,2.

54.Ps. 38:10.

55.Phil 2:2.

56.In Acta 3,4-5. (NPNF 11, 22-23). John also spoke much earlier in his career about the gravity of the responsibility that a shepherd of souls incurred before God in De sac 4,9.

57.In Col 3; In Acta 8,3.

58.In Acta 8,3.

59.Jaroslav Pelikan, *The Emergence of the Catholic Tradition (100-600)* (Chicago: The University of Chicago Press, 1971) 25.

60.De sac 3,9.

61.In 1 Tim 5.

62.De sac 2,4; 3,4-7.

63.De sac 3,17.

64.In 1 Cor 16,6; De sac 3,17.

65.In In 1 Cor 3,6 he affirmed that these appointments were to the deaconate but in In Acta 15,1 he concluded otherwise. See also the discussion in J. Lecuyer, "Saint Jean Chrysostome et l'Ordre du Diaconat." *Melanges B. Botte* (1973): 295-310; and Thomas Halton, "The Kairos of the Mass and the Deacon in John Chrysostom." In *Diakonia: Studies in Honor of Robert T. Meyer* (Washington, DC: The Catholic University of America Press, 1986) 53-59.

66.In Eph 11.

67.Rosemary Radford Ruether. "Mothers of the Church: Ascetic Women in the Late Patristic Age." In *Women of Spirit*. (New York: Simon and Schuster, 1979) 73.

68.In Eph 20; In Col 10.

69.Elizabeth Clark. "Ascetic Renunciation and Feminine Advancement: A Paradox of Late Ancient Christianity." *The Anglican Theological Review* 63 (1981): 245; and Anne Ewing Hickey, *Women of the Roman Aristocracy as Christian Monastics*. (Ann Arbor, MI: UMI Research Press, 1987) passim.

70.Sozomen. *Ecclesiastical History*. 8,24.

71.Vita Olympiadis 1-6. The history of Olympias as a wealthy woman widowed at a young age is similar to Melania the Elder and Paula who were ascetic, celibate companions of Rufinus and Jerome. Elizabeth Clark discusses some of these similarities in "Authority and Humility: A Conflict of Values in Fourth-Century Female Monasticism." *Byzantische Forschungen* 9 (1985): 17-33. which is reprinted in *Ascetic Piety and Women's Faith*. (Lewiston, N.Y.: Edwin Mellen Press, 1986) 209-228. For a further discussion of the significance of Olympias see Joseph Bousquet, "Vie d'Olympias la Diaconesse." *Revue de l'Orient Chrétien* 11 (1906): 225-250.

72.Vita Olympiadis 6;

73.Vita Olympiadis 14; Palladius. *Dialog.* 57-61.

74.Ep ad Olym 8; 17. A.G. Martimort, *Deaconesses: an historical study* (San Francisco: Ignatius Press, 1986) 136-137.

75.A summary of the content and a discussion of their chronological relation to the events of John's exile is given in G. Bardy, "La Chronologie de Lettres de Saint Jean Chrysostome à Olympias." *Melanges de Science Religieuse* 2 (1945): 271-284.

76.In Rom 30-32.

77.*Apostolic Constitutions*. 3,15.

78.Con e q sub.

79.*Apostolic Constitutions*. 8,19.

80.*Apostolic Constitutions*. 8,20. The translation used is from Elizabeth Clark, *Ascetic Piety and Women's Faith*. (Lewiston, N.Y.: Edwin Mellen Press, 1986.) 49-50.

81.In Jn 88,1; In Gal 2:8. However, John saw the rock upon which the church is built as Peter's faith not Peter himself (In Mat 54,3).

82.In Heb Arg,1; In Gal 2.

83.Ep ad Innocent 1; 2. See also the discussion in J. MacDonald, "Innocent I: His life and letters." (B. Litt. thesis. Oxford University, 1957) 192, 196. P.R. Coleman-Norton concludes from the second letter that Chrysostom is only addressing Innocent as a "brother-bishop." ("The Correspondence of St. John Chrysostom with Special Reference to His Epistle to Pope Innocent I." *Classical Philology* 24 (1929): 284).

84.Malcolm Green, "The Papacy of Innocent I." (D. Phil. diss. Oxford University, 1973) 55.

CHAPTER 11
THE PHILOSOPHICAL LIFE

The True Philosophy

John studied under the pagan rhetor Libanius and was a youth during the attempted revival of the classical religious observances under Julian. When he preached to audiences in Antioch, a center for Julian's attempted revival, and later at Constantinople, he presented the Christian life as the true philosophy. He used the term "philosophy" to describe the properly lived Christian life.[1] Key elements in this life were spiritual alertness and the avoidance of a slothful attitude in spiritual things.[2] The standard for this philosophical life was Christ. When John extolled the virtue of his friendship with Basil, he noted how this friendship furthered his relationship with God. What hindered the friendship was John's lack of spiritual commitment.[3] As John pointed out in a study of Paul's shepherding techniques in his first letter to the Corinthians, those who were outside of the Church cannot live the Christian life.

> Did not Paul care for them that were without as well? Yes, he cared for them; but it was not till after they received the Gospel and he had made them subject to the doctrine of Christ, that he laid down laws for them. But so long as they despised it was superfluous to speak the precepts of Christ to those who knew not Christ Himself.[4]

Christians, however, must follow Christ's precepts strictly.[5] We follow Christ of our own free will.[6] Our will must lead us to follow Christ in our words and our actions, and the key to the true philosophy is moderation.[7] When we train children we must lay down limits for them, to teach them that human emotions and urges must not be allowed to reign unchecked.[8] Emotions such as grief were good when directed toward our sin but could become destructive in excess.[9] Anger clouded the reason and destroyed Christians as it ruled their lives.[10] Materialism was another excess that hindered spiritual growth. We are exhorted to leave the care of our material needs in the hands of God who is better able to meet these needs. When Christians lived extravagantly and consumed more than needed, they perverted the philosophical life.[11]

Another measure of the spirituality of Christians as they pursued the philosophical life was their response to evil. In a homily just before the tax revolt in 387, John spoke prophetically to a congregation that was soon to learn of the consequences of evil in a society.

> For of the diversified and manifold affliction which befalls the saints, I have reasons eight in number to declare unto your love. Therefore let all direct themselves to me with the strictest attention, knowing there will be no pardon nor excuse left us hereafter for stumbling at the things which happen, if after all, when there are so many reasons, we are just as much perplexed and disturbed as if there were not one to be found.
>
> The first reason then is, that God permits them to suffer evil, that they may not too easily be exalted into presumption, by the greatness of their good works and miracles.
>
> The second, that others may not have a greater opinion of them than belongs to human nature, and take them to be gods and not men.
>
> The third, that the power of God may be made manifest, in prevailing and overcoming and advancing the word preached, through the efficacy of men who are infirmed and in bonds.
>
> The fourth, that the endurance of these themselves may become more striking, serving God, as they do, not for a reward; but showing even such right-mindedness as to give proof of their undiminished good will towards Him after so many evils.
>
> The fifth, that our minds may be wise concerning the doctrine of a resurrection. For when you see a just man and one abounding in virtue, suffering ten thousand evils, and thus departing the

present life, you are altogether compelled, though unwillingly to think somewhat of the future judgment....

The sixth, that all who fall into adversity may have a sufficient consolation and alleviation, by looking at such persons, and remembering what sufferings have befallen them.

The seventh, that when we exhort you to the virtue of such person and we say to every one of you, "Imitate Paul, emulate Peter," you may not on account of the surpassing character of their good works, slothfully shrink from such an imitation of them, as deeming them to have been partakers of a different nature.

The eighth, that when it is necessary to call any blessed, or the reverse, we may learn whom we ought to account happy, and whom unhappy and wretched.[12]

The themes of properly bearing injury and God's use of temptation in our lives were emphases of John's preaching.[13] The bearing of evil revealed the philosophical life because it displayed an eternal perspective. Living philosophically was the way for all Christians, not just for those who practiced poverty and virginity.[14]

The Christian who does not practice this life becomes an obstacle to the salvation of others.[15] John lamented that sometimes unbelievers acted in a more philosophical way than those in the Body of Christ.[16] No one can claim that there were material obstacles to piety such as poverty. This life is a spiritual state that can empower any station of life. The only hindrances were spiritual weakness and a clouded mind, and both of these were of our own choosing.[17]

The Need for Discipline

A theme consistently applied in John's works was the freedom of the will as a gift from God enabling men and women to break bad habits, form new habits, and thereby train themselves in righteousness. John applied this belief in his ministry consistently and expected results. To catechumens he taught that the evil habit of swearing can be changed.

> If you live very soberly, if you are extremely vigilant and intent on your salvation, I do not think it will take more than ten days to set yourselves completely free from the wicked habit of swearing. But if, after the ten days we should find ourselves still swearing, let us impose a penalty on ourselves and let us fix a really great punishment and sentence for our transgression. What, then, is the sentence? I shall not fix that, but I enjoin you yourselves to decide on the reckoning.[18]

When he preached through the book of Acts at Constantinople, he fixed a penalty for his congregation for the offense of swearing that was evidently prevalent in the marketplace. After stating that we have the power to change our habits, he announced his sentence for those who could not or would not reform.

> Where, with a loud and clear voice, I proclaim to all and testify that those who are notorious for this transgression who utter words which come of the evil one, for such is swearing, shall not step over the threshold of the Church. Let this present month be the time allowed you for reforming in this matter.... I know many will laugh, but it is better to be laughed at now then wept for hereafter.... Now if this law were of my making, at me would be the laughing; but if Another be the Lawgiver, the jeering passes over to Him.[19]

Christians need to control their tongues because idle words degenerate into swearing easily.[20] John also believed that conflict should not be avoided if it proved needful in reforming the city.

> But since our discourse has now turned to the subject of blasphemy, I desire to ask one favor of you all, in return for this my address, and speaking with you, which is, that you will correct on my behalf the blasphemers of this city. And should you hear any one in the street, or in the middle of the forum, blaspheming God; go up to him and rebuke him; and should it be necessary to inflict blows, spare not to do so. Smite him on the face; strike his mouth; sanctify your hand with the blow, and if any should accuse you, and drag you to the place of justice, follow him there;

and when the judge on the bench calls you to account, say boldly that the man blasphemed the King of angels! For if it be necessary to punish those who blasphemed an earthly king much more so those who insult God. It is a common crime, a public injury; and it is lawful for every one who is willing to bring forward an accusation. Let the Jews and Greeks learn, that the Christians are the saviors of the city; that they are its guardians, its patrons, and its teachers. Let the dissolute and the perverse also learn this; that they must fear the servants of God too; that if at any time they are inclined to utter such a thing, they may look round every way at each other, and tremble even at their own shadows, anxious lest perchance a Christian, having heard what they said, should spring upon them and sharply chastise them.[21]

Christians are clearly able to change their lives by resolution of their will.[22] They must discipline themselves to avoid corrupting their minds, which act like pilots of ships or generals over soldiers.[23] An example of this principle was seen in the case of lust. John told his audience that they had the ability to guard themselves against this sin.[24]

Spiritual Disciplines

In order to keep the soul nourished and capable of spiritual growth, John recommended a daily routine in his final instructions to those to be baptized. This routine centered on confession of sin and attendance at the meetings of the church.[25] In this routine, the believer was to rise early and seek the nourishment of the soul as he would also feed the body.[26]

The philosophical life of the Christian was the way to true wisdom.[27] The Christian must do all to the glory of God and live in a manner bringing honor to God.[28] The Christian who lived wrongly blasphemed God.[29] The philosophical life was a life focussed on the things of eternity and not consumed with the pleasures of this world. The Christian's life was not one of ease. An eternal focus allowed one to endure suffering and not become engrossed or focussed on the present life.[30] Trials and affliction help the Christian attain that spiritual focus.

For when the fear of death is urgent, like a fire consuming all things besides, it obliges the soul to philosophize, and to take thought for the future. The desire for wealth, the love of gain, and of bodily pleasures no longer possesses it. These things passing away like clouds, leave the judging faculty clear, and grief entering in softens the heart. For nothing is so opposite to philosophy, as a life of pleasure; nor, on the other hand, is anything so favorable to philosophy as affliction.[31]

Prayer was an important aspect of the Christian life for John. It blocked the assaults of demons and the attacks of the Devil and fortified the child of God for his spiritual service.[32] Christians should pray for the sick, those in harsh slavery in the mines, heretics, and the demon-possessed.[33] John also requested prayer for the Church as she was torn asunder by pride.[34] Prayer worked changes in the one who came to God humbly. It relieved hatred and, when done in conjunction with almsgiving, made the heart of the child of God more conformed to His will.[35] Prayer should focus on the spiritual life and its needs. Christians should only pray for their "daily bread" when they request the meeting of physical needs.[36]

John often exhorted his audience on the values of reading the Scriptures. On of his most pointed comments came as an application in his sermon on the Samaritan woman who spoke with Christ at the well.

Let us now after this be ashamed, and blush. A woman who had five husbands, and who was of Samaria, was so eager concerning doctrines, that neither the time of day, not her having come for another purpose, nor anything else led her away from enquiring on such matters; but we not only do not enquire on such matters but towards them all our dispositions are careless and indifferent. Therefore everything is neglected. For which of you when in his house takes some Christian book in hand and goes over its contents, and searches the Scriptures? None can say that he does so, but with most we shall find draughts and dice, but books nowhere, except among a few. And even these few have the same disposition as the many; for they tie up their books, and keep them always in cases, and all their care is for the fineness of the parchments, and the beauty of the letters, not for reading them. For they have not bought them to obtain advantage and benefit from them but take pains about such matters to show their wealth and pride. Such is the excess of vainglory. I do not hear any one glory in that he knows the content, but that he has a book written in letters of gold. And what gain, tell me, is this? The Scriptures were not given for this only, that we might have them in books, but that we might engrave them on our hearts.... Be not offended at my exhortation. If any one ought to be offended, it is I who often speak and am not heard, not you who are always hearing and disobeying.[37]

He exhorted Christians to own their own Bibles and noted that while the Jews were commended to suspend their holy books from their hands the Christian was to place the books in his home and engrave them on their hearts.[38] However, he did allude to the fact that women wore gospel portions around their necks, a practice that he compared to wearing phylacteries.[39]

The benefits from reading the written word of God were obvious. The Ethiopian Eunuch found salvation while reading the sacred books.[40] However, a mere perfunctory reading of the text was not acceptable for John. He demanded that the Scriptures be studied with an attitude of prayer and with great attention.[41] He was concerned about the lack of knowledge of the Scriptures among his congregation. He noted while preaching both in Antioch and Constantinople that many in his flock had not heard of the book of Acts.[42] He also noted that many in his audience did not know how many letters Paul had written.[43]

This lack of knowledge of the Scriptures, in those who would be God's people, was inexcusable. Reading of the Bible could prevent sinning.[44] We need to search the Scriptures to attain salvation.[45] John also clearly emphasized that the reading of the sacred texts was not for the monk only but for those who lived in the world and felt the barbs of Satan and heard his songs enticing them when they sat in the theater. They need to admonish themselves with the inspired books and hear the songs of the Psalms instead.[46] The reading of the Scriptures made one wise and rich spiritually, and its neglect had disastrous results.

John believed that even if Christians heard the Scriptures without acting on them it was beneficial, because what was heard would serve as a basis for the convicting work of God's Spirit.[47] The reader of God's word does not have the right to pick and choose among the writings. All passages are significant. Even the smallest portions of the text are important. John criticizes the Samaritans for their rejection of all but the books of Moses.[48] The knowledge of the Word of God serves as a base for the Christian life and is a great source for the nurture of the soul.

John believed that worship required preparation of the soul to benefit from the time before God. He taught that a daily time of almsgiving with prayer should be kept and a "little chest" be put by the place of prayer at home for this practice.[49] Part of preparation for worship was the keeping of the Sabbath as a day away from work.[50] The distraction of business did not promote the attentive worship that nurtured the soul.

Another aspect of the Christian's daily routine of prayer was to receive food with thanksgiving.

> The time after dinner is the time for thanksgiving, and he who gives thanks should not be drunk but sober and wide awake. After dinner let us not go to bed but to prayer, or we may become more irrational than the irrational beasts.
>
> I know that many will condemn what I say, thinking that I am introducing a strange new custom into our life; but I will condemn more strongly the wicked custom which now prevails over us. Christ has made it very clear that after taking nourishment at table we ought to receive not sleep in bed but prayer and reading of the divine Scriptures.[51]

Regular reading of the Scriptures is a further preparation for worship. Not only was the reading of Scripture promoted in general but the reading of the texts before the worship service was seen as beneficial for the soul.

What then is it that I require of you? That each of you take in hand that section of the Gospels which is to be read among you on the first day of the week, or even on the Sabbath, and before that day arrives, that he sit down at home and read it through and often carefully consider its contents, and examine its parts well, what is clear, what is obscure, what seems to make for the adversaries, but does not really so; and when you have tried, in a word, every point so go to hear it read. For from zeal like this will be no small gain both to you and to us. We shall not need much labor to render clear the meaning of what is said, because your minds will be already made familiar with the sense of the words, and you will become keener and more clear-sighted not for hearing only nor for learning but also for the teaching of others.[52]

Christians can aid their discipline by the practice of fasting. It was part of the spiritual training they should give to their children. Children should be taught to do this two days per week, Wednesday and Friday.[53] However, they should fast in accord with their strength.[54] Jesus is the great example in this.[55] Christians should also follow Christ's example and realize that real fasting was abstaining from sins as well as from food.[56] Fasting must be done for God's sake and not for public display.[57]

Suffering may lead to grief and despair. However, an eternal focus lifted Christians beyond the present circumstances to attempt to look at life's events from a divine perspective. They must not succumb to despair but must be confident that God is using trials in their lives to promote spiritual growth.[58]

Friendship

Even though John lived as a hermit for two years, he considered friendship an important aspect of the Christian life. The philosophical life was lived in a community and thrived on spiritually beneficial social relationships.

Nothing is so injurious to mankind as to undervalue friendship; and not to cultivate it with the greatest care, as nothing, on the other hand, is so beneficial, as to pursue it to the utmost of our power.[59]

In the first paragraphs of his treatise on the priesthood John reflected on his friendship with Basil during their periods of education and monastic retreat. His picture of that relationship was one where Basil sacrificed greatly for John's spiritual growth.[60] When he preached on friendship he saw it as the greatest of human relationships, surpassing that of family, and marked by total care for each other in Christ.

> I wish to give you the example of friendship. Friends, that is, friends according to Christ, surpass fathers and sons. For tell me not of friends of the present day, since this good thing also has passed away with others. But consider, in the time of Apostles, I speak not of the chief men, but of the believers themselves generally. "All," he says, "were of one heart and soul: and not one of them said that anything of the things which he possessed was his own... and distribution was made to each, according as any one had need."[61] There were then no such words as "mine" and "your." This is friendship, that a man should not consider his goods his own, but his neighbor's, that his possessions belong to another; that he should be as careful of his friend's soul, as of his own; and the friend likewise.[62]

In sum, the philosophical life was one of moderation with an eternal focus. Excesses lead to sin and must be shunned. It is a life in community where each sought the spiritual good of another. It was true friendship and piety marked by caring and discipline.

1.In 1 Cor 7,20. An overview of John's use of this term is given in A.A. Packard, "Chrysostom's True Christian Philosophy." *Anglican Theological Review* 45 (1963): 396-406.

2.In Gen 10,20 and In Acta 29.

3.De sac 1,1-4.

4.In 1 Cor 16,2. (NPNF 90).

5.Among those portions of John's work that discuss the standard of Christlikeness are In Mat 31,5; In 1 Cor 25,3; and In Mat 50,4.

6.In 1 Cor 16,11.

7.Ad vid jun 7; In Jn 80,1; In Mat 57,4-5.

8.In Mat 10,8; In 1 Cor 8,8; In 2 Cor 20,3; De inani gloria 27f; and In 2 Cor 30,4 fin.

9.In 1 Cor 38,8.

10.De sac 3,14; In Heb 1,4.

11.In Jn 80,3; 81,3; Q nemo 1; Ad pop Anti 1,28; and In Mat 68,5.

12.Ad pop Ant 1,14 (NPNF 9, 336-337).

13.In 1 Cor 16,10 and In Acta 18,1 are good examples of this element in his preaching.

14.In Mat 45,3.

15.In Jn 72,5; In Mat 32,11; In 1 Cor 6,8.

16.In 1 Cor 26,8.

17.De laud s Paul 5.

18.Cat ill 9,46. (Harkins. *Baptismal Instructions*. 146). In De inani gloria 33 John told parents that two months could suffice to train the tongue of a child toward godly speech.

19.In Acta 8,3. (NPNF 11, 53). In In Acta 10,4 John reiterated his threats.

20.In 1 Cor 44,7; De inani gloria 28f; Cat ill 9,34f; 9,42; 10,18; and In Eph 17. In In Acts 10,4 John stated that this habit can be changed easily because it is an affair of the mouth.

21.Ad pop Anti 1,32. (NPNF 9, 343).

22.Passages where the formation of habits and change by resolution of the will were addressed include Cat ill 1,25; In 1 Cor 28,2; In 2 Cor 2,7; Ad pop Anti 13; De inani gloria 30; In Heb 24,9; In Mat 11,10; and 17,6.

23.In Mat 20,3; and In 1 Cor 17,5 fin.

24.In 2 Cor 7,7-8 .

25.Cat ill 8,16.

26.Other passages in John's works where he addressed early rising include In Acta 26,3, where it is noted that the soul is purer earlier in the day, and that this was the habit of Christ. Similar references are in In Acta 35,3 and 36,1.

27.In Jn 58,1 and Cat ill 4,13.

28.Cat ill 1,45; 4,17 and 6,8.

29.In Jn 67,3.

30.In Phil 13.

31.In 2 Tim 5 (NPNF 13, 495).

32.De incomp die 4,40; 45. Cat ill 7,25.

33.De incomp die 3,31.

34.De inani gloria 1.

35.In 1 Tim 6; and In 1 Cor 43,7.

36.In Jn 43,2.

37.In Jn 32,3. (NPNF 14, 114). The series of homilies on John's Gospels was given on weekday mornings and the numerous applications to read the

Scriptures might reflect a more leisured audience. (Other passages with similar applications are In Jn 11,1; 21,1; 41; 53,3; In Gen 35,1 and 35,7.) However, there are similar exhortations in passages which clearly were delivered to a broader audience, and although some of the applications rebuked those who bought expensive books, a problem confined to those who could afford books with letters of gold, the basic thrust of the passages was reading the Scriptures as a duty of the Christian. William V. Harris (*Ancient Literacy.* Cambridge: Harvard University Press, 1989. 304 n 92, 313) believes that Chrysostom's "quite atypical congregation" (304) explains these exhortations.

38. In Jn 53,3.

39. In Mat 72,2.

40. In Acta 19,4.

41. In Jn 21,1; 41,1; and 58,1.

42. In Acta 1,1. This series was preached in Constantinople. John made the same complaint in In princ Act 3 (cited in NPNF 11, 1) which was preached about ten years earlier in Antioch.

43. In Rom arg,1.

44. De Laz 3; In Rom arg,1.

45. In Jn 53,3. In De Laz 3 John concluded that it is not possible to be saved without the reading of the Scriptures.

46. In Mat 2,10.

47. In Mat 2,11. Other passages extolling the profitability of the Scriptures include In Jn 37,1 and In Gen 9,2.

48. In Jn 30, 2; 31,2; and In Gen 15,4. This is discussed in Boniface Ramsey, *Beginning to Read the Fathers* (New York: Paulist Press, 1985) 39.

49. In 1 Cor 42,7. Further preparation is exhorted in In Mat 51; 73; and In Eph 3.

50. In Jn 3,1; In Mat 5,1.

51.De Laz 1. (Roth. *On Wealth and Poverty*. 27).

52.In Jn 11,1. (NPNF 14, 38).

53.De inani gloria 79.

54.Ad pop Anti 3,8. A rest from the lenten fast was provided to make it easier (In Gen 11,5) and even if Christians fail to keep the lenten fast they should not be ashamed to go to church (In Gen 10, 1f).

55.In Mat 13,1.

56.Ad pop Anti 3,8.

57.Adv Jud 4,3,3; In Mat 20,1; and Cat ill 5,1. Fasting should be done to prepare for the Eucharist but not to prepare for the superstitious feasts of the Jews, Adv Jud 3,3,6f; 4,1,1. We should do our good deeds in private as was the sacrificing of Isaac by Abraham, In 1 Tim 13.

58.In Jn 78,1; 79,1, 3; K. M. Peterson, "Despair: Exploring Christian and Existential Responses." (M. A. thesis. Western Conservative Baptist Seminary, 1984) 20-22.

59.In 1 Tim 2,1. (NPNF 13, 412).

60.De sac 1,1f.

61.Acts 4:32,35.

62.In 1 Thess 2. (NPNF 13, 331). Other portions of John's work where he addressed friendship included In Acta 40,3; 40,4; In Col 1; In Mat 60,3; De Chris prec 67; and Ad Theo 1,2. See Caroline Dermot Small, "The Understanding of Friendship in the Works of Selected Church Fathers of the Fourth and Fifth Centuries A.D. with Reference to Classical Ideas on Friendship." (D. Phil. diss. Oxford University, 1984).

CHAPTER 12
THE ETHIC OF LOVE

Deeds Done in Love Last for Eternity

Love should motivate the Christian because deeds done in love will survive the return of Christ to the earth when all things will be made new. When preaching on the thirteenth chapter of First Corinthians, John pointed out to his congregation that faith and hope will no longer be as they are now when Christ returns, because Christians will not need to see only with the eyes of faith and look toward a future hope. Rather, the presence of Christ will reward their faith and fulfill their hope. But even after this, love will exist and those things done lovingly will carry great reward in the eternal kingdom.[1] Love is even more powerful than miracles.[2] When Christians love, they follow the great example laid before them. The primary example is the love of God.[3] But there are also the examples of the faithful who have gone before.[4] Love is a great unifying force in the Body of Christ as Christians follow the examples of love they become examples for others and the entire body grows toward godliness.

One can even use deception in a loving manner, as John contended he did when he avoided ordination and allowed Basil to be taken into the service of the Church.[5] John even believed that Christ used deception in a loving manner when, just before His ascension, He did not tell the disciples of his plans to restore the kingdom.[6]

Love leads to peace and reconciliation. John reminded his congregation that when two are at enmity, the one who first acts lovingly and brings about the reconciliation is the one who receives the reward.[7] The consummate expression of love in reconciliation is working for the salvation of another. John addressed this theme often when he preached from the book of Acts while Archbishop at Constantinople. He declared, "Nothing is more frigid than a Christian, who cares not for the salvation of others."[8] He exhorted his audience to bring others with them to the assembly. He also asked the rich who owned lands to construct oratories where the gospel could be preached to their workers.[9]

John expanded the notion of working for the salvation of others to the more general theme of the spiritual edification of others when preaching on the concept of the Body of Christ in Paul's first letter to the Corinthians.

> Don't you see the foundation and rule of Christianity? How, as it is the artificer's work to build, so it is the Christian's to profit his neighbors in all things.[10]

Almsgiving

A form of love and edification that received extraordinary emphasis in John's writings was almsgiving. Even in the context of John's high view of celibate consecration to God, he stated that almsgiving is greater than virginity.[11] The amount was less important than our attitude and the amount will be judged only in relation to our resources.[12] John occasionally suggested a percentage of one's income that should be given to the poor. At one point he advocated giving one third.[13] At another point he said that his audience should give as much to the poor as they do to the children of their mistresses and concluded that one-half of one's income would be appropriate.[14] He also told his audience to give half as much to Christ in the poor as they gave to dancers, prostitutes, and flatterers.[15] Because the amount was not an issue, the poor themselves were not exempt from the mandate to give.[16] In addition, the working class should also contribute to the needs of those less fortunate than themselves.[17] Alms were not given to all; they were not for those who were able to support themselves.[18] However, Christians should not let doubt as to whether the recipient is worthy prevent them from performing this necessary spiritual task. They should not inquire more than is necessary.[19]

Wealth was given to meet needs, not for extravagance.[20] Giving to the poor and showing that we serve God and not Mammon is such a central spiritual exercise to the Christian's experience that John could remark, "I have often said that almsgiving has been introduced not for the sake of the receivers but of the givers, for the latter are they which make the greatest gain."[21] Almsgiving was an act of worship[22] and was necessary to obtain the forgiveness of postbaptismal sins.[23] Without the giving of alms one cannot be saved.[24]

Humility and Pride

Pride nullified acts of love and an attitude of humility must mark the true servant of God. John believed that a heavenly focus and a concern for others witnessed in the true Christian philosophical life was an antidote for the universal tendency toward pride. Humility comes with a heavenward focus because we see our identity in Christ and a perspective on life that minimizes earthly attainments.[25] In his instructions to parents on childrearing John began with a lament on the way pride has afflicted the Body of Christ, tearing it apart like an animal of prey would dismember a carcass.[26] Pride is at the root of great sin and disorder in the Church and John believed that the pulpit must be used against this plague on God's people.[27] John saw Paul's use of the Body of Christ imagery in Romans and First Corinthians as a remedy for this sin.[28] Common membership in this body superceded any other fact of life that might differentiate among God's people.

Pride is a temptation for Christians even when they are about the Lord's work. If they succumb to pride and broadcast their service for God they lose their reward. The more good they do the less they should say about themselves so as to reap the greatest glory from God.[29] Good deeds such as fasting, prayer, and alms can make them proud.[30] However, the Bible gives examples of humble people who were great by the world's standards. The Ethiopian Eunuch was one who came to Christ demonstrating his humility.[31]

The Christian life is one which fights pride and clings to humility. The tendency toward pride is great, and when one succumbs to it all spiritual value even to work done in the service of the Church is wasted from an eternal perspective. It is truly the great enemy of spirituality.

The Christian, the Devil and the World

There were other enemies to the practice of love by God's people. John warned the catechumens that they must be prepared to do battle with their adversary the Devil. Demons were real for John and there were many instruments that were used by Satan in his contest with the people of God.[32] The Devil even used pickpockets to distract the people who had come to the church for spiritual nourishment.

> But he [the Devil] did send robbers and pickpockets to mingle among you and had them ready on more than one occasion to snatch from the many people gathered here the money which they had tied up in their purses. And this has happened in this church many times to many people. But I do not wish this to continue to happen. Not do I wish your eagerness to hear me to be quenched because, as has happened to many of you, you have lost your money. Therefore, I counsel and advise all of you that nobody come into the church carrying money. In that way, your eagerness to hear the homily will not become for these thieves an opportunity for evildoing. Then the pleasure which comes to you from spending your time here will not be affected by the theft of your money.

> The devil contrived this not to make you poorer but to let the loss of your money make you feel deeply disgusted and lead you away from your eagerness to hear the homily. He once stripped Job of all his possessions not to make him poorer but to strip him of his piety.[33]

The preacher competed with the world on many fronts.[34] The calendar was still marked with days that lead people to sin. The first day of the year was filled with Satanic temptation. When John began his series of homilies on the parable of the Rich Man and Poor Lazarus he complimented his audience for shunning its revelry.

Yesterday, although it was the feast-day of Satan, you preferred to keep a spiritual feast, receiving our words with great good will, and spending most of the day here in church, drinking a drunkenness of self-control, and dancing in the chorus of Paul. In this way a double benefit came to you, because you kept free of the disorderly dance of the drunkards and you revelled in well-ordered spiritual dances. You shared a drinking bowl which did not pour out undiluted wine but was filled with spiritual instruction. You become a flute and lyre for the Holy Spirit. While others for the devil, you prepared yourselves by your occupation here to be spiritual instruments and vessels. You allowed the Holy Spirit to play on your souls and to breathe His grace into your hearts. Thus you sounded a harmonious melody to delight not only mankind but even the powers of heaven.[35]

In addition to the calendar there was the ever present danger of astrology. The wonder of the stars attracted many in his audience. John countered that stars were not signs to guide life. John felt it necessary to make this particularly clear when he spoke about the heavenly light that appeared to the three kings of the East at the birth of Christ. It was not an astrological sign but a miracle from God.[36]

There were many entertainments that distracted the people from a spiritual focus. John saw carnival entertainments as frivolous and not nourishing to the soul. In his condemnations he mentioned performers who juggled swords, balanced a child on a pole resting on their faces, and tight rope walkers who entertained the people.[37]

Athletic events were very potent distractions from spiritual matters. Athletic competition formed an important part of city life in both Antioch and Constantinople and served as a focus for forces that could even undermine government stability.[38] John lamented that attendance at the divine worship had fallen off while many had gone to attend the horse races at the circus.

I have no idea what I shall say to you today. I see that since the Feast of Pentecost the attendance at divine services has fallen off,

the Prophets are neglected, the Apostles are little valued, the
Fathers are set aside... There is divine service once a week, and
even this day you cannot spend without the cares of business.
Some say they are poor and must take care of making their living,
while others have urgent business. As a matter of fact the whole
city is at the circus... No poverty stands in the way there, no
urgent work, no illness, no weakness of the feet, nothing of these
is able to hold back the unruly passion. The old men run with
the youths to the betting in order to find a place, and expose
their grey hairs to shame and ridicule. And if they occasionally
come here to the Church, they experience seizures, and listening
to the sermon gives them fainting spells.[39]

He often mentioned the addiction of the people in the city to the races
and other athletic games and lamented how this distracted them from the
meetings of the church and the care of their own souls.[40]   The Olympic
Games were often used as a source of illustrations in his sermons, usually
with the application that the prizes and benefits given by God to those who
pursued holiness were greater than the prizes awarded in athletic contests.[41]

The manifestation of worldliness under the control of the devil that
received the strongest barbs from John was undoubtedly the theatre. The
dancing and mockery of life that it contained was particularly annoying to
him. For John dancing was an instrument of the devil and was responsible
for the beheading of John the Baptist.[42] The theatre was also a vehicle for
the public display of wealth by the rich and used by them to gain the
applause of the people.[43] The theatre was destructive to marriages and to
the morals of the people in general.[44]

Seductive displays of feminine beauty also attracted the censure of
John's preaching. John discussed current tastes in beauty in his sermons
citing hair "tastefully plaited in the Persian fashion,"[45] a woman "displaying
flashing gold and precious gems about her throat,"[46] and "women who
corrupt their faces with colorings and paintings."[47]   He reminded his
congregation that physical beauty and youth does not last twenty years

whereas godliness lasts "into the heavens."[48]

When he pleaded for Theodore to abandon his intended marriage and return to monastic contemplation, he cited the fading character of physical beauty in graphic terms.

> For the groundwork of this bodily beauty is nothing else but phlegm, and blood, and humor, and bile, and the fluid of masticated food. For by these things both eyes and cheeks, and all the other features, are supplied with moisture; and if they do not receive that moisture, daily ascending from the stomach and the liver the skin becoming unduly withered, and the eyes sunken, the whole grace of the countenance forthwith vanishes; so that if you consider what is stored up inside those beautiful eyes, and that straight nose, and the mouth and the cheeks, you will affirm the well-shaped body to be nothing else than a whited sepulchre that parts within are full of so much uncleanness. Moreover when you see a rag with any of these on it, such as phlegm or spittle, you cannot bear to touch it with even the tips of your fingers, no, you cannot even endure looking at it; and yet are you in a flutter of excitement about the storehouses and depositories of these things.[49]

Another source of temptation in the world was represented by the occult and magic. John urged the new Christians to avoid them and scolded his congregation for using diviners to help them search for lost money.[50] In his homilies directed against those in his congregation with Judaizing tendencies, who used the synagogues as a source of spiritual power, John condemned the use of Jewish rituals as a source of magic.[51]

Some of the superstitions of his day John found to be vulgar as well as blasphemous.

> Let me give you another example that is still more ridiculous. I am ashamed and I blush to say it, but still I am forced to speak for the sake of your salvation. If a virgin chances to meet you, you say the day is an unsuccessful one; but if you happen to meet a prostitute, the day is lucky and good and filled with an abundance of business. Are you hiding your face? Did you beat your brow and bend your head down to the ground? But do not

do this while I am talking; do it when you are doing the things of which I speak.[52]

Amulets were condemned as foolishness and no source of power when compared to the true power of the cross of Christ.[53] Also, lunatics were not caused by the moon but by the torment of people by demons.[54]

For John the world was a place of spiritual warfare. The prizes and losses were of eternal consequence and Christians were to always view their lives as under attack. If they were to live for God they must be ever vigilant and aiming toward godliness. There was never any time in the Christian life for complacency or slothfulness. The Christian would either live powerfully for Christ or be on the brink of spiritual disaster.

1.In 1 Cor 34,5.

2.De sac 2,5.

3.The relationship between love for God and love for people on earth in John's writings is discussed in Thomas Barrosse, "The Unity of the Two Charities in Greek Patristic Exegesis." *Theological Studies* 15 (1954): 375-384. He concludes that John's logic was that if we love God, we will do what He wants. He wants us to love our neighbor. We must then love our neighbor.

4.De laud s Paul 3. Krister Ottoson, "Love of God in Saint John Chrysostom's Commentary on the Fourth Gospel." *Church Quarterly Review* 166 (1965): 315-323. 315.

5.De sac 1,8.

6.In Acta 2,2.

7.De Chris prec. Other passages where John addressed this issue include In Heb 31,1 and In Mat 62.5.

8.In Acta 20,4. Other passages where he addressed the Christian working for the salvation of others include: Cat ill 6,18; In Heb 30,6; In Mat 59,6; and In 1 Cor 25, 5.

9.In il Si esur 3-4. John addressed the setting up of oratories in In Acta 18,4.

10.In 1 Cor 36,4. He also addressed this theme in In 2 Cor 25,3; In Heb 30,2-3; In Acta 20,4; De sac 3,10; In 2 Thess 5,4; and In Mat 77,5-6. The use of spiritual gifts to edify the body was addressed in In 1 Cor 29ff. Yves Congar, *Lay People in the Church* (Westminster, MD: Christian Classics, 1985), 357.

11.In Mat 46,4.

12.In Heb 1,4; 32,8. Other passages where John addressed this issue include: In Mat 5,9; In 1 Cor 15,11; 15,15; 21,9-11; and 43,7.

13.In Jn 79,5.

14.In Mat 66,4. In De inani gloria 12 John referred to the money spent on the sponsorship of theater in the city by the rich for the fleeting applause of the crowds. He then directed his words to those in his audience "who refuse to hand over a trifling sum to Christ when He is poor and lacking the barest sustenance; and what the pagans spend on harlots and mimes and dancers in return for a shout of applause, this our Christian will not give for the sake of the eternal kingdom."

15.In 2 Cor 19,3.

16.De pet mat 11; In Mat 64,1.

17.In 1 Cor 43,7.

18.In 2 Thess 5.

19.De Laz 2; In Heb 11,10.

20.In 1 Tim 7.

21.In Phil 15.

22.In 2 Cor 20. Yves Congar, *Lay People in the Church*. (Westminster, MD: Christian Classics, 1985), 135n.

23.In Jn 73,2; 81,3.

24.In Phil. 3,4; In 2 Tim 6; In Jn 7,2; In Mat 77,6; 78,1; In Acta 25, 2-3 fin; and In 2 Cor 17,3.

25.In 1 Cor 1,6.

26.De inani gloria 1f. In In 2 Cor 27,4 John uses a very similar illustration to attack divisiveness in the Church.

27.In Jn 3,6; In Il Pater s p 1f.

28.In Rom 21; In 1 Cor 31,1.

29.In Mat 3,8; 19,3. An example of doing good without drawing attention to ourselves is seen in Matthew who does not name himself in his gospel (In Mat 30,1).

30.In Mat 19,1.

31.In Acta 19,3.

32.Cat ill 12,33f; Adv Jud 1,6,6.

33.De incomp die 4, 46-47. (Harkins. *On the Incomprehensible Nature of God*. 134).

34.In Jn 1,1.

35.De Laz 1. (Roth. *On Wealth and Poverty*. 19).

36.In Mat 6, 1-4. M.L.W. Laistner, *The Intellectual Heritage of the Early Middle Ages* (New York: Octagon Books, 1983), 67. Tertullian (De idol 9,3) believed that the Magi were the last to practice astrology properly. Chrysostom denied that the light over Bethlehem at the birth of Christ was a star. He considered it a supernatural light akin to the pillar of fire during the wilderness wanderings of the Israelites. For a more extended discussion of this point see A. Dihle ("Astrology in the Doctrine of Bardesanes," 168).

37.In Heb 16,9.

38.The Nika Revolt in 532 almost ended the reign of Justinian. For a discussion of this revolt and the Hippodrome factions behind it see J. B. Bury, *A History of the Later Roman Empire from the Death of Theodosius I to the Death of Justinian* (New York: Dover, 1958) 2, 39-48. This phenomena is discussed more fully in Alan Cameron, *Circus Factions: Blues and Greens at Rome and Byzantium* (Oxford: Clarendon, 1976).

39.De Anna. (Carroll. *Preaching the Word*. 105-6).

40.Cat ill 1,43; 6,1; 6,14; De Consub 1; In Gen 7,1.

41.Cat ill 3,9; De laud s Paul 6; In Heb 14,10; 17,8. Diana Bowder, "Paganism and Pagan Revival: Constantius II to Julian." (D. Phil. diss. Oxford University, 1976) 519-520; John Alexander Sawhill, *The Use of Athletic*

Metaphors in the Biblical Homilies of Saint John Chrysostom. Princeton: The University Press, 1928.

42.In Mat 48,4; In 2 Cor 28,4.

43.De inani gloria 4.

44.In Mat 37,8; 48,5; De inani gloria 4; In Acta 42,fin.   Ronald Gagne, Thomas Kane, and Robert VerEerke. *Introducing Dance in Christian Worship* (Washington: The Pastoral Press, 1984), 50. A Rain, "Saint Jean Chrysostome et la Vie de Famille de son époque." *Christianskoje Ctenije* (1895) 225-248; 315-344; and "Saint Jean Chrysostome et les Theatres de son époque." *Christianskoje Ctenije* (1896) 172-193.

45.De inani gloria 2.

46.De inani gloria 2. Later in this homily he cited long hair and a necklace as ways in which parents made their young sons look effeminate and pervert their spirituality and stimulated in them a love of riches (De inani gloria 16).

47.In Mat 20,1.

48.In Heb 28,15.

49.Ad Theo 1,14. (NPNF 9, 103-104).

50.Cat ill 1,39; In 1 Thess 3.

51.Adv Jud 1.7.5f; 8,5,6; 8,7,9; 8,7,1-5; 1,3,4f; 3,1,1,etc.

52.Cat ill 12,55. (Harkins. *Baptismal Instructions.* 190).

53.Cat ill 12,57 and 11,25.

54.In Mat 57,3. Other superstitions are condemned in In Eph 12; and Cat ill 11,25.

Equalities and Inequalities

John's view of the sexes reflects the complex theological and social convictions of his era as well as strong personal prejudice.   When examined it appears to be a collection of contrasts that yields few consistently applied principles.   These inconsistencies arose when he sought to apply a Christian critique to the mores of his era and remained part of that era while trying to be prophetic to it.

He clearly viewed women as the inferior sex. He saw them as more easily deceived, following Eve.[1]   Sins such as gluttony were especially dishonoring and evil in women.[2] However, not all of the differences between the natures of the two sexes were perceived by John to magnify men. Women were more inclined to pity as witnessed by the women at Christ's burial.[3]   Women also received special consideration from God because of their inferiority.   Christ appeared to women first as an act of mercy to the sex that was most condemned.[4]

As John preached on the first chapters in Genesis, his views take on a very sexist tone. He viewed the first man as created in the image of God and saw this image as not being given to the entire race but to males alone.[5] His examples of the heroes of the faith were men and not women.[6] He did not see man in Genesis used in a corporate sense so that the admonition to rule the earth is only given to men.   Therefore "man commands everything whereas woman is subservient- hence Paul's words about man, that he is constituted in God's image and glory whereas woman is man's glory."[7]   In applying the truths taught in the Fall as recorded in Genesis, chapter three, John expanded his concept of male superiority because of the greater guilt that was assigned to the woman.[8] Eve was created as an equal but did not properly use her freedom as a helpmate. She "misused her power."[9]

However, in contests of the soul, celibacy, and martyrdom, women can compete with men on the same level. When preaching on Ignatius, the second century martyr-bishop of Antioch, he mentioned the recent feast of the martyr Pelagia. Comparing their feasts he said, "The persons are different: The table one. The wrestlings are varied: The crown one. The contests are manifold: The prize is the same." He later concluded that, unlike pagan athletic games, both men and women can compete because "here the contest is wholly concerning the soul, the lists are open to each sex, for each kind the theater is arranged."[10]

Creation and the Fall

When comparing these observations with his words on the creation and the fall it appears that he did not see the source of the fundamental inequality between the sexes as being in form but rather in headship. In his Genesis homilies he concluded from the account of the creation that man is created in God's image but sees the woman as created as man's glory. It might be concluded from this that woman is inferior in soul, but the reason that followed explained the area of inferiority as in the place of each in the rule of the created order. He gave the reason for this as based in God's purpose for the ruling of creation.

> You see, since it is on the basis of command that the image was received and not on the basis of form, man commands everything whereas women is subservient- hence Paul's words about man, that he is constituted God's image and glory, whereas women is man's glory. If, however, he had been speaking about form, he would not have distinguished between man and woman being identical in type, after all.[11]

However, when commenting on Paul's principle of headship in First Corinthians, John saw the submission of woman to man as sourced in the fall, not in creation.

> But the head of the woman is the man; and the head of Christ is God.[12] Here the heretics rush upon us with a declaration of inferiority, which out of these words they contrive against the

Son. But they stumble against themselves. For if the man be the head of the women and the head be the same substance with the body, and the head of Christ is God, the Son is of the same substance with the Father....

But do you understand the term "head"... For had Paul meant to speak of rule and subjection, as you say, he would not have brought forward the instance of a wife, but rather of a slave and a master. For, what if the wife be under subjection to us? it is as a wife, as free, as equal in honor....

For with us indeed the woman is reasonably subjected to the man: since equality of honor causes contention. And not for this cause only, but by reason also of the deceit which happened in the beginning. Wherefore you see, she was not subjected as soon as she was made; nor when He brought her to the man, did either she hear any such thing from God, nor did the man say any word to her: he said indeed that she was "bone of his bone and flesh of his flesh."[13] But of rule or subjection he nowhere made mention to her. But when she made ill use of her privilege and she who had been made a helper was found to be an ensnarer and ruined all, then she is justly told for the future, "your desire shall be to your husband."[14]

Another area where John saw the result of the Fall restrict women was in the realm of teaching. Women were not to teach in the Church. Why? "Because she taught Adam once and for all, and taught him badly. . . . Therefore let her descend from the professor's chair."[15]

Equality brings disorder. An orderly society must have defined authority and clear lines of power. Since the Fall there has been subjection in the created order and the subjection of woman to man is a part of this natural ordering of creation. There can be equality of form and substance but not of authority. A consistent principle for Chrysostom is that democracy brings anarchy.

Further, in order that the one might be subject, and the other rule, for equality usually brings strife, he suffered it not to be a democracy, but a monarchy, and as in an army, this order one may see in every family. In the rank of monarch, for instance, there is the husband; but in the rank of lieutenant and general, the wife, and the children too are allotted a third station in command. Then after these a fourth order, that of the servant.[16]

John felt compelled to mention and sought to explain the rule of Candace among the Ethiopians. He treated it as an exception to the norm of order and stated that, "there women bore rule of old, and this was the law among them."[17] It became for the Ethiopians a stabilizing norm. Seen in light of John's ethnocentric view of the world and the superiority of his Greek culture, a deviating norm among the Ethiopians was not overly troubling, even if it required an explanation. Consistent with this principle of headship was the fact that women were excluded from the priesthood, and John made some negative comments about their intrusion into church politics.[18] In addition to the principles of male headship and equality of honor and substance, John saw the principle of mutual interdependence applying to the relationship between the sexes. Both male and female were essential parts of God's administration of his creation.[19]

The source of the inferiority of women to men was the need for order in a fallen world. This need was manifested in institutions such as the family and the empire. Democracy caused anarchy. For a society to function there must be order and submission.

<u>Revolutionized Lives Bring Liberation</u>

A serious question for John concerned the circumstances under which true equality could achieved and the subservient position of women be eliminated. He addressed this in various contexts. As seen earlier, martyrdom, where the ultimate contest of the soul was waged, was an arena where equality prevails. A second instance of equality was seen in the early church in Jerusalem.

"Men and brethren," says Peter. For if the Lord called them brethren much more may he. .... See the dignity of the church, the angelic condition! No distinction there, neither male nor female. I would that the churches were such now. None there had his mind full of some worldly matter, none was anxiously thinking about household concerns. Such a benefit are temptations, such the advantage of afflictions.[20]

For John, all the members of the Jerusalem assembly as they awaited the coming of the Spirit at Pentecost were addressed as men even though there were clearly women present. John noted that they did not have household concerns. It may be that he assumed celibacy in this church but it was much more likely that he saw the equality as arising from their communal living. Later in this series he recommended communal living to his audience in the church at Constantinople.[21] This was consistent with his principle that the differences arise from the need for social order after the Fall and the image of God as revealed in his notion of headship. Communal living for John seemed to break down the elements in the social structure that mandated the subservient position of women. He did not pursue this notion, moving on to the replacement of the fallen Judas, but this was a curious application of some of his basic understandings on the subject of the image of God and the need for order in society.

The primary vehicle for the elimination of the inequality between men and women was the call to celibacy.[22] The celibate life also provided an opportunity for those with means to engage in traveling in the form of pilgrimages to holy places and visits to the dwellings of famous ascetics.[23] Married women would not have been allowed to travel without their husbands, but for the celibate these pilgrimages were a source of praise and fame as well as freedom. The celibate Egeria's diary of her travels, kept for fellow nuns back home, provides posterity with the account of her journey to Mount Sinai, Palestine, and Asia Minor. Among the many things she saw on her pilgrimage were the spot where Lot's wife was turned into a pillar of salt and the correspondence between Jesus and King Abgar of Edessa as well as numerous shrines to the saints and places visit by the Messiah.[24]

John attempted to balance a conviction that celibacy is the superior calling with the fact that marriage was instituted by God and forbidding marriage was a clear violation of scriptural principles. He concluded a discussion of this topic in his homilies on 1 Timothy with the following attempt at a balance. "He that forbids, does it once for all, but he who recommends virginity as a higher state, does not forbid marriage, because he prefers virginity."[25] John also preferred widowhood over digamy, the remarriage after the death of the first partner.[26]

In John's view much of the inferior and subservient role of women as tied to their role in marriage and often spoke of the virgin as "playing the man" or acting "manly."[27] Clearly, for John, marriage was entangling, especially for women, and celibacy was a great liberator. John's advocacy of virginity as a divine vocation and its key role in the life of the individual and the Church gave great pastoral responsibility to the priests as they cared for the virgin.[28] The virgin was not in the oppressive social structure that was instituted to order life in a fallen world. Her vulnerability was a burden that the priests bore but the result was that the virgin became "manly" in her service in the church, rising above the limitations of her sex.

The Virgin Mary was held up as an example to the celibate. John believed that her marriage with Joseph was never consummated.[29] However, Mary was not perfect. She acted presumptuously at the wedding at Cana when she brought her request to Christ.[30] Her position as the mother of Christ afforded her no special position in His kingdom unless she also came to Him for salvation. When Christ was told that His mother and brothers wished to speak with Him he responded that those who were His disciples were His mother and brothers.[31] John saw in this the primacy of obedience in becoming a follower of Christ.

> And this He said, not as being shamed of his mother, nor denying her that bore Him for if He had been ashamed of her, He would not have passed through that womb. But as declaring that she has no advantage from this, unless she do all that is required to

be done. For in fact that which she had essayed to do was of superfluous vanity, in that she wanted to show the people that she had power and authority over her Son, imagining not as yet anything great concerning Him, whence also her unseasonable approach....

For if she is profited nothing by being His mother, were it not for that quality in her, hardly will any one else be saved by his kindred.[32]

John's view of Mary reflected her human failings and need for a Savior with the rest of the race. His view made her a model for the celibate woman but was out of step with most of his contemporaries whose views laid the base for the later Mariological doctrines. Even though he highlighted her weaknesses, John pointed out the relationship she had with her Son. He was quick to point to the example of Jesus as showing great love in His care for her when He was on the cross and provided for her in the home of the Apostle John.[33] In John's sermons she emerged as a model for the woman liberated from the oppression of her sex because even though she was a mother to the Savior, she did not enter fully into marriage and remained the archetypical virgin for the Church.

1.In Gen 16,4; 16,11.

2.In Acta 27,2.

3.In Jn 86,1.

4.In Mat 88.

5.In Gen 8,10.

6.In Gen 12,21.

7.In Gen 8,10.

8.In Gen 17, passim. Chrysostom's sexism has also been discussed by Elizabeth Clark, *Ascetic Piety and Women's Faith* (Lewiston, N.Y.: Edwin Mellen Press, 1986), 26-27, 41-42, 44; "Sexual Politics in the Writings of John Chrysostom." *The Anglican Theological Review* 59 (1977): passim; and Robert Hill, *Saint John Chrysostom: Homilies on Genesis 1-17* (Washington, DC: Catholic University of America Press, 1986), 12.

9.In 1 Cor 26,2;

10.In s. Igna 1.

11.In Gen 8,11.

12.1 Cor. 11:3.

13.Gen 2:23.

14.Gen 3:16. In 1 Cor 26,2-3. (NPNF 12, 150-151).

15.S Gen 4,1. The translation used is from Elizabeth Clark, *Ascetic Piety and Women's Faith*. (Lewiston, N.Y.: Edwin Mellen Press, 1986.) 31.

16.In 1 Cor 34,6. (NPNF 12, 204)

17.In Acta 19,1.

18.De sac 3,9 .

19.In Gen 15, 3.

20.In Acta 3,1. (NPNF 11, 18).

21.In Acta 9, 3-4.

22.Anne Ewing Hickey, *Women of the Roman Aristocracy as Christian Monastics* (Ann Arbor, MI: UMI Research Press, 1987) passim. This is also the theme in Elizabeth Clark's "Ascetic Renunciation and Feminine Advancement: A Paradox of Late Ancient Christianity." (*The Anglican Theological Review* 63 (1981): 240-257.) passim. reprinted in *Ascetic Piety and Women's Faith*. (Lewiston, N.Y.: Edwin Mellen Press, 1986.) 175-208. Virginia Burrus in *Chastity as Autonomy*. (Lewiston, N.Y.: Edwin Mellen, 1987.) passim. discusses the renunciation of sexual relations with husbands and suitors in various apocryphal acts of the apostles, which is an earlier expression of these themes. These acts show that the realization that the oppression of women in the home and in society in general was, to a great degree, a product of their sexual relationships. If they could be liberated from their union to their husbands, then a considerable element of their subordinate position in society could be eliminated. Chastity in the apocryphal acts and monastic celibacy in later eras were vehicles within the Christian community for a woman to leave an oppressive position in society.

23.Elizabeth Clark, *Ascetic Piety and Women's Faith*. (Lewiston, N.Y.: Edwin Mellen Press, 1986.) 47-48.

24.*Egeria's Travels* translated by John Wilkinson (London: SPCK, 1971). The pilgrimage is discussed in the context of other such journeys in Elizabeth Clark, *Ascetic Piety and Women's Faith*. (Lewiston, N.Y.: Edwin Mellen Press, 1986.) 47-48.

25.In 1 Tim 12,2. Derrick Sherwin Bailey, *Sexual Relations in Christian Thought* (New York: Harper and Row, 1959), 20.

26.In 1 Tim 7,4; In Tit 2,1; In Mat 68; 69; De vir 3; 25; and Ad vid jun 2f. This point is discussed by Elizabeth Clark, *Jerome, Chrysostom and Friends* (Lewiston, N.Y.: Edwin Mellen Press, 1979); *Women in the Early Church* (Wilmington, Del.: Michael Glazier, 1983); Yves Congar, *Lay*

People in the Church (Westminster, MD: Christian Classics, 1985), 86.
Thomas Cuming Hall, *History of Ethics Within Organized Christianity* (NY:
Charles Scribner's Sons, 1910), 208; and Daniel Callam, "The Origins of
Clerical Celibacy." (D. Phil. diss. Oxford University, 1977).

27.John taught that women were frail in In Heb 29,5 and counted manli-
ness as a virtue in In Jn 32,1.

28.De sac 3,17.

29.In Mat 5,5.

30.In Jn 21,2-3. Chrysostom's criticism of Mary was so atypical of the
fathers that he is labeled "odd man out" in one survey of the history of the
doctrine of the Virgin Mary (Hilda Graef, *Mary: A History of Doctrine and
Devotion* (New York: Sheed and Ward, 1963) 74.

31.Mat 12:46-49.

32.In Mat 44,1. (NPNF 10, 278-279).

33.In Jn 85,2 .

The Virtues of Family Life

When John preached against the debauchery of the theater of his day, he saw the deviate sexuality of the stage as a plot against the marriages in his congregation.[1] He also admonished his supposedly civilized audience in Antioch to imitate the "barbarians" who do not seek after such entertainments and continued the application of his message on the virtue of family life and the evils of the attack on it through the theater.

> You have a wife, you have children; what is equal to this pleasure? You have a house, you have friends, these are the true delights; besides their purity, great is the advantage they bestow. For what, I pray you, is sweeter than children? What sweeter than a wife, to him that will be chaste in mind?

> To this purpose, we are told, that the barbarians uttered on some occasion a saying full of wise severity. I mean, that having heard of these wicked spectacles, and the unseasonable delight of them; "Why these Romans," they say, "have devised these pleasures as though they did not have wives and children;" implying that nothing is sweeter than children and wife, if you are willing to live honestly.[2]

The family also nurtured spirituality and after we retire from the service of preaching and the Eucharist we should not return to business but to our homes and read our Bibles with our families.[3] In this way the home became a teacher in the life of the church.[4]

The marriage relationship was one of great intimacy. This intimacy was its strength but also a source of potential weakness.[5] Marriage was a great entangler of lives and also brought with it great pressure toward worldliness. John exhorted his congregation to a marriage marked by male leadership combined with compassion and a mutual pursuit of holiness. The wife was not an equal partner in the marriage.[6] John pointed out that when

Paul preached on family and social relationships, he required the same fear of wives for their husbands as he did of slaves for their masters.[7]

John clearly believed in the superiority of the celibate state. "If any marry thus, with these views, he will be but a little inferior to monks; the married but little below the unmarried."[8] John's advocation of virginity was predicated on his view of marriage. He saw it as an oppressive force for both parties but especially for the wife. The background of the wife must be carefully investigated.[9] The bride and the groom would not see each other until the wedding.[10] The marriage ceremony, in John's opinion, was more of Satan than of God and absurdities and superstitions were the norm.

> But when marriages are solemnized, such ridiculous things take place as you shall hear immediately, because the most part, possessed and beguiled by custom, are not even aware of their absurdity, but need others to teach them. For dancing, and cymbals, and flutes, and shameful words and songs and drunkenness and revellings and all the Devil's great heap of garbage is then introduced.

> I know indeed that I shall appear ridiculous in finding fault with these things and shall incur the charge of great folly with the generality, as disturbing the ancient laws, for, as I said before, great is the deceptive power of custom. But nevertheless, I will not cease repeating these things, for there is surely a chance, that although not all yet some few will receive our saying and will choose to be laughed to scorn with us, rather than we laugh with them such a laughter as deserves tears and overflowing punishment and vengeance.

> For how can it be other than worthy of the utmost condemnation that a girl who has spent her life entirely at home and been schooled in modesty from earliest childhood, should be compelled suddenly to cast off all shame and from the commencement of her marriage be instructed in imprudence, and find herself put forward in the middle of wanton and rude men and unchaste and effeminate? What evil will not be implanted in the bride from that day forward? Immodesty, petulance, insolence, the love of

vain glory, since they will naturally go on and desire to have all their days such as these. From this our women become expensive and profuse, from this they are void of modesty, from this proceed their unnumbered evils.[11]

He continued by saying that he was not opposed to marriage but to the pagan elements in the ceremonies. He realized that his views would be ill received. "Now I know that I am a troublesome sort of person and disagreeable, and morose, as though I were curtailing life of some of its pleasure."[12] He also objected to what he considered perverse customs that accompanied the birth of children.

Then after the marriage if perchance a child is born, in this case again we shall see that same folly and many practices full of absurdity. For when the time comes for giving the infant a name, caring not to call it after the saints as the ancients at first did, they light lamps and give them names, and name the child after that one which continues burning the longest, from thence conjecturing that he will live a long life....

The women in the bath, nurses and waiting maids take up mud and smearing it with the finger make a mark on the child's forehead, and if one ask, What means the mud and the clay? the answer is, "It turns away an evil eye, witchcraft and envy." Astonishing! what power in the mud! what might in the clay! what mighty force is this which it has? It averts all the hosts of the devil. Tell me, can you help hiding yourselves for shame.

Now among the Greeks such things should be done is no wonder, but among the worshippers of the Cross, and partakers in unspeakable mysteries, and professors of such high morality that such unseemliness should prevail, this is especially to be deplored again and again.[13]

John assumed that the marriages would be arranged by parents for their children and recommended that this be done when the children were young to prevent immorality.[14] Marriage was used to control sexual passion.[15] Parents should not use marriage to further their own social position or that of their children. Marrying for money leads to disaster.[16]

However, even though marriage had great entanglements and cares, it must never be used as an excuse for spiritual lethargy.[17] Many of the great heroes of Scripture were married.[18]

> I also always entreat you, and do not cease entreating you, not only to pay attention here to what I say, but also when you are at home, to persevere continually in reading the divine Scriptures. When I have been with each of you in private, I have not stopped giving you the same advice. Do not let anyone say to me those vain words, worthy of a heavy condemnation, "I cannot leave the courthouse, I administer the business of the city, I practice a craft, I have a wife, I am raising children, I am in charge of a household, I am a man of the world; reading the Scriptures is not for me, but for those who have been set apart, who have settled on the mountaintops, who keep this way of life continuously." What are you saying, man? That attending to the Scriptures is not for you, since you are surrounded by a multitude of cares? Rather it is for you more than for them. They do not need the help of the divine Scriptures as much as those do who are involved in many occupations. The monks who are released from the clamor of the marketplace and have fixed their huts in the wilderness, who own nothing in common with anyone, but practice wisdom without fear in the calm of that quiet life, as if resting in a harbor, enjoy great security; but we, as if tossing in the midst of the sea, driven by a multitude of sins always need continuous and ceaseless aid of the Scriptures. They rest far from the battle, and so they do not receive many wounds; but you stand continuously in the front rank, and you receive continual blows. So you need more remedies. Your wife provokes you, for example, your son grieves you, your servant angers you, your enemy plots against you, your friend envies you, your neighbor curses you, your fellow soldier trips you up, often a law suit threatens you, poverty troubles you, loss of your property gives you grief, prosperity puffs you up, misfortune depresses you, and many causes and compulsions to discouragement and grief, to conceit and desperation surround us on all sides, and a multitude of missiles falls from everywhere. There

we have a continuous need for the full armor of the Scriptures.[19]

John sought to be prophetic to his congregation as he preached on marriage. He criticized cultural and legal norms that he believed did not conform to Scripture. In the legal climate of his era, the man was given freedom to violate the Scriptural mandates against adultery where similar behavior by women was proscribed. John preached the unpopular notion that adultery was the same for men and women and cited the law of the empire as being contrary to the will of God on this issue.[20]

Education of Children

John was an educated man and his widowed mother had sacrificed greatly to provide for him the best of pagan learning. Even though he critiqued and even renounced many facets of non-Christian wisdom he believed strongly that the education of the young must be purposeful and broad.[21] The excesses avoided at the marriage celebration set the climate of moderation and the true Christian philosophy for the family.[22] Raising children properly was a blessing to the family, especially for women.[23] John told his audience that raising a child in a proper godly manner did not mean that the child was going to become a monk or a virgin.[24]

The education process began at home. For John, because of the sex-differentiated roles in society, the mother led in the training of daughters and the father supervised the education of his sons.[25] John deemphasized corporal punishment. The child should know that the parents would use the rod, but they should not resort to it often as that would alienate the child and cause him to despise their discipline.[26] Education did not necessarily end with training in the home. There was a place for the wisdom of the non-Christian world. He specifically mentioned the use of rhetoric in education, a skill that formed a significant part of the base of his ministry.[27] His own course of study under a pagan rhetor, followed by a period of monastic asceticism heavily influenced his prescription for the families of his congregation. He saw the possibility of a Christian paideia based on the nurturing

ministry of the monks as a formative period in the life of the youth who
would later serve in secular pursuits.[28]

Widows

Marriage and remarriage were separate issues for John. He did not
forbid marriage, and he spoke out against the Valentinians and Manichees
who undervalue this divine institution.[29] He exhorted his congregation, "And
you, are you unable to practice virginity? Be chaste in marriage."[30]

Even though John would not forbid marriage he did recommend against
remarriage for those who were widowed. As he told the young widow in a
poignant letter, she could relieve herself of the cares of widowhood or a
second marriage if she entered the service of the Church and did not
remarry.[31] During this time there were 3,000 widows on the roles at Antioch,
and their contribution to the Church's ministry was significant.[32] John noted
that the standards were stricter for widows than for virgins, and that they
were held in great honor both in the Church and before the divine throne.[33]

Homosexuality

In John's view, homosexuality was a detestable perversion of both the
body and the soul. It was a perversion of the human sexual roles that were
to find their outworking in marriage. As he commented on the "unnatural
affections" in the first chapter of Paul's letter to the Romans,[34] he reasoned
that there were two levels of sin involved. There was the bodily perversion
of homosexuality and there was also the "unnatural affections" which was an
orientation of the soul. He believed that the latter were worse because "the
soul is more the sufferer in sins, and more dishonored, than the body in
diseases."[35]

Clerical Cohabitation

Another problem that he faced was the cohabitation by members of
the clergy with virgins. This arrangement of spiritual partnership was a
scandal in the church and John preached against it. When John began his
attack on this relationship, he classed it as a new innovation.

In our ancestors' era, two justifications were given for men and women living together. The first, marriage, was ancient, licit, and sensible, since God was its legislator.... And the other, prostitution, of more recent origin than marriage, was unjust and illegitimate, since it was introduced by evil demons. But in our time, a third way of life has been dreamed up, something new and incredible which greatly perplexes those who wish to discover its rationale. There are certain men who apart from marriage and sexual intercourse take girls inexperienced with matrimony, establish them permanently in their homes, and keep them sequestered until ripe old age, not for the purpose of bearing children (for they deny that they have sexual relations with the women), nor out of licentiousness (for they claim that they preserve them inviolate). If anybody asks the reason for this practice, they have plenty and start rehearsing them; however, I myself think that they have not found a single decent plausible excuse.[36]

The relationship may have had pure motives, but John believed that the weaknesses of the people involved and the tremendous temptations toward immorality made these idealistic unions impractical on earth. He also believed that the relationship brought dishonor on the Church as outsiders perceived these unions as perverse.[37] He also saw these relationships as dangerous because they wrongly applied the liberating remedy of celibacy. Married women aged quicker than virgins and this served to ease sexual desire among the married. However women in these relationships preserved their youth and the men who lived with them were constantly tempted by their youthful sexuality.

Since sexual intercourse is not hindered in a relationship with a legitimate wife, it serves to still passion and often leads the man to satiation, greatly reduce his desire. And besides this, the birth pangs, parturition, the bearing and rearing of children, and prolonged sicknesses with their aftereffects beseige the body, cause the bloom of youth to fade, and produce a diminution of the sting of pleasure. But with the virgin, nothing of this sort happens, for their is no intercourse which can restrain and relax the frenzy of nature, nor do labor pains and childrearing dry up her flesh; to the contrary, these virgins stay in their prime for a long time, since they remain untouched. After the birth and care of children, the bodies of married women become feeble, but these women retain their beauty until they are forty, rivalling the virgins being led to the nuptial chamber![38]

He also noted the effeminate characteristics it bred in the men involved.[39]

Throughout his treatise against these unions, there is a tone of pastoral frustration as John attempted to persuade people to abandon these relationships. At one point, he vented his frustration in the following dramatic terms.

For when the virgins invade the marketplace or when a conversation takes place about them at home, the people who discuss this strange coupling, if they wish to signify the female companion of such a man, do not call her his mother (for she did not give birth to him), nor his sister (for she did not unloose the same birth pangs), nor his spouse (for she does not dwell with him according to the law of marriage), nor any other relation's name upon which we can agree and which is legitimate; instead, they call her by a term which is shameful and ludicrous. For my part, I will not even suffer to pronounce it, so much do I despise and spurn the very name. Even the expression "living together" offends me.[40]

Work and Labor

John did not share a worldview that disparaged the labor of the artisan or even the slave. Work preserved people from the spiritual ills caused by laziness and exemplified by the leisured class. Work also was a vehicle for demonstrating the love of God to others as the worker provided for the needs of his fellow citizens.[41] He viewed the work of the lower classes of society as a source of strength to both the family and the society in general. He often spoke of the folly of an owner being proud of the craftsmanship of his possessions. The artisan should rather take the credit. Children should be taught this and learn not to despise the work of the laborer.[42] Many types of artisans are mentioned in his sermons and he had a somewhat romantic view of their place in society. He portrayed them as the exploited pillars of the urban community. He also gave the impression that there was some mobility in society for those who were not of the poorest classes, and that artisans had some control over their work and the arrangement of apprentices for their sons.[43]   John believed that the worker could nourish his soul in a similar way to the ascetic.   "Let no one therefore, of those who have trades be ashamed... For to be supported by continual hard work is a sort of asceticism."[44]   He pointed out workers in the Scriptures as examples to his flock. The Ethiopian Eunuch was an example of one who did common work but showed great a great desire for godliness.[45]

1.In Mat 37,8; In 1 Thess 5,4.

2.In Mat 37,9. (NPNF 10, 250).

3.In Mat 5,1; In Gen 2,13.

4.Rowan A. Greer, *Broken Lights and Mended Lives: Theology and Common Life in the Early Church* (University Park: Pennsylvania State University Press, 1986), 109-110; A. C. Repp, "John Chrysostom on the Christian Home as a Teacher." *Concordia Theological Monthly* 22 (1951): 937-948; and S. R. Williams, "The Household in the Early Church with Comparative Selective References to the Pagan Culture of the Roman World." (B. Litt. thesis. Oxford University, 1978).

5.In Eph 20.

6.In Eph 13; 20. Derrick Sherwin Bailey, *Sexual Relations in Christian Thought* (New York: Harper and Row, 1959), 62.

7.In Eph 22.

8.In Eph 20. (NPNF 13, 151). John made similar comments in In Col 10.

9.Cat ill 1,15.

10.Cat ill 1,12; 11,1.

11.In 1 Cor 12,11. (NPNF 12, 69). Similar references to abuse at the wedding ceremony are contained in In il Prop; In 1 Tim 9; In Col 12; and De inani gloria 88.

12.In 1 Cor 12,11.

13.In 1 Cor 12, 13-14. (NPNF 12, 71) A similar reference to pagan customs at birth is in In Col 8, fin.

14.De inani gloria 81; In Mat 59,7.

15.In 1 Thess 5. John is unclear on the purpose of intercourse. In In Titus he allowed that it is broader than for procreation as it is permitted for the elderly, but in In 1 Thess 5 and In il Prop he seemed to limit it to procreation. In Con e q sub 1 he stated that it reduced desire and stilled passion. In In Gen 15,14 he speculated that no intercourse was needed before the Fall. John T. Noonan, *Contraception: A History of Its Treatment by the Catholic Theologians and Canonists* (New York: New American Library, 1965), 104, 110.

16.In Eph 20; In Mat 74,4; Ad Theo 2,5.

17.Cat ill 7,28; In Heb 7,11; In 1 Cor 19,3.

18.In Mat 55,8.

19.De Laz 3,1. (Roth. *On Wealth and Poverty*. 58-59). See also De sac 6,5 and In Mat 2,10.

20.In 1 Thess 5; In 1 Cor 19,3.

21.In Eph 21; In 1 Tim 9; De Anna 1; De inani gloria 16f; In Mat 59,7. The education program must be a guided gradual pattern of education so as not to burden their level of understanding. cf De inani gloria 52. This point is discussed in Stephen D. Benin, "Sacrifice as Education in Augustine and Chrysostom." *Church History* 52 (1983): 8.

22.In 1 Cor 12,13, In Col 8,fin.

23.In 1 Tim 9.

24.In Eph 21.

25.De inani gloria 90.

26.De inani gloria 30.

27.In Col 4.

28.In Adv op 3 John argued before Christian parents that training under the monks was beneficial for the children who would later serve in the city in secular pursuits. He also proposed a Christian paideia with monastic roots. This aspect of John's thought in this early treatise is developed in David G. Hunter's "John Chrysostom's *Adversus Oppugnatores Vitae Monas-*

ticae: Ethics and Apologetics in the Late Fourth Century." (Ph.D. diss. The University of Notre Dame, 1986.) p. 183f.

29.In 1 Tim 12.

30.This was a frequent application in John's sermons before his congregations in Antioch and Constantinople. See In Mat 7,7; 45,3; In Rom 30,3; In Eph 20,9; In Phil 12,3; In 2 Thess 6,4; In 2 Tim 10,5; In Tit 2; In Heb 7,4; In Gen 12,4; In il: Vidi dom 4,2, 6,1; Adv op 3,13;

31.In Jn 63; In 1 Thess 5,2; De vir 40; In il Vid elig 5, 6; De n iter; In Acta 49,4; In 1 Thess 6,2; In 1 Tim 10,1; In Tit 2,1.

32.In Mat 66,2.

33.In 1 Tim 14; In 1 Cor 19,7; In Jn 70,2.

34.Romans 1:26-27.

35.In Rom 4,1.   Bernardette Brooten, "Patristic Interpretations of Romans 1:26." *Studia Patristica* 18 (1985) vol. 1. 287-292;   Chrysostom condemned the rampant homosexuality of the philosophical schools of Antioch in Adv op 3,8. This is discussed by John Boswell in *Christianity, Social Tolerance and Homosexuality* (Chicago: University of Chicago Press, 1980) 131-132. Boswell believes that the condemnations of the Church Fathers were delivered against ritualistic cult homosexual prostitution or pederasty. As David F. Wright points out in "Homosexuals or Prostitutes." *Vigiliae Christianae*. 38 (1984): 125-153 Boswell's reasoning is based on a faulty analysis of the evidence. W.L. Peterson in "Can *arsenokoitai* be translated by 'Homosexuals'?" *Vigiliae Christianae* 40 (1986): 187-191 attempts to counter some of Wright's reasoning, asking whether the modern concept of homosexuality can be transported into ancient texts. Wright .has countered Peterson's objections in "Translating *arsenokoitai*," *Vigiliae Christianae*. 41 (1987): 396-398.

36.Con e q sub 1 (Clark. *Jerome, Chrysostom and Friends*. 164-165).

37.Con e q sub 2f.

38.Con e q sub 1 (Clark. *Jerome, Chrysostom and Friends*. 166).

39.For a fuller discussion of the phenomenon and Chrysostom's response to it see Elizabeth Clark, "John Chrysostom and the Subintroductae." *Church History* 46 (1977): 171-185, reprinted in *Ascetic Piety and Women's Faith*. (Lewiston, N.Y.: Edwin Mellen Press, 1986.) 265-290.

40.Con e q sub 4 (Clark. *Jerome, Chrysostom and Friends*. 220).

41.Eric Osborn, *Ethical Patterns in Early Christian Thought*. (Cambridge: Cambridge University Press, 1976) 120-121. For a more complete treatment see Lucien Daloz, *Le Travail Selon Saint Jean Chrysostom* (Paris: P. Lethielleux, 1959).

42.De inani gloria 13. E.M. Thomas, "Guilds of Craftsmen and Small Traders in the Ancient World (exclusive of Egypt) from the Earliest Greek Times to the End of the Fifth Century A.D." (B. Litt. thesis. Oxford University, 1934); A.H.M. Jones, *The Greek City from Alexander to Justinian* (Oxford, Oxford University Press, 1940), 192, 194f; Cod Theo 14,3,1.7; 14,4,1.8; R.M. Price, "The Role of Military Men in Syria and Egypt from Constantine to Theodosius II." (D. Phil. diss. Oxford University, 1973).

43.In Mat 1,5; 26,6; 88,4; De Anna 5,3; De Laz 2,3; De bap Chris 1; In Rom 17,5. This point is developed in W. Ceran, "Stagnation and Fluctuation in Early Byzantine Society." *Byzantinoslavonica* 31 (1970): 198-201.

44.In 1 Cor 5,11.

45.In Acta 19,3.

> And I know well, that to many I am overly minute in busying
> myself about these things; I shall not however refrain from this.
> For the cause of all our evils is this, such faults being at all count-
> ed trifling, and therefore disregarded.[1]

John made this point to his audience after criticizing the extravagant tastes
of the rich, which by their "vulgar ostentation" perverted the work of the
craftsmen such as sandal makers, cooks, and builders.[2] He continued in the
homily to criticize the morals of the youth of the city.[3] The preacher must
critique the society and challenge it to be more faithful to the biblical
standards of conduct. The Scriptures were not only set forth in exposition
but were also held up as a mirror to judge the people and to lead them to
the true philosophy, to live a heavenly life on earth.

One of the areas of Chrysostom's life that Palladius felt the need to
defend was his refusal to engage in the social life of the capital. Not only
did he refuse to banquet with the rich, but he also did not entertain the
clergy to their expectations. Palladius' foil in the dialogue in defense of
John's life argues that John could have followed the example of Christ eating
with the twelve and provided for his clergy. Palladius defended John by
noting that the priests expected a feast served at their demand and to take
food away from the poor and sick for this purpose would be most unChrist-
like.[4]

Social Issues

Abortion was commonly used to terminate the pregnancies of prostitutes in John's day, and he spoke out against this evil as an example of sin
leading to further sin.

> Why sow where the ground makes its care to destroy the fruit?
> Where there are many efforts at abortion? Where there is
> murder before the birth? For even the harlot you do not allow
> to continue as a mere harlot but make her a murderer also. You

see how drunkenness leads to whoredom, whoredom to adultery, adultery to murder; or rather to something even worse than murder. For I have no name to give it, since it does not involve a thing born, but prevents its being born. Why then do you abuse the gift of God and fight with His laws, and follow after what is a curse as if a blessing, and make the chamber of procreation a chamber for murder, and arm the woman who was given for childbearing for slaughter.[5]

Slavery was a firmly established institution in John's day. However, this did not exempt this practice from the critique of the prophetic preacher. In the introduction to his three homilies on Paul's letter to Philemon, John gave a conservative analysis to the plight of the "race of slaves."

But it is useful for you to learn that this epistle was sent upon necessary matters. Observe therefore how many things are rectified thereby. We have this one thing first, that in all things it becomes one to be earnest. For if Paul bestows so much care upon a runaway, a thief, and a robber, and does not refuse and is not ashamed to send him back with such commendations....

Secondly, that we ought not abandon the race of slaves, even if they have proceeded to extreme wickedness....

Thirdly, that we ought not to withdraw slaves from the service of their masters.

Let me also say one other thing. He teaches us not to be ashamed of our domestics, if they are virtuous. For if Paul, the most admirable of men, speaks thus much in favor of this one, much more should we speak favorably of ours.[6]

He did temper his remarks about slavery with a reminder that from an eternal perspective "slavery is nothing but a name. The lordship that is according to the flesh is brief and temporary; for whatever is of the flesh, is transitory."[7] He also told parents to teach their children that slavery was not part of God's original creation but was a result of sin. This shows both the transitory nature of the institution and the awesome consequences of sin.

Teach him the facts of natural society and the difference between slave and free man. Say to him: "My son, there were no slaves of old in the time of our forebears, but sin brought slavery in its train; for when one insulted his father, he paid this penalty, to become his brother's bondsman."[8]

Slavery was not a block to piety. Just as Onesimus could be useful as a slave and returned to his master as a fellow-Christian yet still a slave, so also Joseph as a slave was freer than his master's wife who was a slave to sin.[9] People who reject the truth are more confined than slaves.[10]

In addition to seeing the institution of slavery as a seedbed for illustrating spiritual truth, John also preached against the abuse of slaves as part of his prophetic call to the city for misuse of all forms of wealth.[11]

Private Property

John's preaching on wealth must be viewed in the context of his teaching on property and ownership. Ultimate ownership belongs to God alone and all possession by man was conditional, a form of stewardship. The issue was not absolute control of property because of ownership but rather ascertaining God's will in the use of property.[12] The words "mine own" are a "curse and abominable... brought in by the Devil."[13] The love of money seen in the concept of absolute ownership corrupts the soul.[14]

In addition to preaching out against a view of property that included absolute control and ownership, John also spoke out prophetically against two other abuses in his society, usury and unjust contracts. He contended that when Christ spoke about not refusing the one who would borrow from you,[15] He did not mean the system of John's day involving a contract with interest.[16] He also noted that many of the cares of the rich were tied up in their concerns about interest, contracts, and securities for loans.[17] John also called for the rich to give to the poor by cancelling unjust contracts made with them.[18]

Abuse of Wealth

The city was a place of wealth and power. The upper class could show their wealth and power by great displays.[19] John described the church as having a revenue of "one of the lowest among the wealthy" and yet able to support the 3,000 widows and virgins on its rolls in addition to those who serve in the hierarchy. It was also able to carry out its ministries to the prisoners, sick, and poor. This analysis of the distribution of assets is a striking commentary on the concentration of wealth in his day.[20]

Wealth was also a force that compromised the ministry of the Church and constrained its prophetic voice.

> Therefore it is not possible for us to open our mouths, when the state of the church is no better than that of the worldly men. Have you not heard that the apostles would not consent so much as to distribute the money that was collected without any trouble? But now our bishops have gone beyond agents, and stewards, and hucksters in their care about these things; and when they ought to be careful and thoughtful about your souls, they are vexing themselves every day about these things, for which innkeepers, and tax-gatherers, and accountants, and stewards are careful.

> For I suppose that by the grace of God they that assemble here amount to the number of 100,000[21], and if each bestowed one loaf to some one of the poor; all would be in plenty; but if one farthing only, no one would be poor; and we should not undergo so many revilings and jeers in consequence of our care about money. For indeed the saying, "sell thy goods and give to the poor, and come and follow me"[22] might be seasonably addressed to the prelates of the church with respect to the property of the church.

> Hence great neglect of the Scriptures, and remissness in prayers, and indifference about all other duties; for it is not possible to be split into two things with due zeal.[23]

Earlier, in his treatise *On the Priesthood*, he lamented the difficulty of maintaining balance with the pressure of dealing with the church's finances.[24] He concluded at a number of points in his homilies that an overemphasis on finances had led the church to abandon its proper ministry.[25]

When he preached from the book of Acts on the life of the early Christian community, while Archbishop of Constantinople, he advocated the principle of communal ownership. He estimated that the wealth held by the those in the Christian community in the capital city amounted to at least 200,000 pounds of gold. He asserted that the 50,000 poor of the city could be easily cared for and that food preparation would be more efficient if meals were taken in common. He cautioned his audience that he was only proposing this and closed this illustration wishfully, "If God grant life, I trust that we will soon bring you over to this way of life."[26]

As John preached on pride and childrearing he saw that a self-indulgent materialism contributed to both wrongful self elevation and to the destruction of young children as they learned spiritually destructive habits. Christians should use their material resources to demonstrate their values and beliefs in the same way as the pagans do.

> At this point I direct my discourse to the faithful among us who refuse to hand over a trifling sum to Christ when He is poor and lacking the barest sustenance; and what the pagans spend on harlots and mimes and dancers in return for a single shout of applause, these our Christian will not give for the sake of the eternal kingdom.[27]

John then proceeded to demonstrate that all expenditures greater than one's needs were a misuse of the wealth God has given. He concludes with the rule: "clothing to cover us, a roof and walls, shoes these belong to the necessities, but all other possessions are superfluous."[28]

As John preached against wrongful use of wealth he attempted, at times unsuccessfully, to maintain his stance that the abuse of wealth, not its possession, was sin. Christians should never be self indulgent with what has been entrusted to them by God.[29] Money should be used for eternal gain. In addition to giving it to others, it can be invested strategically for the Kingdom of God. The rich can promote the salvation of those who work for them by setting up oratories for preaching on their estates.[30] Christians must use their wealth to benefit others and always control it and not let it control them.[31]

Wealth is perverted when it is not used to advance the Church or to meet basic human needs. After complaining on the impracticality of silk shoe laces because the wearing of them focuses the attention of the wearer on the ground so he can avoid soiling his treasured laces instead of focusing on heaven, John suggested that the shoes could be worn around the neck or on the head so they will not be soiled. When the response was laughter, he answered that he was inclined to weep for their madness because they would rather soil their bodies than their shoes, totally losing the functionality, and hence, the rationality, of clothes.[32] He entered into this tirade on style over function when he remarked on the moderation of the disciples in only having five loaves and two fishes between twelve men.[33] Near the end of the homily he laments on the youths of his day.

> For I suppose no general prides himself so much on his legions and trophies, as our profligate youths on the decking out of their shoes, on their trailing garments, and on the dressing of their hair; yet surely all these are the work of other people, in their trades.[34]

Consistent themes in John's condemnation of ostentation were the sin inherent in abandoning of functionality and the fact that an owner is foolish enough to think that he can take pride in the craftsmanship of an object. Throughout his preaching on the subject, the craftsman is the hero and the victim of the ostentation of the rich. His true function was perverted; he was the creator of what is worn or displayed, but he received no credit.[35]

Not only did John preach against those who wore expensive clothing, but he also preached against those husbands who displayed their wealth by adorning their wives.[36] John viewed this as degrading to the wife because the husband made her equal to his horse who also served as a vehicle to display his treasures.[37] He taught the catechumen that the adorning of women should be avoided and at one point concluded that it is almost blasphemous.

> I wish you women to abstain not only from other hurtful practices, but also from the habit of painting your faces and adding to them, as if the workmanship were defective. By doing so you insult the Workman.[38]

He concluded at another point that physical beauty lasts only twenty years before old age and the wrinkles it brings.[39]

Wealth that was not used to further the work of the church or to meet basic needs turned against the one who held on to it wrongly. Wealth held in this way clouded the mind and blocked the full appreciation of spiritual things.[40] A specific example of this consequence that riled the preacher was the practice of the rich talking over matters of business during the divine worship.[41] Wealth held wrongly "mars the garment of righteousness."[42] When preaching of Paul's injunction in Ephesians, chapter five, verse five, that no covetous man shall have any inheritance in the kingdom of God, he warned his congregation that "the statement is not hyperbolical, it is true."[43] He continued by showing that this teaching of the apostle was built firmly on the foundation of Christ's teaching on the subject.

> If then it is not possible to serve God and Mammon, they who serve Mammon[44] have thrown themselves out of the service of God; and they who have denied His sovereignty, and serve lifeless gold, it is plain enough that they are idolaters.[45]

Two assumptions that seem to lie at the base of much of John's preaching on money were his beliefs that wealth is always gotten at another's expense and that it is always gotten wrongly if the circumstances are closely examined. He exhorted his audience to invest in the Kingdom of Heaven because there "our wealth comes not from another's loss."[46] His preaching on the second point was marked by an ethical dilemma, as he concluded that even though the wealth was obtained wrongly by an ancestor, the present holder of the property did not sin in its accrual. In the end he did "not urge this argument too closely" but declared that owned property was not primary because the more important things are clearly held in common. To show this, he used an example from his own culture of the centrally important marketplace, which was the most important location in the city but was not private property as well as examples from creation.

> Tell me, then, whence art thou rich? From whom did you receive it and he who transmitted it to you? From his father and his grandfather. But can you, ascending through many generations, show the acquisition just? It cannot be. The root and origin of it must have been injustice. Why? Because God in the beginning made not one man rich and another poor. Nor did He afterwards take and show to one treasures of gold, and deny to the other the right of searching for it.. But He left the earth free to all alike....

> But I will not urge this argument too closely. Let your riches be justly gained, and without rapine. For you are not responsible for the covetous acts of your father. Your wealth may be derived from rapine, but you were not the plunderer. Or granting that he did not obtain it by robbery, that his gold was cast up somewhere out of the earth....

> Mark the wise dispensation of God. That He might put mankind to shame, He has made certain things common as the sun, air, earth, and water, the heaven, the sea, the light, the stars, whose benefits are dispensed equally to all as brethren....

> Why is it that there is never a dispute about a market place? Is it not because it is common to all? But about a house, and about property, men are always disputing. Things necessary are set before us in common; but even in the least things we do not observe a community. Yet those greater things He has opened freely to all, that we might thence be instructed to have these inferior things in common. Yet for all this, we are not instructed.[47]

Gluttony and Drunkenness

An abuse of wealth that John often saw as illustrative of the dehumanizing, carnal nature of excess in any form was gluttony. When food is consumed above the level of need, John remarked "the increase of luxury is but the multiplication of dung."[48]   He pointed out with great illustrative flourish that all that is increased by excess consumption is excrement.   One's spiritual desires were lessened as one put over-nourishment of the body ahead of any desire for food for the soul.[49]   In addition to dulling the soul, gluttony also clouded the mind and made men irrational.[50]   And finally, it also affected the body. It was bad for health and caused disease.[51]   The rich man rising late in the day burdened by excess, was vividly portrayed for John's audience.

> But this man, rising from his bed when the noon sun has filled the market-place, and people are tired of their several works, then this man gets up, stretching himself out just as if he were indeed a hog in fattening, having the fairest part of the day in darkness.   Then he sits there for a long time on his bed, often unable even to lift himself up from last evening's debauch, and having wasted still more time in this listlessness proceeds to adorn himself, and issues forth, a spectacle on unseemliness with nothing human about him, but with all the appearance of a beast with a human shape: his eyes rheumy from the effect of wine, while the miserable soul, just like the lame is unable to rise, bearing about its bulk of flesh, like an elephant.[52]

Drunkenness was another example of excess and, like all other sin, a matter a choice.   It was "a self-chosen demon; it eclipses reason, renders understanding barren, it feeds its fuel to our carnal passions."[53]   John's thoughts regarding excess in general were applied in this area.   Excess was not part of the true Christian philosophy and therefore dehumanized men and especially women, the weaker sex.   It attacked the entire being in both body and soul.   In the immaterial soul both the mind and the spirit were affected; the mind was clouded and the spirit was turned from God.   There were also effects in the physical body that undermined spirituality.   For example, excessive alcohol consumed at meals prevented one from giving thanks to God as one ought after eating from His provision.[54]   Excess quickly became compulsion and obsession.

> When wine-tipplers get up each morning, they start their
> meddlesome probing to discover where they will find the day's
> drinking-bouts, carousals, parties, revels, and drunken brawls; they
> busy themselves searching for bottles, mixing bowls, and drinking
> cups.[55]

Class Distinctions

The prophetic role of the bishop necessarily applied this view of moderation and a needs-based consumption to the class structure of the city. There were the rich and the poor, and John often reminded his audience, which contained all classes, to develop a broader focus than the immediate. He alluded to the vacillations of politics and the quick downfall of those who had been in power and concluded that the fate of the rich is often worse than that of the poor.

> How such a one's splendid and famous mansion fell down; How
> is it so entirely desolate that all things that were in it have come
> into hands of others; How many trials have taken place daily
> about this same property, what a stir; How many of that man's
> relations have died either beggars or inhabitants of a prison.[56]

The life of a rich man was a life full of care for his wealth and how he could preserve and expand it. He must always be on the look out for robbers and others who would attack his fortune.[57] The rich must even be watchful of those who would call themselves friends as they might only be attracted by wealth and power. John pitied the man who had "parasites" for friends.[58]

John reminded his audience that Christ identified with those who were poor by this world's standards.[59] He also said that he would rather sit with the poor like Christ than with the rich.[60] John even contended that Paul was of lowly birth but rose to be the greatest of Apostles.[61] The rich should not only refrain from oppressing the poor but should provide a room for the poor and so serve Christ.[62]

John was consistent with his theme of moderation as the key to the

Christian philosophy when he concluded that "he who can live on a little is far greater than he who cannot."[63] The prophetic role of the bishop in the city was based on John's firm belief that the moderate, philosophical Christian life was best for the individual in society and best for society as whole. It strengthened an individual's relationship with God and attacked divisive forces in society. The bishop was the advocate for this transforming force.

1.In Mat 49,5. (NPNF 10, 307).

2.In Mat 49,5.

3.In Mat 49,7-8. He returned to this theme later in the series in In Mat 59,7.

4.Palladius. *Dialogue*. 13.

5.In Rom 24, fin. (NPNF 11, 520).

6.In Philemon, Arg. (NPNF 13, 546).

7.In Eph 22. (NPNF 13, 157).

8.De inani gloria 71; (Laistner. *Christianity and Pagan Culture*. 115). John was most probably alluding to the incident of Noah and Ham as recorded in Genesis 9.

9.In 1 Cor 19,5.

10.In Eph 12, fin.

11.In 1 Cor 40,6 is an example of this theme in his preaching.

12.In 1 Cor 10,7. A summary of the views of various Church Fathers against an absolute view of ownership is given in Dale Vree, "Radical Bishops." *New Oxford Review* October, 1984. 22-25.

13.In Eph 20. John's view of possession is discussed by Charles Avila, *Ownership: Early Christian Teaching* (Maryknoll, NY: Orbis, 1983) 85-87.

14.In Jn 69,1. John believed that differences in wealth among the people of the world could only be explained by evil avarice, because in the beginning when God created the world there was no such inequality. In 1 Tim 12. This point is discussed in George Wolfgang Forell, *History of Christian Ethics* (Minneapolis: Augsburg, 1979) 148-149.

15.Mat. 5:42.

16.In Mat 18,3.

17.In Mat 56,8.

18.In Mat 54,9. He also pointed out that debtors are shamed by being forced to wear wooden collars in In Col 8.

19.These included public sponsorship of theatre as mentioned in De inani gloria 4. The wealth of the city of Antioch was attested, among many literary allusions, by the fine domestic mosaics which have been excavated at the site. W. F. Albright, "Explorations and Excavations in Palestine and Syria." *American Journal of Archaeology* 40 (1935): 166.

20.In Mat 66,3-4.

21.Probably the sum of the congregations in Antioch out of a total population of about 250,000.

22.Mat. 19:21.

23.In Mat 85,4. (NPNF 10, 510).

24.De sac 3,16.

25.In Mat 85,4; In 1 Cor 21,11.

26.In Acta 11,3.   Other examples in John's preaching where he used the extreme wealth of the rich to further an application are In Mat 70,2 fin and In Acta 11,3 (In Mat was at Antioch and In Acta was in Constantinople.) Richard Schlatter (*Private Property: The History of an Idea.* 39) notes John's preaching of socialism in Constantinople in In Acta 11,3f and compares it to Jerome (Ep 130,14) and Augustine (Ep 147,4) who permitted private property but held that it was better to hold material goods in common.   Barry Gordon ("The Problem of Scarcity and the Christian Fathers: John Chrysostom and some Contemporaries," 109) believes that this emphasis in Chrysostom can be attributed to the general economic decline of the era as well as theological commitments.

27.De inani gloria 12. (Laistner. *Christianity and Pagan Culture.* 91).

28.De inani gloria 13. Other passages where John developed this thought include: In Eut 2,3; Ex in Ps 47; 48; In Mat 63,4; In 1 Cor 21,6; In Jn 65,3; and In 1 Thess 12, 3-5. This is discussed in Walter Sherwig, *Rich and Poor in Christian Tradition* (London: Burns, Oates and Washbourne, 1948), 35.

29.Elizabeth Clark, *Ascetic Piety and Women's Faith* (Lewiston, N.Y.: Edwin Mellen Press, 1986) 209f.

30.In Acta 18,4.

31.De Laz 2; 7; In 1 Cor 10,7; 13,8.

32.In Mat 49,7.

33.Mat 14:17.

34.In Mat 49,7. (NPNF 10, 309).

35.A beautiful example of John's condemnation of abused wealth is in In Col 7 where he was appalled that some women desired silver chamber pots while the poor were starving in the city.

36.In Mat 18,2 is another example of general preaching against expensive clothing. In Eph 13 and In Heb 28,14-15 are examples of his preaching against husbands who adorn their wives.

37.In Phil 10 John cited the lack of utility of adorning either a wife or a horse and both were condemned.

38.Cat. ill. 1,37. (Harkins. *Baptismal Instructions*. 38).   He also addressed this in Cat ill 1,34 and 12,42f.

39.In Heb 28,15.

40.Sections of John's writings that deal with this theme in general terms include In Jn 16,4; Cat ill 2,5; In Heb 33,9; In Mat 21,1; 63,1-2; In 1 Cor 11,10; In 1 Cor 16,9; 23,8; and Q nemo 1f. In In Mat 44,6 he stated further that wealth can cloud the mind and made people effeminate.

41.In Mat 88, fin.

42.In Eph 13.

43.In Eph 13.

44.cf Mat. 6:24.

45.In Eph 18. (NPNF 13, 133-4).

46.In Jn 54,3.

47.In 1 Tim 12. (NPNF 13, 447-8).

48.In 1 Tim 13. See also In 1 Cor 17,1.

49.In Jn 45,1. John saw the Jews as an example of this in Adv Jud 1,2,5.

50.In Jn 18,2.

51.Q nemo 8; In Jn 22,3. In In Acta 27,2 John stated that gluttony was especially bad in women. In 1 Cor, 39,17-18 he stated that it prevented people from growing to their full height.

52.In Acta 35,3. (NPNF 11, 222).

53.Cat ill 5,9.

54.De Laz 1. John continued his attacks on drunkenness in De Laz 1 and in In Mat 57,5 asked the question: "what is viler than a drunken woman."

55.Adv Jud 5,1,2. (Harkins. *Discourses Against Judaizing Christians*. 97).

56.In 1 Cor 11,10. (NPNF 12, 63).

57.In Phil 2.

58.In Col 1.

59.In Mat 48,8-9; 50,4; De inani gloria 12; Ad pop Anti 2,22.

60.In Col 1. In Mat 69,3. He also saw poverty as "the procurer of heaven" in In Phil 10 (NPNF 13, 233).

61.De laud s Paul 5.

62.In 1 Cor 40,6. John invited the rich to make a room for Christ in the poor in their homes. In Acta 40,2.

63.In Heb 2,fin.

CHAPTER 16
THE BISHOP AND UNBELIEF

John's Apologetic

The task of defending the Faith was a duty for all Christians.[1] Christians
must use Scripture as well as reason in their defense of the Faith, but as
they use reason they must avoid the negative example of the Apostle Thomas
in his refusal to believe until confronted with irrefutable evidence.[2] John
made use of reason to suggest proofs for Christians' beliefs but they were
usually so tied to allusions to Scripture that he seemed to have little faith in
the use of reason apart from the Bible.[3]

John's basic apologetic for the Christian faith was fourfold. A first
line of defense for the faith was the worldwide spread of the Gospel.

> That the Persian, the Sarmatian [an ancient people of Eastern
> Europe], the Moor and the Indian should be acquainted with the
> purification of the soul and of the power of God, and His
> unspeakable mercy to men, and the severe discipline of faith and
> the visitation of the Holy Spirit, and the resurrection of bodies,
> and the doctrines of life eternal. For in all these things and in
> whatever is more than these, the fisherman, initiating by Baptism
> divers races of Barbarians, persuaded them to live on high
> principles.[4]

In addition to the worldwide spread of the Gospel, its indestructibility
under persecution and the resoluteness of the Christians as they faced their
pagan foes were seen by John as evidences of its truth. This steadfastness
of the Christians showed the difference between the truth of their convictions
and the errors of their opponents. "Error is such that it is dissipated even
without opposition, but the truth prevails in the midst of hostile forces."[5]

> Our doctrine, which you say is fiction, has been assailed by
> tyrants, kings, orators of invincible eloquence, as well as by
> philosophers, sorcerers, magicians, and demons, and "their tongues
> against them are made weak" according to the prophetic saying,
> and "the arrows of children are their wounds."[6] Emperors

benefitted from their attack upon us only insofar as they gained a reputation for savagery worldwide. They were carried away by their anger against the martyrs into inhuman cruelty and did not realize that they were incurring untold disgrace. The philosophers and talented orators had a great reputation with the public on account of their dignity and their ability to speak. After the battle against us they became ridiculous and seemed no different from foolish children. From so many nations and peoples, they were not able to change anyone, wise ignorant, male, female, or even a small child. The estimation of what they wrote is so low that their books disappeared a long time ago, and mostly perished when they first appeared. If anything at all is found preserved, one finds it being preserved by Christians.[7]

Closely related to these two and usually mentioned in conjunction with them is the fact that the apostles who were of a humble state in society formed the base for the spread of the faith. In talking about Peter as he rose to speak at Pentecost, John contrasted him to the philosophers.

Without experience, without skill of the tongue, and in the condition of quite ordinary men, matched against juggling conjurors, against impostors, against the whole lying throng of sophists, of rhetoricians, of philosophers grown moldy in the Academy and the walks of the Peripatetics, against all these they fought the battle out. .... And Plato, who talked a great deal of nonsense in his day is silent now, while this man utters his voice everywhere; not only among his own countrymen alone but also among the Parthians, Medes, and Elamites, and in India, and in every part of the earth, and to the extremities of the world. Where now is Greece, with her big pretensions? Where is the name of Athens? Where is the ravings of the philosophers? He of Galilee, he of Bethsaida, he, the uncouth rustic, has overcome them all. Are you not ashamed- confess it - at the very name of the country of him who has defeated you? ...

Why then, it is asked, did not Christ exercise His influence upon Plato, and upon Pythagoras? Because the mind of Peter was much more philosophical than their minds.[8]

John then continued by showing that Peter's mind was more philosophical because he was more disposed to receive the grace of God. Plato, on the other hand, was one marked by shifting vanity and perverse thoughts. He proposed a republic where virgins went naked, sexual relations were unrestrained by the bonds of marriage, and the family was set aside.[9]

A final element in John's apologetic for the faith was fulfilled prophecy. He saw the "books of the Jews" as containing proofs of the validity of the Christian faith.

> I must bring forward as evidence the books of the Jews, who crucified him. I must go through the Scriptures, over which the Jews kept such careful guard, and set before the eyes of those who are still unbelieving the predictions and testimonies about Christ these books contain.[10]

He then proceeded to outline many instances of prophecies and allusions from the prophets fulfilled in the coming of Christ.

Reaching Out to Unbelief

Christians must reach out to those who live in unbelief outside the Church. John spoke of the travels of the apostles in the book of Acts and then commented that those in his audience did not need to travel to reach those outside the Church. He pointed out that there were those in his congregation who owned villages and fields and that they ought to build a church and bring in a member of the clergy to preach to their laborers. He contrasted their unwillingness to do the task of eternal significance with their great willingness to build a house for the emperor with no expense spared. He chided them for not providing for the souls of their laborers while providing baths, taverns, markets, and fairs to meet their baser needs and stimulate their drunkenness and covetousness. He implied that a priest might stimulate them to virtue and in the end might make the enterprise more profitable. He also pointed out the dynamics of the investment from an eternal perspective.

> Look not at the cost, but calculate the profit. Your people over there cultivate your field. You cultivate their souls. They bring

to you your fruits. You raise their souls to heaven.[11]
John also encouraged monks to engage in missionary work and thereby nourish the souls of others in addition to their ascetic disciplines designed to benefit their own spirituality.[12]

John presented Paul as an example in the task of confronting the pagan community with its multiplicity of gods.[13] John was aware of pagan challenges to the faith and mentioned Celsus and Plotinus in his homilies.[14] Pagan religions cannot be sanctified or redeemed. Even the presence of the Septuagint in the temple of Serapis in Alexandria did not sanctify this pagan edifice.[15] Pagan gods cannot save and act beneath the morality of the true God; they are, in fact, demons.[16]

Even though there was no further imperial attempt to suppress Christian ascendancy, it is clear that the empire did not immediately become Christian even among the high-ranking government officials. Just before the year 400, Flavian Nicomamchus, a praetorian prefect, restored worship of the gods in Rome and reestablished the Altar of Victory that had been removed earlier by Gratian. Other officials used opportunities of imperial weakness or periods of revolt to persecute the Christians during John's ministry and period of exile.[17]

During John's time in the capital city he had to deal with Gothic soldiers and officials who represented unbelief in two forms. Some still adhered to tribal religions and others had embraced Christianity through Arian missionaries.[18] He was opposed to the Arian faith of the Goths but felt that preaching the Trinitarian Gospel to them was superior to forced conversion.[19] The historian Theodoret noted that John himself preached to the Goths and, as was often the case in his ministry, felt the burden of the example of the Apostle Paul in this mission.

> Also, like Paul, feeling that he was a debtor to all men, he sent able preachers to Scythians and Goths, and he himself, through an interpreter, preached to the Goths who resided in Constan-

tinople.[20]

<u>Heretics</u>

Unbelief, as seen in the heretical sects of John's era, presented seemingly innumerable challenges to the bishop protecting his flock.   Any analysis of John's view of heresy must be prefaced by an understanding of his view of truth.   The quest for truth is not evolutionary, moving from partial truth or untruth to truth.   Rather, truth has come first 'through revelation while error is a deviation, usually a conscious deviation, from truth.   He saw scriptural support for this view in Christ's parable of the wheat and the tares in Matthew 13:24-30.   The wheat is sown and the tares are added afterward by the servants of the enemy.   John saw Christ making a comment on the nature of truth in this parable.

> And He signifies also that the error comes after the truth, which the actual event testifies.   For so after the prophets, were the false prophets; and after the apostles, the false apostles; and after Christ, Antichrist, for unless the Devil sees what to imitate, or against whom to plot, he neither attempts, nor knows how.[21]

Christians should not be offended or surprised at the existence of heretics because they have been with the Church since the time of the Apostles.[22] Truth, revealed truth, is preexistent, and when people do not respond in submission to this truth but set up their reasoning as a source of knowledge, then divisions arise.

> You see, whenever people are unwilling to take the consequences of following the norm of Sacred Scripture, wishing to make room for the vagaries of private reasoning, they upset their sense of balance and undermine the solid orthodoxy of dogmas with endless disputes and questioning.[23]

In addition to appealing to the revealed truth in the Scripture, John also appealed to the dogmas of the church, usually an appeal in areas of doctrine decided at the Councils of Nicea (325) and Constantinople (381).   In his eighth homily on Genesis he again used the analogy of wheat and tares and described Arian teaching as "those noxious ailments springing up like weeds among the dogmas of the Church."[24]

A second element common to all heresies in addition to a departure from revealed truth was deviation from a proper view of Christ. In John's sixth homily of Paul's letter to the Philippians, he addressed the Kenosis Passage. He announced that many heresies are defeated by this passage.

> Rouse yourselves then to behold so great a spectacle, so many armies falling by one stroke, lest the pleasure of such a sight should escape you.[25]

He then compared the sight to a chariot race where all of the drivers are overthrown by the victor as he dashes alone toward the finish amid the applause and cheers of the crowd. John proceeded to name a large catalog of heretics who were refuted by the Kenosis Passage. He included Arius, Paul of Samosata, Sabellius, Marcion, Valentinus, Manes, and Appolinarius as well as others. The tone of the passage was that all heresies were, at base, Christological. He drew a similar conclusion from conflicts with adherents of pagan religions in his second homily on Colossians.

> But if one must reason with a Greek, the discussion should not begin with this [sin, and judgment]; but whether Christ be God, and the Son of God, whether those gods of theirs be demons. If these points be established, all others follow; but, before making good the beginning, it is vain to dispute about the end.[26]

He exhorted his congregation that in "our contest with heretics, we must make the attack with minds in vigor, that they may be able to give exact attention."[27] In his pastoral ministry John often mentioned various heretical groups, usually with the basic aims of providing members of his flock with answers against their proselytizing efforts. He gave them explanations for their objections to the true faith and sought to convince his audience that they were rejecters of revealed truth.

The followers of Marcion were misled in their truncated canon. In the first chapter of Galatians Paul condemned those who bring another gospel, but the Marcian interpretation of this as necessitating the rejection of three of the four canonical gospels was clearly wrong. They were misled by the phrase "which is not another Gospel... as diseased people are injured even by healthy food... it is clear that the four Gospels are one Gospel... Paul is not speaking of the number but of the discrepancy of the things spoken."[28]

John saw the Arians as having the same basic problem as the Jews; they reject the Christ of the true faith.[29] John warned new Christians not to listen to them but to have an answer. He then proceeded to give them a quick apologetic for the Arian error.

> You must have these articles of faith accurately fixed in your minds, that you may not be easily overwhelmed by the deceits of the Devil. But if the Arians wish to trip you up, you should know for sure that you must block up your ears to what they say. Answer them with confidence, and show them that the Son is like in substance to the Father. For it is the Son Himself who said: As the Father raises up the dead and gives them life, even so the Son also gives life to whom He will.[30] And in all things He shows that He has equal power with the Father.[31]

The charge of easy forgiveness plagued John in his ministry. He believed strongly in the power of anyone to repent from their sin at any time and resented the teaching of the rigorist Novatians who saw no recourse on earth for some sinners. John remarked tauntingly to his congregation, "Where then be those who would cut off repentance?" and then gave a call for repentance from the people.[32] At another point he referred sarcastically to them as the "pure."[33]

Other heretical movements John condemned in his homilies include those of Paul of Samosata,[34] Sabellius the Libyan,[35] Apollinarius of Laodicea,[36] Mani,[37] and the Gnostics.[38] In a letter to Olympias shortly before his death he lamented the errors of a monk named Pelagius. It cannot be known for sure if this was the founder of the teaching that bears his name.[39]

1.In Jn 17,4.

2.In Jn 87,1. This principle was also addressed in De incomp die 1,26; 5,30; 5,40; In Col 4; and In Jn 23,3.

3.In Col 5; In Rom 3; 5; Ad pop Anti 9,5.

4.In 1 Cor 7,20 (NPNF 12, 43).   See also De s Bab c Jul 10 and Con Jud et gen 13.

5.De laud s Paul 4.

6.Psalm 63(64):8-9.

7.De s h Bab 11. (Schatkin and Harkins. *St. John Chrysostom- Apologist.* 81-82). This line of reasoning was also used in Con Jud et gen 15.

8.In Acta 4,3-4. (NPNF 11, 29-30).

9.In Acta 4,4. Other passages that deal with the humble status of the apostles include De s Bab c Jul 16; 18; Con Jud et gen 6; In 1 Cor 4,4; 5,5; and 7,18.

10. Con Jud et gen 2.1. (Schatkin and Harkins. *St. John Chrysostom-Apologist.* 191). A catalog of fulfilled prophecy follows.

11.In Acta 18,5. (NPNF 11, 118). Paragraphs four and five of the homily deal with the illustration in its entirety.

12.Ep 49, 53-54, 123, 126. (cited in Jedin. *History of the Church.* 2, 366).

13.In Acta 38,1.

14.In 1 Cor 6,6.

15.Adv Jud 1,6,1.

16.De s Bab c Jul 3.

17.In Mat 1,5; Hubert Jedin ed., History of the Church. (NY: Seabury, 1980) II,212; and Donald Attwater. Saint John Chrysostom: The Voice of Gold. (Milwaukee: Bruce, 1939) 11.

18.Friedrich, Otto. *The End of the World: a history* (New York: Coward, McCann and Geoghegan, 1982); A.H.M. Jones. *The Later Roman Empire, 284-602: A Social, Economic, and Administrative Survey.* 3 vols. (Oxford, 1964); Thompson, E.A. "Christianity and the Northern Barbarians." In *The Conflict Between Paganism and Christianity in the Fourth Century.* 56-78. ed by A. Momigliano. (Oxford: Clarendon, 1963); Pirenne, Henri. *Mohammed and Charlemagne* (Totowa, NJ: Barnes and Noble, 1980).

19.Ad pop Anti 2,3; In il: Vidi dom 4,4-5; Socrates. *Ecclesiastical History.* 6,5; and Sozomen. *Ecclesiastical History.* 8,4; 8,7-9.7.

20.Theodoret *Ecclesiastical History.* 5,30; 5,31. See also a discussion of this in Thomas S. Burns, *A History of the Ostrogoths* (Bloomington: Indiana University Press, 1984), 149; R. Henderson, "Missions of the Early Christian Church, II: Chrysostom." *The Catholic Presbyterian* 6 (1881): 188; Hubert Jedin, ed. *History of the Church.* (NY: Seabury, 1980) II, 194 (quoting Ep ad Olym 9,5).

21.In Mat 36,1.

22.In Acta 33,3.

23.In Gen 14,6. (Hill. *Homilies on Genesis 1-17.* 184). In In Gen 13,13 John also cited Scripture as the norm, "So, I beg you, block your ears against all distractions of that kind, and let us follow the norm of Sacred Scripture." John also believed that heresies arose when people measured "divine things by human reasoning" In 2 Tim 2. cf. In Gen 9,1.

24.In Gen 8,12. John also uses the phrase "it is said" in In 1 Cor 38,5 when he speaks of the tradition of Christ's ordination of his brother James as the first bishop of Jerusalem.

25.In Phil. 6,1. (NPNF 13, 206).

26.In Col 2. (NPNF 13, 269).

27.In Phil 11. (NPNF 13, 234). cf. Cat ill 1,22.

28.In Gal 1:7. (NPNF 13, 7). The Marcionites were also addressed in In Heb 3,2; In Mat 7,5; 43,2; 49,2; In Phil 6; 7; and Con Anom 8.

29.Adv Jud 3,3,3.

30.John 5:21.

31.Cat ill 1,22. (Harkins. *Baptismal Instructions*. 31). Numerous passages in which the Arians are mentioned include In Gen 15,10; In Jn 82,2; In Heb 2,1-2; In Phil 6; and In Col 3. Also see discussion in Paul Harkins. *Saint John Chrysostom: On the Incomprehensible Nature of God*. Washington: Catholic University of America Press, 1984. 15f.

32.In Gal 3:4. (NPNF 13, 25).

33.In Eph 14.

34.In Heb 2,2; 3,2; In Mat 7,5; In Eph 11; In Phil 6; In Jn 8,1; and 39,3.

35.In Jn 75,1; 82,2; and In Heb 2,1-2;. In In Phil 6 (NPNF 13, 206) Sabellius was cited as teaching that the Father, Son, and Holy Spirit were mere names. In Cat ill 1,22 the catechumens are counseled to avoid their teaching and given an apologetical answer for it.

36.In Phil 6. In In Phil 7 (NPNF 13, 214) John said that "I must now speak against such as deny that He [Christ] took on a soul."

37.In Phil 6; Con Anom 8,9; In Mat 16,3; 49,2; 55,7; In 1 Cor 38,3; and, 39,4. Samuel Lieu, "The Diffusion and Persecution of Manichaeism in Rome and China." (D. Phil. diss. Oxford University, 1981).

38.Con Anom 8; In Mat 16,3; 16,8; and, 55,7.

39.(NPNF 11,332).

CHAPTER 17

JOHN AND THE JEWS

The unbelief that drew from John a special and at times a quite vehement response was the unbelief of the Jews of his day. His homilies against the Jews have been cited as baseless anti-Semitism. However, his apologetic against the Jews must be viewed in a more complete context.

The New World of the Fourth Century

The fourth century was a new religious world for the Christian and the Jew. It was the first century of the new relationship between Christianity and Judaism, as this was the first time the Christians were in power.[1] John was reacting in this context to what he viewed as a major pastoral problem, the subversion of the faith of the members of his flock. Judaism was far more active and successful in proselytism in John's era than in others.[2] If the members of his congregation were not becoming full followers of the Jewish faith they were apparently willing to integrate Jewish practices into their piety to form a syncretistic worship that was not compatible with Christian orthodoxy. John found it necessary to denounce those in his flock who were fasting with Jews and using oaths mediated through Jewish rituals in their business dealings.[3]

The Reign of Julian

Also, the relationship between the Jews and the Christians in the final decades of the fourth century was further complicated by the aftermath of the reign of Julian and his program against the faith of Constantine. Under Julian, the Jews were free for the first time since the days of Alexander Severus who died in 235 A.D.[4] Immediately after he ascended to the undisputed imperial dignity upon the death of his cousin Constantius II who persecuted the Jews and Christian sects who did not agree with his Arian understanding of the Christian faith, Julian proclaimed a general religious amnesty.[5] Julian, although he did not accept monotheism in any form and condemned it in the Jews, numbered Jews among his acquaintances and addressed the Patriarch Hillel II in most friendly terms.[6] As part of his program of religious freedom as well as his particular friendship with various Jewish leaders and his antipathy toward the Christians, Julian proposed to sponsor the rebuilding of the temple in Jerusalem. In a letter to Patriarch Hillel II, he cited the persecution of the Jews by Constantius and the proposed taxation that Julian had abolished upon the death of his rival for the throne. He asked for the prayers of the Jews as he embarked on his ill-fated Persian campaign.[7]

When Julian left for the Persian campaign that would cost him his life on March 5, 363, the rebuilding of the temple had hardly begun.[8] The attempt to rebuild the temple was halted both by the death of the emperor and the report of miraculous divine intervention thwarting the construction.[9]

> What of our own times? Did not the flame leaping from the foundations of the temple at Jerusalem burn up those who were attempting to restore it and cause the survivors to cease from impious enterprise without converting them, however, or making them abandon their blind ways?[10]

The association of the Jews with the apostate emperor served to further alienate the Christian bishops from the Jewish community when Julian died after only two years in power. John was an adolescent in Antioch during Julian's reign and undoubtedly remembered the unsettling environment of the emperor's time in Antioch and the comparative favoritism he showed toward the Jews. Julian's good will toward the Jews was probably perceived as an assault upon Christianity rather than genuine feelings of respect toward Jewish religion. In a letter on the duties of a priest, he disparaged those who only worship one God and insulted those who "are so zealous that they will suffer want and famine rather than taste swine's flesh or anything strangled or even killed by accident..."[11]

John versus the Jews in Antioch and Constantinople

John's comments about the Jews in his sermons must be viewed in their specific contexts. His series of homilies against Christians with Judaizing tendencies, preached as a priest, must be viewed in light of the religious situation in Antioch where there was much competition for converts between the two communities. Also, Antioch was a center for Julian's proposed revitalization of the state religions, and the memory of his repudiation of Christianity and his aid to the Jews in the attempted rebuilding of their temple was still vivid. In Constantinople, when he preached on the book of Acts, his words had a far less censorious tone. He did not condemn the ministry of the Apostles in the temple in Jerusalem and referred to them as Jews.[12] He condemned in no uncertain terms Judaizing tendencies in his congregation in Antioch, but while preaching in Constantinople he mentioned that Peter and John lived as Jews for expediency and did not condemn it.[13] He even postulated the salvation of Gamaliel solely on the basis of his words of moderation in Acts, chapter five.[14]

John's preaching on the passages in the book of Acts was consistent with another important theme in his interpretation of Scripture and his understanding of piety. This was the theme of timeliness. The Jews were clinging to practices that God had once used but had clearly chosen to use no longer. To use them in the face of God's obvious choice was rebellion, nothing else. The destruction of Jerusalem and its temple should have been proof enough for the world to see that the rituals and worship of the Old Covenant was no longer a part of God's program.[15]

> It was not my sole purpose to stitch shut the mouths of the Jews. I also was anxious to give you more extensive instruction in the teachings of the Church. Come now, and let me give you abundant proof that the temple will not be rebuilt and that the Jews will not return to their former way of life. In this way you will come to a clearer understanding of what the Apostles taught, and the Jews will be all the more convicted of acting in a godless way. As witness I shall not produce an angel, not an archangel, but the very Master of the whole world, our Lord Jesus Christ. When he came into Jerusalem and saw the temple, he said: "Jer-

usalem will be trodden down by many nations, until the times of many nations be fulfilled."[16] By this he meant the years to come until the consummation of the world. And again, speaking to his disciples about the temple, he made the threat that a stone would not remain upon a stone in that place until the time when it be destroyed. His threat was a prediction that the temple would come to a final devastation and completely disappear.

But the Jew totally rejects this testimony. He refuses to admit what Christ said. What does the Jew say? "The man who said this is my foe, I crucified him, so how am I to accept his testimony?" But this is the marvel of it. You Jews did crucify Him. But after He died on the cross, He then destroyed your city; it was then that He dispersed your people; it was then that He scattered your nation over the face of the earth. In doing this He teaches us that He is risen, alive, and in heaven.[17]

John also noted that the Jews had tried to rebuild the temple three times: in the time of Hadrian, in the time of Constantine, and, most recently, in the time of Julian. That they failed was proof that the prophecy of Christ would stand until His return.[18]

The religious context at Antioch in the last half of the fourth century saw a strong Jewish community flourishing in the city. Members of the Christian congregation embraced various Jewish rituals. The city contained the tomb of the Maccabean martyrs that had been claimed as Christian martyrs by the Church, but whose Jewish origins were obvious.[19] The Christian hierarchy might have imperial support in occupying the Maccabean site but the reclamation of the Old Testament as a Christian book blurred the distinction between the communities. To some on the periphery of the Christian community the Jews seemed to be more in touch with the ritual and powerful world of Moses and the prophets. Their incorporation of Jewish ritual into their piety greatly angered John, and his series of homilies against these tendencies are replete with condemnations of the Jews and their religious practices.

This series of homilies was preached in Antioch probably just before 390 A.D. around the beginning of the Jewish year. Many Christians were celebrating the holidays of the Jews and attending their synagogues.[20] It was natural for some in the church in the city to blur the distinction between the two communities. They both claimed the Maccabees, and they shared a view of the books of the Old Covenant as sacred writings.[21] People were forcing those in the church to swear their oaths at the synagogues and some were fasting with the Jews.[22] John preached against this reverence for the synagogue and the role it regularly played in the lives of some of his flock.[23]

In John's works the case against the Jews is built on three levels: the level of theology, the level of apologetic tactic, and the level of personal insult. John had good theological reasons for his denunciation of the Jews. For him, the most important was their role in the crucifixion of Christ.

> But I must get back to those who are sick [the Judaizing Christians]. Consider then, with whom they are sharing their fasts. It is with those who shouted: "Crucify Him, Crucify Him,"[24] with those who said: "His blood be upon us and upon our children."[25]... Is it not strange that those who worship the Crucified keep common festival with those who crucified him?[26]

They were also given the Scriptures and therefore, when they rejected Christ, they did it with full knowledge of the truth in active rebellion.[27] In addition to rejecting truth, they perverted the Scriptures in their rejection of Christ.[28] Finally, in addition to their murder of Christ, they also had to answer for killing some of the prophets that God sent to them.[29]

On the level of apologetic tactic, John tried to present the Jewish community as on the same level as the pagans because in their rejection of the truly divine Christ, they, like the pagans, were not worshipping the true God. In reality they worshipped demons.[30]

On the final level, in what can be called little more than baseless personal insult, the Jews were seen as ungrateful,[31] cheaters at trade,[32] and those who abandoned the poor.[33] They also preyed on the women, the

weaker vessels, in the Christian community.[34]   A charge that strained
credibility was that of killing their own children. But John made that charge
although the only evidence he could adduce to support it was the testimony
of the Old Testament Scriptures that some of the Jews of that era participated in the infant sacrifice to Canaanite deities.[35]

In summary, John's reference to the Jews in his homilies was heavily
colored by the context in which he spoke. In Antioch where there was great
competition between the two communities for the souls of the city, and the
combination of Jewish rituals with Christian faith was a serious threat to his
flock, he was vehement in this denunciation even to the point of baseless
insult. In Constantinople where no such danger seemed to exist, his words
are much more tempered and even conciliatory in his treatment of the Jews
in his homilies on the book of Acts.

1.Jacob Neusner, *Judaism in the Matrix of Christianity* (Philadelphia: Fortress, 1986). A dated but still useful overview of the view of the Jews expressed in the writings of the Church Father is given by S. Krauss in "The Jews in the Works of the Church Fathers." *The Jewish Quarterly Review* 5 (1893): 122-157; 6 (1894): 82-99, 225-261. An overview which focuses more on the fourth century is contained in Wayne A. Meeks and Robert L. Wilken. *Jews and Christians in Antioch in the First Four Centuries of the Common Era* (Missoula, MT: Scholars Press, 1978) 59f. Rosemary Radford Ruether "Judaism and Christianity: Two fourth-century religions." *Studies in Religion* 2 (1972): 1-10. R. E. Taylor, "Attitudes of the Fathers toward Practices of Jewish Christians." *Studia Patristica* 4 (1959): 504-511. Johannes Quasten, "The Conflict of Early Christianity with the Jewish Temple Worship." *Theological Studies* 2 (1941): 481-487. M. Wiles, "The Old Testament in Controversy with the Jews." *Scottish Journal of Theology.* 8 (1955): 113-126. Robert L. Wilken, "The Jews and Christian Apologetics After Theodosius I *Cunctos Populos.*" *Harvard Theological Review* 73 (1980): 451-471 and *John Chrysostom and the Jews: Rhetoric and Reality in the Late Fourth Century.* Berkeley: University of California Press, 1984. A. Malina, "Jewish Christianity or Christian Judaism." *Journal for the Study of Judaism* 7: 46-57. A. Lukyn Williams, *Adversus Judaeos: a bird's-eye view of Christian Apologiae until the Renaissance* (Cambridge: The University Press, 1935) 133-137.

2.Bernard J. Bamberger, *Proselytism in the Talmudic Era* (New York: KTAV, 1968), 272. The significant position of the Jewish community in the economic society and the social position of their "patriarch" in the city of Antioch is discussed by Carl H. Kraeling, "The Jewish Community at Antioch." *Journal of Biblical Literature* 51 (1932): 130-160.

3.Adv Jud 2; 3; 8.

4.Michael Adler, "The Emperor Julian and the Jews." *The Jewish Quarterly Review* 5 (1893): 594. Fred Allen Grissom, "Chrysostom and the Jews: Studies in Jewish-Christian Relations in Fourth-Century Antioch." (Ph. D. diss. Southwestern Baptist Theological Seminary, 1978) 134-140.

5.Ammianus Marcellinus. *History* 22,5; Sozomen *Ecclesiastical History*. 5,5; and Socrates *Ecclesiastical History*. 2,23 Kallistos Ware, "Christian Theology in the East 600-1453." In *A History of Christian Doctrine*. edited by H. Cunliffe-Jones. 181-225. (Edinburgh: T and T Clark, 1978), 184.

6.Michael Adler, "The Emperor Julian and the Jews." *The Jewish Quarterly Review* 5 (1893): 594, 598-9.

7.The letter is translated in Michael Adler, "The Emperor Julian and the Jews." *The Jewish Quarterly Review* 5 (1893): 622-624.

8.M. Avi-Yonah, *The Jews of Palestine: a political history from the Bar Kokhba War to the Arab conquest* (New York: Schocken Books, 1976), 199.

9.M. Avi-Yonah, *The Jews of Palestine: a political history from the Bar Kokhba War to the Arab conquest* (New York: Schocken Books, 1976), 202.

10.De laud s Paul 4. (Halton. *In Praise of Saint Paul*. 56).

11.Ep 63 cited in Michael Adler, "The Emperor Julian and the Jews." *The Jewish Quarterly Review* 5 (1893): 598-599. On pages 601f Adler also discusses Julian's criticism of Jewish dietary laws, his disparaging of Hebrew and use of the Greek text of the Hebrew Scriptures, his condescending remarks about Moses, Abraham and other prophets as well as his assertion of the superiority of Homer and other classical literature to Jewish "fables." Julian's mixed motives are also discussed by C. B. Armstrong in "The Synod of Alexandria and the Schism at Antioch in A.D. 362." *The Journal of Theological Studies* 22 (1921): 206-221, 347-355 and Robert Browning, *The Emperor Julian* (London: Weidenfeld and Nicolson, 1975), 165-169.

12.In Acta 7,2.

13.In Acta 8,1.

14.In Acta 14,1.

15.Adv Jud 4,6,1; and 6,3,6. This element of John's apologetic is discussed in J. L. Makowski, "The Element of *'akairos* in John Chrysostom's Anti-Jewish Polemic." *Studia Patristica* 12 (1975): 222-231.

16.Lk 21:24.

17.Adv Jud 5,1,6-7. (Harkins. *Discourses Against Judaizing Christians*. 99-100). Cf also Adv Jud 5,5,4f; and 5,12,1f. John saw the spread of the Gospel in the Roman world during the life of Paul as fulfilling the prophecy in the Olivet Discourse. This interpretation is also seen in In Mat 75 and 76.

18.Adv Jud 6,2,2; Con Jud et gen 16f.

19.Julian Obermann, "The Sepulchre of the Maccabean Martyrs." *Journal of Biblical Literature* 50 (1931): 250-265.

20.Adv Jud 1,1,5. He interrupted his series on the incomprehensible nature of God (De incomp die) to preach these homilies.

21.Adv Jud 1,5,8f.

22.Adv Jud 1,3,4.

23.Adv Jud 1,2,7; 1,5,3f; and, In Gen 12,1.

24.Lk 23:21.

25.Mt 27:25.

26.Adv Jud 1,5,1. (Harkins. *Discourses Against Judaizing Christians*. 18). Cf. also Adv Jud 1,7,5; 8,5,4; and In Jn 84,1.

27.In Jn 8,1 and Adv Jud 1,2,1f.

28.In Gen 8,6-8 Con jud et gen 7; and Ex in Ps 109 cited in Hill. *Homilies on Genesis 1-17*. 108.

29.Adv Jud 1,5,5f.

30.Adv Jud 1,6,3-7.

31.Con Jud et gen 4.

32.Adv Jud 1,7,1.

33.Adv Jud 1,7,1.

34.Adv Jud 2,3,4.

35.Adv Jud 1,6,7-8.

CHAPTER 18
THE CHRISTIAN HOPE

The Surety of God's Justice

When John commented on the priesthood of Christ as expressed in the fourth chapter of the book of Hebrews, he followed the writer of the book in exhorting his listeners to hold fast to their profession. He then identified the profession of the Christian as the belief in the "resurrection, that there is retribution, that there are good things innumerable, that Christ is God and that the Father is right."[1] A consistent theme in John's preaching is the need to prepare in this life for the life to come. We will face God when we depart and we must be prepared to face Him and His judgment.[2]

The clear implication of John's understanding of the basic Christian profession for his audience was that they must be sure to depart this life in righteousness.[3] If the Christian departed after baptism but in sin, he would receive no rewards in the eternal kingdom and would have despair and sadness in heaven.[4] We must also keep a heaven-centered righteousness. If Christians receive rewards for their acts of service for God here on earth, then their reward in the presence of God will be diminished.[5] The perspective that John wanted in his flock also focussed in the resurrection and the fact that death is not a cessation. It was this message of comfort that he gave to the widow facing the death of her husband.[6] John applied this teaching of resurrection and judgment to the concern of his congregation that the souls of the departed wandered the cosmos as demonic forces.

> Nor is it indeed possible for a soul, torn away from the body, to wander here any more. For "the souls of the righteous are in the hands of God."[7] and if so of the righteous, then those children's souls also; for neither are they wicked; and the souls too of sinners are straightway led away hence. ....
>
> Whence it is evident that after their departure hence our souls are led away into some place, having no more power of them-

selves to come back again, but awaiting that dreadful day.[8]

Christian funerals should reflect this confidence in the resurrection and judgment. Christ rose naked so we do not need an expensive funeral.[9] We should mourn fallen souls not dead bodies.[10] A funeral is not a time of fear for the Christian with a proper perspective.[11]

However, there was always the possibility of apostasy. Christians in this life could not be sure that they would enter the kingdom unless they held fast until death. John was concerned for his own salvation and pointed out that not even the Apostle Paul was sure that he would enter the eternal Kingdom.

> "Lest by any means, having preached to others, I myself should be rejected."[12] Now if Paul feared this who had taught so many, and feared it after his preaching and becoming an angel and undertaking the leadership of the whole world; what can we say?

> For "think not" says he, "because you have believed, that this is sufficient for your salvation: since if to me neither preaching nor teaching nor bringing over innumerable persons, is enough for salvation unless I exhibit my own conduct also unblamable, much less to you."[13]

Christians must live in light of eternity and lay up treasure in the eternal Kingdom. They can invest in this kingdom by giving to the poor and pursuing virtue. The rewards which are available in the Kingdom of Heaven are greater than those that can be earned in the service of any king on earth.[14] Paul lived in a heavenly manner on earth and the Christian who lives in this light should not fear.[15] John wrestled with these two, seemingly contradictory, beliefs: Christians must diligently work out their salvation if they were to enter the kingdom and Christians should not fear. He saw the struggle in Paul and in his own life and concluded that the duty of each Christian was to live in a godly manner and to commit their eternal future to God, the righteous Judge. He noted there was good and bad in all and God will reward each.[16]

With this sober view of the consequences of sin in this life, John could liken the perspective of the preacher with that of others who constantly lived in the presence of death and destruction.

> For neither naval pilot, nor wrestler with wild beasts, nor gladiator, needs to be adjusted mentally to death and slaughter as much as the one who undertakes the preaching office. The dangers are greater, the opponents more formidable, as here slaughter is not concerned with trivia. Heaven is the prize, hell is the penalty for those who lose, the destruction or salvation of the soul. That is the set-up not merely for the preacher of the Gospel but for the ordinary layman, since every man is commanded to take up his cross and follow.[17]

For John, the present is sweet only to those with no heavenly perspective.[18] John proclaimed to an audience that included the very rich and the very poor that the dwellings of the godly in heaven would surpass the palaces of the rich in this world.[19] An eternal perspective lifts the Christian's eyes off the present circumstances and looks at the one enduring question: What is a person's status before God? We should not grieve for the dead and have joy for the living but should rather focus on whether they are saved from their sins.[20] For John, excess grief at a funeral belied a hope of the resurrection.[21]

Christ's return to the earth will be preceded by a forerunner as was his first coming.[22] The endtimes will be an era dominated by the Antichrist, of whom Nero was a type.[23] The Antichrist will be destroyed as God revealed to the prophet Daniel. John believed the four kingdoms that figured in the prophecy of Daniel were the Babylonians, Persians, Greeks, and Romans.[24]

The Reality of Heaven and Hell

John's seemingly central focus on hell and its punishments and the judgment awaiting all people must be balanced with another theme of his preaching. This theme was that being rejected by God and not going eternally into His presence was a far more awesome consequence of a godless life than the torments of hell.

> Now I know that many tremble only at hell, but I affirm the loss
> of that glory to be a far greater punishment than hell.... Yet
> though one suppose 10,000 hells, he will utter nothing like what
> it will be to fail of that blessed glory, to be hated of Christ, to
> hear "I know you not."[25]

The righteous judgment of God will determine the eternal fate of those
who stand before Him. No one who fails this judgment will enter heaven
with His people.[26] For John, there is no hope of purgation or any repentance after death. This further enforces the importance of living in light of
eternity on earth.

> But there the affliction is more bitter because it is not in hope
> nor for any escape, but without limit and throughout.

> ...for we shall not always hear these things, we shall not always
> have power to do them.... Let us then repent here that so we may
> find God merciful to us in the day that is to come.[27]

In the end all will submit, but the submission that is not of a free will
does not bring divine favor.

> "Every tongue shall confess..."[28] But there is no advantage in that
> submission for it comes not of a rightly disposed choice, but of
> necessity of things...[29]

There is also no option of annihilation. Those who perish will not
cease to exist. When John commented on the words of 1 Corinthians that
some shall be saved "through fire"[30] he taught that those in view in this
passage were those who had failed the divine judgment and would be
preserved for punishment.[31] Those who fail the judgment will be punished
for eternity.

> And when you hear of fire, do not suppose the fire in that world
> to be like this; for fire in this world burns up and makes away
> with anything which it takes hold of; but that fire is continually
> burning those who have once been seized by it and never ceases:
> therefore it is called unquenchable. For those who have sinned
> must put on immortality, not for honor, but to have a constant

supply of material for that punishment to work upon; and how terrible this is, speech could never depict but from the experience of little things it is possible to form some slight notion of these great ones.[32]

Who will stand up and help us when we are punished? There is no one; but it must needs be that wailing and weeping and gnashing our teeth, we shall be led away tortured into that rayless gloom, the pangs no prayer can avert, the punishments which cannot be assuaged.[33]

The reality of hell should be taught in the Church because its teaching and the fear of damnation can keep people from taking their salvation lightly and falling into the eternal fire.

See what advantage is come of fear? If fear were not a good thing, fathers would not set tutors over their children; nor lawgivers magistrates for cities. What is more grievous than hell? Yet nothing is more profitable than the fear of it.[34]

For indeed my heart is troubled and throbs; and the more I see the account of hell confirmed, the more do I tremble and shrink through fear. But it is necessary to say these things lest we fall into hell.[35]

Christians must never forget that the corollary of this teaching is that while they are here, there is hope and repentance. The sinner can always come back to God. Those who hear the word preached must always be watchful lest they depart unfaithful.

While we are here we have good hope; when we depart to that place, we have no longer the option of repentance, nor of washing away our misdeeds. For this reason we must continually make ourselves ready for our departure from here... The future is unknown, to keep us always active in the struggle and prepared for that removal.[36]

John applied this message of watchfulness to himself and could not feel secure in his eternal future. All must take care of their disposition toward God.

For here it is possible to go unto the king, and entreat: but there
no longer; for He permits it not, but they continue in scorching
torment...

What then shall we do there? For to myself also do I say these
things.

But if thou, said one, who art a teacher, speaks so of yourself, I
care no more, for what wonder, should I be punished?

... For tell me; was not the Devil superior to men? Yet he fell
away. Is there any one who will derive consolation from being
punished along with him?[37]

Hell will be even more terrible than what is threatened.[38] There will
also be gradations of punishment in hell.[39] John soberly reminded the
congregation that "God is at no loss for inflictions. For according to the
greatness of His mercy so also is His wrath."[40]

1.In Heb 7,5.

2.In Mat 20,6; 23,10; 81,5; 90,3;. In 1 Cor 9,2-6; 22,4; and 22,4 fin.

3.In Mat 31,6.

4.In Heb 13,9.

5.In 2 Cor 16,5.

6.Ad vid jun 3; See also In 1 Cor 38,5 and In para 8.

7.Wisdom of Solomon 3:1.

8.In Mat 28,3. (NPNF 10, 192). However, in De Laz 2 he stated: "Many of the simpler people think that the souls of those who die by a violent death become demons. This is impossible, quite impossible. It is not the souls of those who die violently which become demons, but the souls of those who live in sin."

9.In Jn 85,5

10.Ad Theo 1,1-3

11.In 1 Cor 12,14

12.I Corinthians 9:27

13.In 1 Cor 24,2. (NPNF 12, 132-133). John stated his concern about his own salvation in In Mat 76,5 and In 1 Cor 9,2. John, probably because of his view of Pauline authorship of the epistle to the Hebrews, also tied the warning passages to the teaching on salvation in the epistle to the Romans.

14.In Mat 1,12. John often asserted that it was important for Christians to keep their eyes on that fearful day of judgment. In Jn 54,4; 76,3; 77,5 ; and In 1 Cor 2,11.

15.De laud s Paul 2 and In Jn 83,1.

16. De Laz 6; In 1 Cor 2,11; In Mat 23,9; In 1 Cor 42,5; and In 2 Cor 10,6-7.

17.De laud s Paul 6. (Halton. *In Praise of Saint Paul.* 101).

18.In Jn 67,1

19.In Jn 56,3

20.In Phil 3.

21.In Jn 62,4.

22.In Mat 57,1.

23.In 2 Thess 1; In 2 Thess 4.

24.In 2 Thess 4.

25.In Mat 23,9 (NPNF 10, 164). Similar comments are made in Ad Theo 1,12.

26.In 2 Cor 10, 6-7.

27.In Phil 13. (NPNF 13, 245). Similar comments are made in In Jn 34,3; Con Jud et gen 8; In Mat 43,5-6; In 1 Cor 9,2f; and 42,5.

28.Phil. 2:9.

29.In Mat 36,3 (NPNF 10, 241).

30.1 Cor 3:15.

31.In 1 Cor 9,5-6.

32.Ad Theo 1,10. (NPNF 9, 98).

33.In 1 Cor 42,5. (NPNF 12,248).

34.Ad pop Anti 15,2. (NPNF 9, 439).

35.In 1 Cor 9,2. (NPNF 12, 50). John preached on similar themes in In Mat 36,4; In Phil 6; In Col 6; In Jn 28,2; In 2 Thess 2.; and Adv Jud 1,4,1.

36.De Laz 2. (Halton. *In Praise of Saint Paul.* 45).

37.In Mat 43,5-6. (NPNF 10, 276-277).

38.In 2 Thess 3.

39.In Eph 4.

40.In Mat 43,5. (NPNF 10, 276).

CHAPTER 19
EPILOGUE

Assessments of John and his impact in the history of Christianity have usually been hagiographic, overlooking some of the flaws that greatly influenced the course of his ministry. He was a passionate man who easily polarized those with whom he came in contact. After his death and rehabilitation, his faults faded and posterity has deemed his piety exemplary.

Chrysostom's pupil, John Cassian, spoke of him as an example for the faithful.

> It would be a great thing to attain to his stature, but it would be hard. Nevertheless even the following of him is lovely and magnificent.[1]

Julian of Eclanum, a younger contemporary of John later banished for refusing to subscribe to the condemnation of Pelagianism, characterized Chrysostom's preaching as marked "rather by exhortation than by exposition."[2] John's sermons were cited by both sides in the Pelagian debates and Augustine made great effort to show that John was not heterodox in his understanding of grace and human nature in his treatise against Julian.[3]

The centuries after his death saw John emerge as a Father of the Church and a venerated preacher whose works were preserved and cited in various contexts from medieval Eucharistic debates to Chaucer's *Parson's Tale*.[4]

Calvin wrestled with the Chrysostom's reputation as an educated rhetorician whose works might be deemed an irrelevant facet of rejected Romanism. Was he a Roman saint who was separated from the common Christian by a sacramental wall? Was his message irrelevant for the Protestants and Reformed of the Reformation era? When Calvin wrote a preface to Chrysostom's homilies, he felt the need to justify their publication in his ministry of restoring the purity of the Church.

Now I am not unaware of an objection that can be raised against me

> at this point: that Chrysostom, whom I am on the point of making
> available to the common people, intended his studies only for the
> learned and the educated. But, on the contrary, unless both the title
> and style of his oratory are lying, this man composed sermons which he
> delivered to the people at large.... Accordingly anyone who maintains
> that he ought to be hidden away among the learned is quite wrong,
> seeing that he has taken pains specifically to be popular.[5]

Calvin then continued with comments that Chrysostom was superior to the
other fathers in arriving at the true sense of Scripture, not obscuring it with
allegorical machinations. He cited Jerome, Origen, and others as examples
of less successful exposition.[6]

Chrysostom was also cited in the Reformation era by polemicists on
both sides in an effort to demonstrate the continuum of their positions with
the Patristic era.[7]

John was also honored as he was placed in a circle of holy fathers in
Dante's *Paradisio* where he stands between Nathan the prophet and Anselm
of Canterbury, two men who, like John, defied their rulers to defend their
convictions.[8]

In sum, John is a reminder and an illustration that historians must
avoid the Scylla and Charybdis of historical reflection. They must avoid a
Whig stance that glories in the present at the expense of the past or
reinterprets the past in light of its contribution to his present.[9] They must
also avoid a "Golden Age" mentality that elevates the past beyond recogni-
tion. John was neither a primitive whose study holds no lessons for the
modern Christian nor was he a saint leading a life without blemish, a
heavenly existence on earth. He was a Christian, thrust into leadership,
serving God and his flock to the best of his ability. He was consumed by his
call to preach and his zeal for the spiritual advancement of his flock.

> Preaching improves me. When I begin to speak weariness
> disappears; when I begin to teach fatigue too disappears. Thus
> neither sickness itself or indeed any other obstacle is able to
> separate me from your love .... My congregation is my only glory.[10]

1.De Incarnatione 7,31. A discussion of this dependence is contained in Rowan A. Greer's *Broken Lights and Mended Lives: Theology and Common Life in the Early Church*. (University Park: Pennsylvania State University Press, 1986.), p. 174. Cassian's view of God's gracious reaching out toward man was dependent on John's fourth homily on the Gospel of John. This specific point of dependence is discussed in Johannes Quasten. *Patrology. Vol. 4.* (Westminster, Md.: Christian Classics, 1986.) p 520.

2.PL 21,960. Cited in Robert Hill. *Saint John Chrysostom: Homilies on Genesis 1-17* (Washington, DC: Catholic University of America Press, 1986) 11.

3.Augustine. *Against Julian* (New York: Fathers of the Church, 1957) 1,6-7; 2,10; 3,17; and 6,22 (p 25-31, 34-36, 39-43, 97, 101, 103, 136, 380). This issue is further discussed in Arthur Kenny, "Was Saint John Chrysostom a Semi-Pelagian?" *The Irish Theological Quarterly* 27 (1960): 16-29 and Francois-Joseph Thonnard, "Saint Jean Chrysostom et Saint Augustin dans la Controverse Pelagienne." *Revue des 'Etudes Byzantines* 25 (1967): 189--218.

4.Citation of Chrysostom in this era is discussed by J. M. Hussey, *The Orthodox Church in the Byzantine Empire* (Oxford: Clarendon, 1986); A. A. Vasiliev, *History of the Byzantine Empire* (Madison: University of Wisconsin Press, 1952); M. L. W. Laistner. *The Intellectual Heritage of the Early Middle Ages* (New York: Octagon Books, 1983); D. Knowles, "The Middle Ages 604-1350" In *A History of Christian Doctrine*. edited by H. Cunliffe-Jones. 227-286 (Edinburgh: T and T Clark, 1978); Robert E. McNally, *The Bible in the Early Middle Ages* (Westminster, Md.: Newman Press, 1959); R. M. Correale, "Source of the Quotation from Chrysostom in the Parson's Tale." *Notes and Queries* 27 (1980): 101-102; and Barry Collett, "A Benedictine Scholar and Greek Patristic Thought in Pre-Tridentine Italy: A Monastic Commentary of 1538 on Chrysostom." *The Journal of Ecclesiastical History* 36 (1985): 66-81.

5.J. H. McIndoe, "John Calvin: Preface to the Homilies of Chrysostom." *Hartford Quarterly* 5 (1965): 21.

6.Ibid. pp. 22-24.

7.Philip Melanchthon, *Melanchthon on Christian Doctrine*. (Loci Communes 1555). Grand Rapids: Baker, 1982. 20; Philip Schaff, *Creeds of Christendom* (Grand Rapids: Baker, 1977) 38, 41; and R.J. Schoeck, "The Use of Saint John Chrysostom in Sixteenth Century Controversies." *Harvard Theological Review* 54 (1961): 21-27.

8.Dante. *Paradisio*. Canto xii.

9.Herbert Butterfield. *The Whig Interpretation of History* (New York: Norton, 1965) v-vi and passim.

10.De terre motu. (Carroll. *Preaching the Word*. 107).

BIBLIOGRAPHY

Adams, Charles Darwin. *Demosthenes and His Influence.* New York: Longmans, Green and Company, 1927

Adler, Michael. "The Emperor Julian and the Jews." *The Jewish Quarterly Review* 5 (1893): 591-651.

Albright, W.F. "Explorations and Excavations in Palestine and Syria." *American Journal of Archaeology* 40 (1935): 154-167.

Alissandratos, Julia. "The Structure of the Funeral Oration in John Chrysostom's Eulogy of Meletius." *Byzantine Studies* 7 (1980): 182-198.

Ameringer, Thomas. *The Stylistic Influence of the Second Sophistic on the Panegyrical Sermons of Saint John Chrysostom: A Study in Greek Rhetoric.* Washington: Catholic University of America Press, 1921.

Amidon, Philip R. "Studies in the Procedure of Church Synods of the Third and Fourth Centuries to the Year 375." D. Phil. diss., Oxford University, 1979.

Anderson, Bonnie S. and Judith P. Zinsser. *A History of Their Own-Women in Europe from Prehistory to the Present.* New York: Harper and Row, 1988.

Anderson, Galusha. "The Elements of Chrysostom's Power as a Preacher." *Decennial Publications of the University of Chicago* 3:51-66.

Armstrong, C.B. "The Synod of Alexandria and the Schism at Antioch in A.D. 362." *The Journal of Theological Studies* 22 (1921): 206-221, 347-355.

Athanassiadi- Fowden, Polymnia. "An Emperor and Hellenism: Studies in the thought and action of the Emperor Julian." D. Phil. diss., Oxford University, 1976.

_____. *Julian and Hellenism.* Oxford: Clarendon Press, 1981.

Attwater, Donald. *Saint John Chrysostom: The Voice of Gold*. Milwaukee: Bruce, 1939.

Aubineau, Michel. "Les Homelies Pascales de Saint Jean Chrysostome" In *Symposium*, 112-119. Thessaloniki: Patriarchal Institute for Patristic Studies, 1973.

Augustine. *Against Julian*. New York: Fathers of the Church, 1957.

_____. *The Confession of Saint Augustine*. Grand Rapids: Baker, 1977.

Avila, Charles. *Ownership: Early Christian Teaching*. Maryknoll, NY: Orbis, 1983.

Avi-Yonah, M. *The Jews of Palestine: a political history from the Bar Kokhba War to the Arab conquest*. New York: Schocken Books, 1976.

Bailey, Derrick Sherwin. *Sexual Relations in Christian Thought*. New York: Harper and Row, 1959.

Baldovin, John Francis. "The Urban Character of Christian Worship in Jerusalem, Rome, and Constantinople from the Fourth to the Tenth Century." Ph. D. diss., Yale University, 1982.

Balsdon, J.P.V.D. *Life and Leisure in Ancient Rome*. New York: McGraw-Hill, 1960.

Bamberger, Bernard J. *Proselytism in the Talmudic Era*. New York: KTAV, 1968.

Barb, A.A. "The Survival of the Magic Arts." In *The Conflict Between Paganism and Christianity in the Fourth Century*. ed by Arnaldo Momigliano, 100-125 Oxford: Clarendon, 1963.

Bardy, G. "La Chronologie de Lettres de Saint Jean Chrysostome à Olympias." *Melanges de Science Religieuse* 2 (1945): 271-284.

_____. "Le Concile d'Antioch (379)." *Revue Benedictine* 45 (1933): 196-213.

Barnes, T.D. "The Baptism of Theodosius II." *Studia Patristica* 29 (1989): 8-12.

_____. "A Law of Julian." *Classical Philology* 69 (1974): 288-291.

_____. *The New Empire of Diocletian and Constantine*. Cambridge: Harvard University Press, 1982.

_____. "Synesius in Constantinople." *Greek, Roman, and Byzantine Studies* 27 (1986): 93-112.

_____. "When Did Synesius Become Bishop of Ptolemais?" *Greek, Roman and Byzantine Studies* 27 (1986): 325-329.

Barnish, S.J.B. "The Fall of Boethius: A study in the relations between late Roman Senator and Barbarian." D. Phil. diss., Oxford University, 1983.

Barringer, Robert. "Ecclesiastical Penance in the Church of Constantinople: A Study of the Hagiographical Evidence to 983 AD." D. Phil. diss., Oxford University, 1979.

Barrosse, Thomas. "The Unity of the Two Charities in Greek Patristic Exegesis." *Theological Studies* 15 (1954): 355-388.

Bartelink, G.J.M. "Philosophie et Philosophe dans Quelques Oeuvres de Jean Chrysostom." *Revue d'Ascetique et de Mystique* 36 (1960): 486-492.

Baudoin, Paule. "*Makrothumia* dans Saint Jean Chrysostom." *Studia Patristica* 22 (1989): 89-97.

Baur, C. *Johannes Chrysostomus und Seine Zeit*. Munich: Hueber, 1930. 2v.

_____. *John Chrysostom and His Time*. Westminster, Maryland: Newman, 1960. 2v.

_____. "Der Kanon des Johannes Chrysostomus." *Theologische Quartalschrift* 105 (1924): 258-271.

_____. "Saint Jerome et Saint Jean Chrysostome." *Revue Benedictine* 23 (1906): 430-436.

Baynes, Norman H. "Alexandria and Constantinople: A Study in Ecclesiastical Diplomacy." *Journal of Egyptian Archaeology* 72 (1926): 148-156.

_____. *Byzantine Studies and Other Essays*. London: Athlone, 1955.

_____. "Constantine the Great and the Christian Church." *Proceedings of the British Academy* (1930): 1-102.

_____. *The Early Church and Social Life*. London: G. Bell and Sons, 1927.

Benin, Stephen D. "Sacrifice as Education in Augustine and Chrysostom." *Church History* 52 (1983): 7-20.

Bickersteth, J.E. "Hyopante: Studies in the Festival of the Purification of Saint Mary the Virgin in the early Byzantine Church." D. Phil. diss., Oxford University, 1952.

Bloch, H. "The Pagan Revival in the West at the End of the Fourth Century." In *The Conflict Between Paganism and Christianity in the Fourth Century*. ed. A. Momigliano, 193-217. Oxford: Clarendon, 1963.

Bobrinskoy, Boris. "L'ésprit du Christ dans les sacraments chez Jean Chrysostome et Augustine."In *Jean Chrysostome et Augustine*. 248-279. Paris: éditions Beauchesne, 1975.

Bonner, Gerald. "The Extinction of Paganism and the Church Historian." *The Journal of Ecclesiastical History* 33 (1984): 339-357.

Boswell, John. *Christianity, Social Tolerance and Homosexuality*. Chicago: University of Chicago Press, 1980.

Boularand, Ephrem. "La Venue de l'Homme à la Foi d'après Saint Jean Chrysostome." *Analecta Gregoriana* 18 (1939): 1-189.

Bowder, Diana. "Paganism and Pagan Revival: Constantius II to Julian." D. Phil. diss., Oxford University, 1976.

Bowersock, G.W. *Greek Sophists in the Roman Empire*. Oxford: Clarendon, 1969.

_____. *Julian the Apostate*. Cambridge: Harvard University Press, 1978.

Brandle, Rudolf. "Jean Chrysostome: l'Importance de Matthew 25:31-46 pour son Ethique." *Vigiliae Christianae* 31 (1977): 47-52.

_____. *Matthew 25:31-46 im Werk des Johannes Chrysostomus*. Tubungen: Mohr, 1979.

Braude, William G. *Jewish Proselyting in the First Five Centuries of the Common Era- The Age of the Tannaim and Amoraim*. Providence: Brown University, 1940.

Breck, John. *The Power of the Word in the Worshipping Church*. Crestwood, NY: St. Vladimir's Seminary Press, 1986.

Brightman, F.E. *Liturgies: Eastern and Western*. Oxford: Clarendon, 1896.

Bromiley, Geoffrey. *Historical Theology: an introduction*. Grand Rapids: Eerdmans, 1978.

Brooten, Bernardette. "Patristic Interpretations of Romans 1:26." *Studia Patristica* 18 (1985) vol. 1. 287-292.

Brown, Peter. *The Body and Society- Men, Women and Sexual Renunciation in Early Christianity*. New York: Columbia University Press, 1988.

_____. *The Cult of the Saints*. Chicago: The University of Chicago Press, 1981.

_____. "Late Antiquity." In *A History of Private Life*. Cambridge: Harvard University Press, 1987.

_____. "The Rise and Function of the Holy Man in Late Antiquity." *Journal of Roman Studies* 61 (1971) 80-101.

_____. *Society and the Holy in Late Antiquity*. Berkeley: University of California Press, 1982.

Browning, Robert. *The Emperor Julian*. London: Weidenfeld and Nicolson, 1975.

_____. "The Riot of A.D. 387 in Antioch: The Role of the Theatrical Claques in the Later Empire." *Journal of Roman Studies* 42 (1952): 13-20.

Bruck, E.F. "Ethics vs Law: Saint Paul, the Fathers of the Church, and the Cheerful Giver in Roman Law." *Traditio* 2 (1944): 97-121.

Brundage, James A. *Law, Sex, and Christian Society in Medieval History*. Chicago: University of Chicago Press, 1987.

Budde, Gerard J. "Christian Charity: Now and Always, the Fathers of the Church and Almsgiving." *The American Ecclesiastical Review* 85 (1931): 561-579.

Burger, Douglas Clyde. *A Complete Bibliography of the Scholarship on the Life and Works of Saint John Chrysostom*. Evanston: the author, 1964.

Burns, J. Patout and Gerald M. Fagin. *The Holy Spirit*. Wilmington, Del.: Michael Glazier, 1984.

Burns, Mary Albania. *Saint John Chrysostom's Homilies on the Statues: A Study of the Rhetorical Qualities and Form*. Washington: Catholic University of America Press, 1930.

Burns, Thomas S. *A History of the Ostrogoths*. Bloomington: Indiana University Press, 1984.

Burrus, Virginia. *Chastity as Autonomy*. Lewiston, N.Y.: Edwin Mellen, 1987.

Burton, G.P. "Powers and Functions of Proconsuls in the Roman Empire 70-260." D.Phil. diss., Oxford University, 1973.

Bury, J.B. *A History of the Later Roman Empire from the Death of Theodosius I to the Death of Justinian*. New York: Dover, 1958.

Bush, Robert Wheler. *The Life and Times of Chrysostom*. London: The Religious Tract Society, 1885.

Butler, Cuthbert. "The Dialogue de Vita Chrysostomi and the Historia Lausaica: Authorship." *The Journal of Theological Studies* 221 (1921): 138-155.

Butler, Howard Crosby. *Early Churches in Syria*. Princeton: The Department of Art and Archaeology of Princeton University, 1929.

Callam, Daniel. "The Origins of Clerical Celibacy." D. Phil. diss., Oxford University, 1977.

Cameron, Alan. *Circus Factions: Blues and Greens at Rome and Byzantium*. Oxford: Clarendon, 1976.

Campbell, William A. "A Byzantine Stadium." *Antioch-on-the Orontes I The Excavations of 1932*. Princeton: Princeton University Press, 1934.

Campenhausen, Hans von. *The Virgin Birth in the Theology of the Ancient Church*. Naperville, Ill.: Alec R. Allenson, 1964.

Carcopino, Jerome. *Daily Life in Ancient Rome: the People and the City at the Height of the Empire*. New Haven: Yale University Press, 1940.

Carroll, Thomas K. *Preaching the Word*. Wilmington, Del.: Michael Glazier, 1984.

Carter, Robert E. "The Chronology of Saint John Chrysostom's Early Life." *Traditio* 18 (1962): 357-364.

_____. "Chrysostom's *Ad Theodorum Lapsum* and the Early Chronology of Theodore of Mopsuestia." *Vigiliae Christianae* 16 (1962): 87-101.

_____. "The Future of Chrysostom Studies: Theology and   Nachleben." *Studia Patristica* 10 (1970): 14-21.

_____. "The Future of Chrysostom Studies: Theology and Nachleben." In *Symposium*, 129-136. Thessaloniki: Patriarchal Institute of Patristic Studies, 1973.

_____. "Saint John Chrysostom's Rhetorical Use of the Socratic Distinction Between Kingship and Tyranny." *Traditio* 14 (1958): 367-371.

Casson, Lionel. *Ships and Seamanship in the Ancient World*. Princeton: Princeton University Press, 1971.

Cayrè, F. *Manual of Patrolgy and History of Theology*. Paris: Desclèe and Company, 1936.

Ceran, W. "Stagnation and Fluctuation in Early Byzantine Society." *Byzantinoslavonica* 31 (1970): 192-203.

Chase, Frederic Henry. *Chrysostom: A Study in the History of Biblical Interpretation*. Cambridge: Deighton, Bell and Company, 1887.

Chesnut, Glenn F., Jr. "The Byzantine Church Historians from Eusebius to Evagrius: A historiographical study." D. Phil. diss., Oxford University, 1971.

_____. *The First Christian Historians*. Macon, GA: Mercer University Press, 1986.

Chitty, Derwas J. *The Desert A City: An Introduction to the Study of Egyptian and Palestinian Monasticism under the Christian Empire*. Oxford: Basil Blackwell, 1966.

Cipolla, Richard G. "The Eucharistic Transformation: A historical and hermeneutical study of transubstantiation." D. Phil diss., Oxford University, 1974.

Clark, Elizabeth. *Ascetic Piety and Women's Faith*. Lewiston, N.Y.: Edwin Mellen Press, 1986.

_____. "Ascetic Renunciation and Feminine Advancement: A Paradox of Late Ancient Christianity." *The Anglican Theological Review* 63 (1981): 240-257.

_____. "Authority and Humility: A Conflict of Values in Fourth-Century Female Monasticism." *Byzantische Forschungen* 9 (1985): 17-33.

_____. *Jerome, Chrysostom and Friends*. Lewiston, N.Y.: Edwin Mellen Press, 1979.

_____. "John Chrysostom and the *Subintroductae*." *Church History* 46 (1977): 171-185.

_____. "Sexual Politics in the Writings of John Chrysostom." *The Anglican Theological Review* 59 (1977): 3-20.

_____. *Women in the Early Church*. Wilmington, Del.: Michael Glazier, 1983.

Clews, Diana. "The Correspondents of Saint Jerome." B. Litt. thesis, Oxford University, 1973.

Cobham, Claude Delaval. *The Patriarchs of Constantinople*. Cambridge: The University Press, 1911.

Cochrane, Charles Norris. *Christianity and Classical Culture: A Study of Thought and Action from Augustus to Augustine*. Oxford: Clarendon, 1940.

Coleman-Norton, P.R. "The Correspondence of St. John Chrysostom with Special Reference to His Epistle to Pope Innocent I." *Classical Philology* 24 (1929): 279-284.

_____. "St. Chrysostom and the Greek Philosophers." *Classical Philology* 25 (1930): 305-317.

_____. "St. Chrysostom's Use of Josephus." *Classical Philology* 26 (1931): 85-89.

_____. "St Chrysostom's Use of the Greek Poets." *Classical Philology* 27 (1932): 213-221.

Collett, Barry. "A Benedictine Scholar and Greek Patristic Thought in Pre-- Tridentine Italy: A Monastic Commentary of 1538 on Chrysostom." *The Journal of Ecclesiastical History* 36 (1985): 66-81.

Coman, J. "Le Rapport de la Justification et de la Charite dans les Homelies de Saint Jean Chrysostome à l'Epitre aux Romans." *Studia Evangelica* 5 (1969): 248-271.

_____. "L'Unitè du Genre Humain d'aprés Saint Jean Chrysostome." In *Symposium*, 41-58. Thessaloniki: Patriarchal Institute for Patristic Studies, 1973.

Congar, Yves. *Diversity and Communion*. Mystic, Conn.: Twenty-Third Publications, 1984.

_____. *Lay People in the Church*. Westminster, MD: Christian Classics, 1985.

Conybeare, Frederick C. "On the Western Text of Acts as Evidenced by Chrysostom." *American Journal of Philology* 17 (1896): 135-171.

Cooper, P. K. "The Third Century Origins of the 'New' Roman Army." D. Phil. diss., Oxford University, 1968.

Correale, R.M. "Source of the Quotation from Chrysostom in the Parson's Tale." *Notes and Queries* 27 (1980): 101-102.

Cunningham, Agnes. *Prayer: Personal and Liturgical.* Wilmington Del.: Michael Glazier, 1985.

D'Alton, J.F. "Saint John Chrysostom in Exile." *Irish Ecclesiastical Record* 46 (1935): 225-238.

Daloz, Lucien. *Le Travail Selon Saint Jean Chrysostom.* Paris: P. Lethielleux, 1959.

Danielou, Jean. "L'Incomprehensibilite de Dieu d'après Saint Jean Chrysostome." *Recherches de Science Religieuse* 37 (1950): 176-194.

_____. *The Ministry of Women in the Early Church.* London: Faith Press, 1961.

D'Arms, John H. "Facing the Future of Graduate Education." *Rackham Reports* 1986-1987. 1-16.

Davies, John Gordon. *Daily Life in the Early Church: Studies in the Church Social History of the First Five Centuries.* London: Lotterworth, 1952.

Davis, R.P. "The Value of *Liber Pontificalis* as Comparative Evidence for Territorial Estates and Church Property from the Fourth to the Sixth Century." D. Phil. diss., Oxford University, 1976.

Dewart, Joanne E. McWilliam. *Death and Reserrection.* Wilmington, Del.: Michael Glazier, 1986.

Dieu, Leon. "Le Commentaire de Saint Jean Chrysostome sur Job." *Revue d'Histoire Ecclesiastique* 13 (1912): 640-658.

_____. "La Mariologie de Saint Jean Chrysostome." *Memoires et Rapports du Congres Marial.* Brussels, 1921. 71-83.

Dihle, A. "Astrology in the Doctrine of Bardesanes." *Studia Patristica* 20 (1989): 160-168.

Donegan, Susan. "John Chrysostom's Exegesis on Romans 5:12-21: Does it Support a Doctrine of Original Sin?" *Diakonia*. 22 (1989): 5-14.

Downey, Glanville. *Antioch in the Age of Theodosius the Great.* Norman: University of Oklahoma Press, 1961.

_____. "The Church at Daphne." *Antioch-on-the Orontes I The Excavations of 1932.* Princeton: Princeton University Press, 1934.

_____. "The Economic Crisis at Antioch Under Julian the Apostate." in *Studies in Roman Economic and Social History in Honor of Allan Chester Johnson.* ed. by P. R. Coleman-Norton. Princeton: Princeton University Press, 1951. 312-321.

_____. "From the Pagan City to the Christian City." *Greek Orthodox Theological Review* 10 (1964): 121-139.

_____. *A History of Antioch in Syria.* Princeton: Princeton University Press, 1961.

_____. "Libanius, Oration in Praise of Antioch." *Proceedings of the American Philosophical Association* 103 (1959): 652-686.

_____. "Philanthropia in Religion and Statecraft in the Fourth Century after Christ." *Historia* 4 (1955): 199-208.

_____. "Polis and Civitas in Libanius and Augustine." *Academie Royale de Belique* 52 (1966): 351-366.

_____. "The Shrines of St. Babylas at Antioch and Daphne." *Antioch-on-the-Orontes II The Excavations 1933-1936.* Princeton: Princeton University Press, 1938.

_____. "The Size of the Population of Antioch." *Transactions of the American Philological Association* 89 (1958): 84-91.

_____. "Themistius and the Defense and Hellenism in the Fourth Century." *Harvard Theological Review* 50 (1957): 259-274.

Dreyfus, Francois. "Divine Condescension as a Hermeneutical Principle of the Old Testament in Jewish and Christian Tradition." *Immanuel* 19 (1984-1985): 74-86.

Duchesne, L. *Christian Worship: Its Origin and Evolution*. 5th ed. London, 1923.

Duckett, Eleanor Shipley. *Medieval Portraits From East and West*. Ann Arbor: The Uniuversity of Michigan Press, 1972.

Dumortier, Jean. "Les Citations Bibliques des Lettres de S Jean Chrysostome à Theodore." *Studia Patristica* 2 (1961): 78-83.

_____. "Les Citations Scripturaires des Cohabitations (PG 47, 495-532) d'apres leur Tradition Maniscrite." *Studia Patristica* 1 (1957): 291-296.

_____. "La Culture Profane de Saint Jean Chrysostome." *Melanges de Science Religieuse* 10 (1953): 53-67.

_____. "L'Education des Enfans au IVe Siecle." Revue de Science Humaines (1947): 222-238.

_____. "Platon et Saint Jean Chrysostome." *Association G. Bude* (1953): 186-189.

_____. "La Question d'Authenticitè des Lettres à Theodore." *Byzantinische Zeitschrift* 51 (1958): 66-72.

_____. *Saint Jean Chrysostome à Theodore*. Paris: Les Belles Lettres, 1966.

_____. *Saint Jean Chrysostome. Les Cohabitations Suspectes*. Paris: Les Editiones du Cerf, 1955.

Dunbar, David G. "The Biblical Canon." In *Hermeneutics, Authority and Canon*. Grand Rapids: Zondervan, 1986.

Dvornik, F. *Early Christian and Byzantine Political Philosophy: Origins and Background. Dunbarton Oaks Studies*, 9. Washington, D.C, 1966.

Ehler, Sidney Z. and John B. Morrall. *Church and State through the Centuries*. New York: Biblo and Tannen, 1967.

Elert, Werner. *Eucharist and Church Fellowship in the First Four Centuries*. Saint Louis: Concordia, 1966.

Eliade, Mircea. *A History of Religious Ideas, Volume 2- From Gautama Buddha to the Triumph of Christianity*. Chicago: University of Chicago, 1982.

Eno, Robert. "Some Patristic Views on the Relationship of Faith and Works in Justification." in *Justification by Faith* edited by H. George Anderson et al. 111-130. Minneapolis: Augsburg, 1985.

_____. *Teaching Authority in the Early Church*. Wilmington, Del.: Michael Glazier, 1984.

Erickson, Craig Douglas. *Participating in Worship*. Louisville: Westminister/ John Knox Press, 1989.

Ettlinger, Gerard H. *Jesus, Christ and Savior*. Wilmington, Del.: Michael Glazier, 1987.

_____. "Some Historical Evidences for the Date of Saint John Chrysostom's Birth in the Treatise *Ad Viduam Iuniorem*." *Traditio* 16 (1960): 373-380.

Evans, Craig. "Patristic Interpretation of Mark 2:26, when Abiathar was High Priest" *Vigiliae Christianae* 40 (1986) 183-186.

Evans, Robert F. *Pelagius: Inquiries and Reappraisals*. NY: Seabury, 1968.

Fee, G.D. "The Text of John and Mark in the Writings of Chrysostom." *New Testament Studies* 26 (1980): 525-547.

Feldman, Hilary. "Some Aspects of the Christian Reaction to the Tradition of Classical Munificence with Particular Reference to the Works of John Chrysostom and Libanius." M. Litt. thesis, Oxford University, 1980.

Festugiere, A.J. *Antioche Paienne et Chretienne*. Paris: de Boccard, 1959.

Finn, Thomas. *The Liturgy of Baptism in the Baptismal Instructions of Saint John Chrysostom*. Washington: Catholic University of America Press, 1967.

Fiorenza, Elisabeth Schussler. *Aspects of Religious Propaganda in Judaism and Early Christianity*. Notre Dame, IN: University of Notre Dame Press, 1976.

Flanagan, M.L. *Chrysostom on the Condescension and Accuracy of the Scriptures*. Nabier: Wellington, 1958.

Forell, George Wolfgang. *History of Christian Ethics*. Minneapolis: Augsburg, 1979.

Fox, Robin Lane. *Pagans and Christians*. San Francisco: Harper and Row, 1986.

Frend, W.H.C. "Church and State. Perspectives and Problems in the Patristic Era." *Studia Patristica* 17 (1982): 38-54

_____. "The Church of the Roman Empire." In *The Layman in Christian History*. ed by Stephen Neill and Hans-Ruedi Weber. London: SCM Press, 1963.

_____. *The Rise of Christianity*. Philadelphia: Fortress, 1984.

_____. "Town and Countryside in Early Christianity." In *Studies in Church History*. ed D. Baker. Oxford: Oxford University Press, 1969. 25-42.

Friedrich, Otto. *The End of the World: a history*. New York: Coward, McCann and Geoghegan, 1982.

Gager, John G. *Kingdom and Community: the Social World of Early Christianity*. Englewood Cliffs, NJ: Prentice-Hall, 1975.

_____. *The Origins of Anti-Semitism*. Oxford: Oxford University Press, 1985.

Gange, Ronald, Thomas Kane, and Robert VerEerke. *Introducing Dance in Christian Worship*. Washington: The Pastoral Press, 1984.

Galtier, Paul. "Saint Jean Chrysostome et la Confession." *Recherches de Science Religieuse* 1 (1910): 209-240, 313-350.

Garnsey, Peter. *Social Status and Legal Privilege in the Roman Empire*. Oxford: Clarendon, 1970.

_____. "Social Status and Legal Privilege in the Second and Third Centuries of the Roman Empire with Special Reference to the Curial Class." D. Phil. diss., Oxford University, 1967.

Garrett, James Leo. "The Priesthood of All Believers: from Cyprian to John Chrysostom." *Southwestern Journal of Theology*. 30 (1988): 22-33.

Geanakopolos, Deno John. "Church Building and Caesaropapism AD 312-565." *Greek, Roman and Byzantine Studies* 7 (1966): 167-186.

Geerard, Mauritii, ed. *Clavis Patrum Graecorum*. Brepols: Turnhout, 1974.

Geerlings, J and Silva N. "Chrysostom's Text of the Gospel of Saint Mark." *Harvard Theological Review* 24 (1931): 121-142.

Gignac, F.T. "The Text of Acts in Chrysostom's Homilies." *Traditio* 26 (1970): 308-315.

Gilliard, Frank D. "Senatorial Bishops in the Fourth Century." *Harvard Theological Review* 77 (1984): 153-175.

Glover, T.R. *The Conflict of Religions in the Early Roman Empire*. Boston: Beacon Press, 1960.

Gnuse, Robert. *You Shall Not Steal*. Maryknoll, NY: Orbis, 1985.

Gonzalez, Justo L. *Faith and Wealth*. San Francisco: Harper and Row, 1990.

Goodspeed, Edgar J. *The Formation of the New Testament*. Chicago: University of Chicago Press, 1926.

Gorman, Michael. *Abortion and the Early Church*. Downers Grove, IL: Inter Varsity Press, 1982.

Gorday, Peter. *Principles of Patristic Exegesis: Romans 9-11 in Origen, John Chrysostom and Augustine*. New York: Edwin Mellen Press, 1983.

Gordon, Barry. "The Problem of Scarcity and the Christian Fathers: John Chrysostom and some Contemporaries." *Studia Patristica* 22 (1989): 108-120.

Gough, Michael. *The Origins of Christian Art*. New York: Praeger, 1974.

Gracey, M.H. "The Roman Army in Syria, Judaea and Arabia." D. Phil diss., Oxford University, 1981.

Graef, Hilda. *Mary: A History of Doctrine and Devotion*. New York: Sheed and Ward, 1963.

Graham, Keith. "The Opposition of the Orthodox Bishops as seen through Basil to Arianism under the Emperor Valens." D. Phil. diss., Oxford University, 1975.

Grant, Robert M. *Early Christianity and Society*. New York: Harper and Row, 1977.

_____. *Eusebius as Church Historian*. Oxford: Clarendon, 1980.

_____. *Gods and the One God*. Philadelphia: Westminister, 1986.

Grant, Robert M. and David Tracy. *A Short History of the Interpretation of the Bible*. Philadelphia: Fortress, 1984.

Greeley, Delores. "The Church as 'Body of Christ' According to the Teaching of Saint John Chrysostom." Ph. D. diss., The University of Notre Dame, 1971.

_____. "Saint John Chrysostom- Prophet of Social Justice." *Studia Patristica* 17 (1982): 1163-1168.

Green, H. Benedict. "The Significance of the Pre-Baptismal Seal in Saint John Chrysostom." *Studia Patristica* 6 (1962): 84-90.

Green, Malcolm. "The Papacy of Innocent I." D. Phil. diss., Oxford University, 1973.

Greer, Rowan A. *Broken Lights and Mended Lives: Theology and Common Life in the Early Church*. University Park: Pennsylvania State University Press, 1986.

_____. *The Captain of Our Salvation: A Study in the Patristic Exegesis of Hebrews*. Tubingen: J.C.B. Mohr, 1973.

Gregory, Timothy E. "Julian and the Last Oracle at Delphi." *Greek, Roman and Byzantine Studies* 24 (1983): 355-366.

_____. *Vox Populi: Popular Opinion and Violence in the Religious Controversies of the Fifth Century A.D.* Columbus: Ohio State University Press, 1979.

Griffiths, D.W. "Saint John Chrysostom: The Fruit of a Worthy Communion." *Priestly Studies* 28 (1961): 30-42.

Grillmeier, Aloys. *Christ in Christian Tradition: Volume 1- From the Apostolic Age to Chalcedon (451)*. Atlanta: John Knox, 1975.

Grissom, Fred Allen. "Chrysostom and the Jews: Studies in Jewish Christian Relations in Fourth-Century Antioch." Ph. D. diss., Southwestern Baptist Theological Seminary, 1978.

Haddad, George. *Aspects of Social Life in Antioch in the Hellenistic-Roman Period*. New York: Hafner, 1949.

Hall, Thomas Cuming. *History of Ethics Within Organized Christianity*. New York: Charles Scribner's Sons, 1910.

Halliday, W.R. *The Pagan Background of Early Christianity*. New York: Cooper Square Publishers, 1970.

Halton, Thomas. *The Church*. Wilmington, Del: Michael Glazier, 1985.

_____. *In Praise of Saint Paul*. Boston: Daughters of Saint Paul, 1964.

_____. "The Kairos of the Mass and the Deacon in John Chrysostom." In *Diakonia: Studies in Honmor of Robert T. Meyer*. Washington, DC: The Catholic University of America Press, 1986. p 53-59.

_____. "Saint John Chrysostom *De Fato et Providentia*: A Study of its Authenticity." *Traditito* 20 (1963): 1-24.

_____. "Saint John Chrysostom on Education." *The Catholic Educational Review* 61 (1963): 163-175.

_____. "Some Images of the Church in Saint John Chrysostom." *American Ecclesiastical Review* 153 (1965): 96-106.

_____. "Two Newly-Edited Homilies of John Chrysostom." *Irish Theological Quarterly*, 43 (1976): 133-138.

Hare, B.W. "Saint John Chrysostom on Education." *Prudentia* 6 (1974): 99-104.

Harjunpaa. Toivo. "Saint John Chrysostom in the Light of His Catechetical and Baptismal Homilies." *Lutheran Quarterly*, 29 (1977): 167-195.

Harkins, Paul. "Chrysostom's Sermo as Neophytes." *Studia Patristica* 10 (1970): 112-117.

_____. "Chrysostom the Apologist: On the Divinity of Christ" In *Kyriakon: Festschriften Johannes Quasten*. Munster: Verlag Aschendorff, 1970. I, 441-451.

_____. "Pre-Baptismal Rites in Chrysostom's Baptismal Catecheses." *Studia Patristica* 8 (1966): 219-238.

_____. *Saint John Chrysostom: Baptismal Instructions*. Westminster, Maryland: Newman Press, 1963.

_____. *Saint John Chrysostom: Discourses Against Judaizing Christians*. Washington: Catholic University of America Press, 1979.

_____. *Saint John Chrysostom: On the Incomprehensible Nature of God*. Washington: Catholic University of America Press, 1984.

_____. "The Text Tradition of Chrysostom's Commentary on John." Ph. D. diss., The University of Michigan, 1943.

_____. "The Text Tradition of Chrysostom's Commentary on John." *Theological Studies* 19 (1958): 404-412.

_____. "The Text Tradition of Chrysostom's Commentary on John." *Studia Patristica* 7 (1966): 210-220.

Harries, Jill. "Bishops, Senators and their Cities in Southern and Central Gaul." D. Phil. diss., Oxford University, 1981.

Harris, Robbie James. "John Chrysostom's Use of the Homily." M.A. thesis, Southern Baptist Seminary, 1957.

Harris, William V. *Ancient Literacy*. Cambridge: Harvard University Press, 1989.

Hatch, Edwin. *The Influence of Greek Ideas and Usages upon the Christian Church*. London: Williams and Norgate, 1904.

Hawkins, Ernest J. and Cyril Mango. "The Mosaics of Saint Sophia at Istanbul: The Church Fathers in the North Tympanum." *Dunbarton Oaks Papers* 26 (1972): 1-41.

Hay, C. "Antiochene Exegesis and Christology." *Australian Biblical Review* 12 (1964): 10-23.

_____. "Saint John Chrysostom and the Integrity of the Human Nature of Christ." *Franciscan Studies* 19 (1959): 298-317.

Heather, Peter. "The Crossing of the Danube and the Gothic Conversion." *Greek, Roman and Byzantine Studies* 27 (1986): 289-318.

Henderson, R. "Missions of the Early Christian Church, II: Chrysostom." *The Catholic Presbyterian* 6 (1881): 185-192.

Henry, P. "From Apostle to Abbot: the Legitimation of Spiritual Authority in the Early Church." *Studia Patristica* 17 (1982): 491-505.

Heron, Alasdair I.C. *Table and Tradition*. Philadelphia: Westminster, 1983.

Herzog, Edward. "Saint Jean Chrysostome et la Confession." *Revue Internationale de Theologie* 10 (1902): 21-36.

Hickey, Anne Ewing. *Women of the Roman Aristocracy as Christian Monastics*. Ann Arbor, MI: UMI Research Press, 1987.

Hill, Carole. "Classical and Christian Traditions in Some Writings of Saint Ambrose of Milan." D. Phil. diss., Oxford University, 1979.

Hill, Robert. "*Akribeia*: a Principle of Chrysostom's Exegesis." *Colloquium* 14 (1981): 32-36.

_____. "Christmas in the Book of Genesis." *Clergy Review* 68 (1983): 445-447.

_____. "On Giving Up Horses for Lent." *Clergy Review* 68 (1983): 105-106.

_____. "On Looking Again at *Sunkatabasis*." *Prudentia* 13 (1981): 3-11.

_____. *Saint John Chrysostom: Homilies on Genesis 1-17*. Washington, DC: Catholic University of America Press, 1986.

_____. *Saint John Chrysostom: Homilies on Genesis 18-45*. Washington, DC: Catholic University of America Press, 1990.

_____. "Saint John Chrysostom's Teaching on Inspiration in Sixth Homily on Isaiah." *Vigiliae Christianae* 22 (1968): 19-37.

_____. "St. John Chrysostom and the Incarnation of the Word in Scripture." *Compass Theology Review* 14 (1980): 34-38.

_____. "St. John Chrysostom's Teaching on Inspiration in His Old Testament Homilies." Ph. D. diss., Pontificiam Universitatem S. Thomas de Urbe, Sidney, 1981.

Hillgarth, J.N. *Christianity and Paganism, 350-750*. Philadelphia: University of Pennsylvania Press, 1986.

Hinson, E. Glenn. "Indentity and Adaptibility: The role of selected ecclesiastical and theological forms in the early Christian mission." D. Phil. diss., Oxford University, 1973.

Hn'ik, Frank M. *The Philanthropic Motive in Christianity*. Oxford: Basil Blackwell, 1938.

Hollinghurst, G.F. "The Ministry of Teaching in the Christian Church to the Death of Saint Augustine." D. Phil. diss., Oxford University, 1954.

Howego, J. "Greek Imperial Countermarks: Studies in the economy of the Eastern Roman Empire." D. Phil. diss., Oxford University, 1983.

Hsaing, P.S. "Saint John Chrysostom on the Priesthood." *The Homiletical and Pastoral Review* 55 (1955): 920-926.

Hubbel, Harry M. "Chrysostom and Rhetoric." *Classical Philology* 19 (1924): 261-276.

Hunt, E.D. "Pilgrimage to the Holy Land in the Fourth and Fifth Century." D. Phil. diss., Oxford University, 1976.

Hunter, David G. "Borrowings from Libanius in the Comparatio Regis et Monachi of Saint John Chrysostom." *The Journal of Theological Studies* 39 (1988): 525-531.

_____. *A Comparasion Between a King and a Monk/ Against the Opponents of the Monastic Life.* Lewiston, NY: Edwin Mellen, 1988.

_____. "John Chrysostom's *Adversus Oppugnatores Vitae Monasticae*: Ethics and Apologetics in the Late Fourth Century." Ph. D. diss., The University of Notre Dame, 1986.

_____. "Libanius and John Chrysostom: New Thoughts on an Old Problem." *Studia Patristica* 22 (1989): 129-135.

Hunter, David G. ed. *Preaching in the Patristic Age.* New York: Paulist, 1989.

Hussey, J.M. *The Orthodox Church in the Byzantine Empire.* Oxford: Clarendon, 1986.

Huttmann, Maude Aline. *The Establishment of Christianity and the Proscription of Paganism.* New York: Longmans, Green and Company, 1914.

Hyatt, M. "The Active and the Contemplative Life in Saint John Chrysostom's Treatise on the Priesthood." *Diakonia* 15 (1980): 185-192.

Jaeger, Werner. *Early Christianity and Greek Paideia.* Oxford: Oxford University Press, 1961.

_____. *Paideia: the Ideals of Greek Culture.* Oxford: Oxford University Press, 1943. 3 vols.

Johnson, Paul. *A History of the Jews*. New York: Harper and Row, 1987.

Jones, A.H.M. *The Cities of the Eastern Roman Provinces*. Oxford: Oxford University Press, 1971.

_____. *Constantine and the Conversion of Europe*. New York: Collier, 1962.

_____. *The Decline of the Ancient World*. New York: Longman, 1966.

_____. *The Greek City from Alexander to Justinian*. Oxford, Oxford University Press, 1940.

_____. *The Later Roman Empire, 284-602: A Social, Economic, and Administrative Survey*. 3 vols. Oxford, 1964.

_____. "Saint John Chrysostom's Parentage and Education." *Harvard Theological Review* 46 (1953): 171-173.

_____. "The Social Background of the Struggle Between Paganism and Christianity." In *The Conflict Between Pagan and Christianity in the Fourth Century*. ed by Arnaldo Momigliano, 17-37. Oxford: Clarendon, 1963.

Jurgens, W.A. *The Faith of the Fathers*. Collegeville, MN: The Liturgical Press, 1979.

Kannengiesser, Charles. "Le mystère pascal du Christ mort et ressusitè selon Jean Chrsostome." In *Jean Chrysostom et Augustine*, 221-246. Paris: Éditions Beauchesne, 1975.

Karmiris, J. "Ecclesiology of the Three Hierarchs." *Greek Orthodox Theological Review* 6 (1961): 135-185.

Keane, H. "The Sacrament of Penance in Saint John Chrysostom." *The Irish Theological Quarterly* 14 (1919): 305-317.

Kelly, J.N.D. *Early Christian Creeds*. NY: David McKay, 1972.

Kennedy, George. *Classical Rhetoic and Its Christian and Secular Tradition From Ancient to Modern Times*. Chapel Hill: University of North Carolina Press, 1980.

_____. *Greek Rhetoric Under Christian Emperors*. Princeton: Princeton University Press, 1983.

Kenny, Arthur. "Was Saint John Chrysostom a Semi-Pelagian?" *The Irish Theological Quarterly* 27 (1960): 16-29.

Kidd, B.J. *The Roman Primacy to A.D. 461*. London, 1936.

Kilmartin, Edward J. "The Active Role of Christ and the Spirit in the Divine Liturgy." *Diakonia* 17 (1983): 95-108.

_____. "John Chrysostom's Influence on Gabriel Qatraya's Theology of Eucharistic Consecration." *Theological Studies* 42 (1981): 444-457.

King, N.Q. *The Emperor Theodusius and the Establishment of Christianity*. Philadelphia: Westminster, 1960.

Klijn, A.F.J. and G.J. Reinink. *Patristic Evidence for Jewish-Christian Sects*. Leiden: Brill, 1973.

Knowles, D. "The Middle Ages 604-1350" In *A History of Christian Doctrine*. edited by H. Cunliffe-Jones. 227-286. Edinburgh: T and T Clark, 1978.

Kraeling, Carl H. "The Jewish Community at Antioch." *Journal of Biblical Literature* 51 (1932): 130-160.

Krauss, S. "The Jews in the Works of the Church Fathers." *The Jewish Quarterly Review* 5 (1893): 122-157; 6 (1894): 82-99, 225-261.

Krauth, C.P. "Chrysostom Considered with Reference to the Pulpit." *The Evangelical Review* 1 (1849): 84-104.

Krtitch, Daniel. "Saint John Chrysostom as the Theologian of Divine Philanthropy." Ph. D. diss., Harvard University, 1969.

Krupp, R.A. "The Effect of the Emerging State-Church on the Ministry of John Chrysostom." M.A. thesis, The University of Portland, 1977.

_____. *Saint John Chrysostom: A Scripture Index*. Lanham, MD: University Press of America, 1984.

Laistner, M.L.W. *Christianity and Pagan Culture in the Later Roman Empire, with John Chrysostom's Address on Vainglory and the Right Way for Parents to Bring Up Their Children*. Ithica: Cornell University Press, 1967.

_____. *The Greater Roman Historians*. Berkeley: University of California Press, 1963.

_____. *The Intellectual Heritage of the Early Middle Ages*. New York: Octagon Books, 1983.

Laporte, Jean. *The Role of Women in Early Christianity*. Lewiston, NY: Edwin Mellen Press, 1982.

Lawrenz, M.E. III. "The Christology of John Chrysostom." *Studia Patristica* 22 (1989): 148-154.

Leddy, J.F. "The Social Legislation of the Roman Empire from Augustus to Constantine." D. Phil. diss., Oxford University, 1939.

Leduc, F. "L'Eschatologie, Une Preoccupation Centrale de Saint Jean Chrysostome." *Proche Orient* 19 (1969): 109-134.

_____. "Peche et Conversion Chez Saint Jean Chrysostome." *Proche Orient* 26 (1976): 34-58; 27 (1977): 15-42; 28 (1978): 44-88.

_____. "Le Theme de la Vaine Glorie Chez Saint Jean Chrysostome." *Proche Orient* 19 (1969): 3-32.

Leroux, Jean-Marie. "Monachisme et Communautè Chrètienne d'après Saint Jean Chrysostome."In *Theologie de la Vie Monastique*, 143-190. Paris: Aubier, 1961.

_____. "Saint Jean Chrysostome et le Monachisme." In *Jean Chrysostome et Augustin*, 125-144. Paris: Éditions Beauchesne, 1975.

_____. "Saint Jean Chrysostome: Mission de l'Esprit dans la Salut de Monde." *Spiritus* 19 (1964): 149-156.

Liebeschuetz, J.H.W.G. *Antioch: City and Imperial Administration in the Later Roman Empire*. Oxford: Clarendon, 1972.

_____. "Did the Pelagian Movement Have Social Aims?" *Historia* 12 (1963) 227-241.

_____. "The Finances of Antioch in the Fourth Century A.D." *Byzantinische Zeitschrift* 52 (1959): 344-356.

_____. "Friends and Enemies of John Chrysostom." in Ann Moffatt, ed. *Maistor: Classical, Byzantine and Renaissance Studies for Robert Browning*. Canberra: Australian Association for Byzantine Studies, 1984. 85-111.

Lienhard, John T. *Ministry*. Wilmington, Del.: Michael Glazier, 1984.

Lietzmann, Hans. *The Era of the Church Fathers*. New York: Charles Scribner's Sons, 1952.

_____. *From Constantine to Julian*. New York: Charles Scribner's Sons, 1950.

Lieu, Samuel. "The Diffusion and Persecution of Manichaeism in Rome and China." D. Phil. diss., Oxford University, 1981.

_____. ed. *The Emperor Julian: Panegyric and Polemic*. Liverpool: Liverpool University Press, 1986.

Lightfoot, C.S. "The Eastern Frontier of the Roman Empire with Special Reference to the Imperial Frontier." D. Phil. diss., Oxford University, 1981.

Maat, William. *A Rhetorical Study of Saint John Chrysostom's De Sacerdotio.* Washington: The Catholic University of America Press, 1944.

MacDonald, J. "Innocent I: His life and letters." B. Litt. thesis, Oxford University, 1957.

MacMullen, Ramsey. *Christianizing the Roman Empire.* New Haven: Yale University Press, 1984.

_____. *Corruption and the Decline of Rome.* New Haven: Yale University Press, 1988.

_____. *Paganism in the Roman Empire.* New Haven: Yale University Press, 1981.

Makowski, J.L. "The Element of *akairos* in John Chrysostom's Anti-Jewish Polemic." *Studia Patristica* 12 (1975): 222-231.

Malina, A. "Jewish Christianity or Christian Judaism." *Journal for the Study of Judaism* 7: 46-57.

Malingrey, Anne Marie. "La Double Tradition Manuscrite de la Lettre de Jean Chrysostom à Innocent." *Traditio* 37 (1981): 381-388.

_____. "Étude d'un Theme Philosophique dans l'Oeuvre de Jean Chrysostome." *Acts du viie Congres de l'Association G. Bude* Paris: Les Belles Lettres, 1964. 289-291.

_____. *Indices Chrysostomici.* New York: G. Olms, 1978.

_____. *Jean Chrysostom: Sur la Providence de Dieu.* Paris: Editions du Cerf, 1961.

_____. *Jean Chrysostom: Sur l'Incomprehensibili de Dieu.* Paris: Editions du Cerf, 1970.

_____. "Le Ministére épiscopal dans L'Oeuvre de Jean Chrysostome." In *Jean Chrysostome et Augustin*, 75-89. Paris: Éditions Beauchesne, 1975.

_____. "Pour Une édition Critique du De Sacerdotio de Jean Chrysostome." *Traditio* 32 (1976): 347-352.

_____. "Problems Souleves par la Realisation d'un Index de Jean Chrysostome." *Revue de l'Organization International pour l'Etude des Langue Anciennes par Ordinateur.* (1970): 45-47.

_____. "La Tradition Latine d'un Texte de Jean Chrysostome (*Quad nemo laeditur*)." *Studia Patristica* 7 (1966): 248-254.

_____. "La Tradition Manuscrite des Homelies de Jean Chrysostome De Incomprehensibili." *Studia Patristica* 10 (1970): 22-28.

Malley, William. *Hellenism and Christianity. Analecta Gregoriana.* 210 (1978).

Markus, R.A. *Saeculum: History and Society in the Theology of St. Augustine.* Cambridge: Cambridge University Press, 1970.

Marrou, H.I. *A History of Education in Antiquity.* Madison: University of Wisconsin Press, 1982.

_____. "Synesius of Cyrene and Alexandrian Neoplatonism." In *The Conflict Between Paganism and Christianity in the Fourth Century.* 126-150. Oxford: Clarendon, 1963.

Martimort, A.G. *Deaconesses: an historical study.* San Francisco: Ignatius Press, 1986.

Matthews, John. *The Roman Empire of Ammianus.* Baltimore: Johns Hopkins University Press, 1989.

McGinn, Bernard, John Meyendorff, and Jean Leclercq, eds. *Christian Spirituality: Origins to the Twelfth Century.* New York: Crossroad, 1987.

McGrath, Alister. "The Development of the Doctrine of Justification during the Patristic and Medieval Periods." B.Div. thesis, Oxford University, 1983.

McGuckin, John A. "The Patristic Exegesis of the Transfiguration." *Studia Patristica* 18 (1985) vol 1. 335-342.

McIndoe, J.H. "John Calvin: Preface to the Homilies of Chrysostom." *Hartford Quarterly* 5 (1965): 19-26.

McKendrick, N.G. *Quod Christus sit Deus*. Ann Arbor: University of Michigan Press, 1966.

McKibbens, Thomas R. "The Exegesis of John Chrysostom: Homilies on the Gospels." *Expository Times* 93 (1982): 264-270.

McKinnon, James. *Music in Early Christian Literature*. Cambridge: Cambridge University Press, 1987.

McNally, Robert E. *The Bible in the Early Middle Ages*. Westminster, Md.: Newman Press, 1959.

Meeks, Wayne A. and Robert L. Wilken. *Jews and Christians in Antioch in the First Four Centuries of the Common Era*. Missoula, MT: Scholars Press, 1978.

Melanchthon, Philip. *Melanchthon on Christian Doctrine. (Loci Communes 1555)*. Grand Rapids: Baker, 1982.

Metzger, Bruce. "Antioch on the Orontes." *Biblical Archaeologist* 11 (1948): 69-88.

Meyer, Louis G. *Alms Gathering by Religious*. Washington: Catholic University of America Press, 1946.

Meyer, Robert T. "Palladius as Biographer and Autobiographer." *Studia Patristica* 17 (1982): 66-71.

_____. *Palladius: Dialogue on the Life of Saint John Chrysostom*. New York: Newman Press, 1985.

Miller, J. Innes. "The Spice Trade Under the Roman Empire from the Accession of Augustus to the Death of Heraclius B.C. 29-641 A.D." D. Phil. diss., Oxford University, 1963.

Mitchell, Leonel A. "The Baptismal Rite in Chrysostom." *Anglican Theological Review* 43 (1961): 397-403.

Momigliano, A. "Christianity and the Decline of the Roman Empire." In *The Conflict Between Paganism and Christianity in the Fourth Century* ed by A. Momigliano, 1-16. Oxford: Clarendon, 1963.

_____. "Pagan and Christian Historiography in the Fourth Century" In *The Conflict Between Paganism in the Fourth Century* ed by A. Momigliano, 79-99. Oxford: Clarendon, 1963.

Moore, H. *The Dialogue of Palladius Concerning the Life of Chrysostom.* London: SPCK, 1921.

Moss, Jean Dietz. *Rhetoric and Praxis.* Washington, D.C.: Catholic University of America Press, 1986.

Muller, H. "The Spiritual Campaign between Christians and Pagans from Lactantius to Augustine." B. Litt. thesis, Oxford University, 1945.

Murphy, F.X. *The Christian Way of Life.* Wilmington, Del.: Michael Glazier, 1986.

_____. "Conflagration: The Eschatological Perspective from Origen to Chrysostom." *Studia Patristica* 18 (1985) vol 1. 179-186.

_____. "The Moral Doctrine of Saint John Chrysostom." *Studia Patristica* 11 (1972): 52-57.

_____. "The Patristic Origins of Orthodox Mysticism." *Mystics Quarterly* 10 (1984) 59-63.

Murray, R.J. "The Use of Conditional Sentences in Saint John Chrysostom's Homilies on the Gospel on St. John." Ph. D. diss., Ohio State University, 1960.

Musurillo, Herbert A. *Jean Chrysostom: La Virginite*. Paris: Editions du Cerf, 1966.

_____. "The Problem of Ascetical Fasting in the Greek Patristic Writers." *Traditio* 12 (1956): 1-64.

Nairn, J.A. "On the Text of the De Sacerdotio of Saint John Chrysostom." *Journal of Theological Studies* 7 (1906): 575-590.

Natali, A. "Christianisme et Cité à Antioche à la Fin de IVe Siecle d'après Jean Chrysostome." In *Jean Chrysostome et Augustin*. 41-59. Paris: Beauchesne, 1975.

Neill, Stephen and Hans-Ruedi Weber. *The Layman in Christian History*. Philadelphia: Westminister, 1963.

Nestle, E. "Chrysostom on the Life of John the Apostle." *American Journal of Theology* 9 (1905): 519-520.

Neusner, Jacob. *Judaism and Christianity in the Age of Constantine*. Chicago: University of Chicago Press, 1987.

_____. "Judaism in Late Antiquity." *Judaism* 15 (1966): 230-241.

_____. *Judaism in the Matrix of Christianity*. Philadelphia: Fortress, 1986.

_____. *Self-Fulfilling Prophecy*. Boston: Beacon Press, 1987.

Neville, Graham. *Saint John Chrysostom: Six Books on the Priesthood*. Crestwood, NY: St. Vladimir's Seminary Press, 1984.

Newman, John Henry, Cardinal. *An Essay on the Development of Christian Doctrine*. Notre Dame, IN: University of Notre Dame Press. 1989. (reprint on 1878 edition).

Nicholson, O.P. "Lactantius: Prophecy and politics in the age of Constantine the Great." D. Phil. diss., Oxford University, 1981.

Neibuhr, H. Richard and Daniel D. Williams, eds. *The Ministry in Historical Perspective*. San Francisco: Harper and Row, 1983.

Noonan, John T. *Contraception: A History of Its Treatment by the Catholic Theologians and Canonists*. New York: New American Library, 1965.

Norman, A.F. *Libanius: Selected Works*. Cambridge: Harvard University Press, 1977.

_____. *Libanius. Selected Works: The Julianic Orations*. Cambridge: Harvard University Press, 1969.

Obermann, Julian. "The Sepulchre of the Maccabean Martyrs." *Journal of Biblical Literature* 50 (1931): 250-265.

Ohleyer, Leo Joseph. *The Pauline Formula Induere Christum with Special Reference to the Works of Saint John Chrysostom*. Washington: Catholic University of America Press, 1921.

Osborn, Eric. *Ethical Patterns in Early Christian Thought*. Cambridge: Cambridge University Press, 1976.

Ostrogoorsky, G. *History of the Byzantine State*. 2nd ed. Oxford: Oxford University Press, 1968.

Ottoson, Krister. "Love of God in Saint John Chrysostom's Commentary on the Fourth Gospel." *Church Quarterly Review* 166 (1965): 315-323.

Pack, Roger A. "Studies in Libanius and Antiochene Society Under Theodosius." Ph. D. diss., The University of Michigan, 1935.

Packard, A.A. "Chrysostom's True Christian Philosophy." *Anglican Theological Review* 45 (1963): 396-406.

Pagels, Elaine. *Adam, Eve, and the Serpent*. New York: Random House, 1988.

_____. "The Politics of Paradise: Augustine's Exegesis of Genesis 1-3 Versus that of John Chrysostom." *Harvard Theological Review* 79 (1985): 67-99.

Palladius. *The Lausiac History of Palladius*. New York: Macmillan, 1918.

Pargoire, J. "Les Homelies de Saint Jean Chrysostome en Juillet, 399." *Echoes d'Orient* 3 (1900): 151-162.

Parker, T.M. *Christianity and the State in the Light of History*. London: Adam and Charles Black, 1955.

Payne, Robert. *The Holy Fire*. Crestwood, NY: St. Vladimir's Seminary Press, 1980.

Pelikan, Jaroslav. *The Emergence of the Catholic Tradition (100-600)*. Chicago: The University of Chicago Press, 1971.

_____. *The Excellent Empire: The Fall of Rome and the Triumph of the Church*. San Francisco: Harper and Row, 1987.

_____. *Jesus Through the Centuries*. New Haven: Yale University Press, 1985.

Peters, F.E. *The Harvest of Hellenism*. New York: Simon and Schuster, 1970.

Peterson, K.M. "Despair: Exploring Christian and Existential Responses." M. A. thesis, Western Conservative Baptist Seminary, 1984.

Peterson, W.L. "Can *arsenokoitai* be translated by Homosexuals?" *Vigiliae Christianae* 40 (1986): 187-191.

Petropoulos, J.C.B. "The Church Father as Social Informant: Saint John Chrysostom on Folksongs." *Studia Patristica* 22 (1989): 159-164.

Phan, Peter C. *Social Thought*. Wilmington, Del.: Michael Glazier, 1984.

Pietri, Charles. "L'Aristocratie Chrétienne entre Jean de Constantinople et Augustin d'Hippone." In *Jean Chrysostome et Augustin*. 283-305. Paris: Beauchesne, 1975.

Pirenne, Henri. *Mohammed and Charlemagne*. Totowa, NJ: Barnes and Noble, 1980.

Pistorius, P.V. *Plotinus and Neoplatonism*. Cambridge: Bowes and Bowes, 1952.

Poon, Michael Nai-Chiu. "The Counsel Against Despair: A Study in John Chrysostom's Ethics." D. Phil. diss., Oxford University, 1984.

Price, R.M. "The Role of Military Men in Syria and Egypt from Constantine to Theodosius II." D. Phil. diss., Oxford University, 1973.

Price, S.R.F. "The Imperial Cult in Asia Minor: Religious Aspects. "D. Phil. diss., Oxford University, 1980.

Quasten, Johannes. "The Conflict of Early Christianity with the Jewish Temple Worship." *Theological Studies* 2 (1941): 481-487.

_____. *Patrology*. Westminster, Md.: Christian Classics, 1983.

_____. *Patrology*. Vol. 4. Westminster, Md.: Christian Classics, 1986.

Quin, Jerome D. "Saint John Chrysostom on History in the Synoptics." *The Catholic Biblical Quarterly* 24 (1962): 140-147.

Racle, P.G. "A la Source d'un Passage de la VIIe Catechese Baptismale de Saint Jean Chrysostome." *Vigiliae Christianae* 15 (1961): 46-53.

Ramsey, Boniface. *Beginning to Read the Fathers*. New York: Paulist Press, 1985.

Rancillac, P. *L'église Manifestation de l'Esprit chez Saint Jean Chrysostome*. Beyrouth: Dar al-Kalima, 1970.

Rashdall, Hastings. *The Idea of Atonement in Christian Thought*. London: Macmillan, 1920.

Raynor, Duncan H. "The Faith of the *Simpliciores*: A Patriarch's Dilemma." *Studia Patristica* 22 (1989): 165-169.

Repp, A.C. "John Chrysostom on the Christian Home as a Teacher." *Concordia Theological Monthly* 22 (1951): 937-948.

Riley, Hugh. *Christian Initiation*. Washington: Catholic University of America Press, 1974.

Ritter, A.M. "Between Theocracy and Simple Life: Dio Chrysostom, John Chrysostom and the Problem of Humanizing Society." *Studia Patristica* 22 (1989): 170-180.

Rogers, Jack B. and Donald K. McKim. *The Authority and Interpretation of the Bible*. New York: Harper and Row, 1979.

Roth, Catharine P. *St. John Chrysostom: On Marriage and Family Life*. Crestwood, NY: St. Vladimir's Seminary Press, 1986.

_____. *St. John Chrysostom: On Wealth and Poverty*. Crestwood, NY: St. Vladimir's Seminary Press, 1984.

Ruether, Rosemary Radford. *Gregory of Nazianzus*. Oxford: Clarendon, 1969.

_____. "Judaism and Christianity: Two fourth-century religions." *Studies in Religion* 2 (1972): 1-10.

_____. "Misogynism and Virginal Feminism in the Fathers of the Church." In *Religion and Sexism*. New York: Simon and Schuster, 1974.

_____. "Mothers of the Church: Ascetic Women in the Late Patristic Age." In *Women of Spirit*. New York: Simon and Schuster, 1979.

Rush, Alfred C. *Death and Burial in Christian Antiquity*. Washigton: Catholic University of America Press, 1941.

Ryan, John A. *Alleged Socialism of the Church Fathers*. St. Louis: B. Herder, 1913.

Ryan, P.J. "Chrysostom: A Derived Stylist." *Vigiliae Christianae* 36 (1982): 5-14.

Sawhill, John Alexander. *The Use of Athletic Metaphors in the Biblical Homilies of Saint John Chrysostom*. Princeton: The University Press, 1928.

Schatkin, Margaret A. "The Authenticity of Saint John Chrysostom's *De Santo Babylos Contra Julianum et Gentiles*." In *Kyriakon: Festschrift Johannes Quasten*. Munster: Aschendorff, 1970.

_____. *Critical Edition and Introduction to Saint John Chrysostom's De Santo Babylos Contra Iulianum et Gentiles*. Ann Arbor: The University of Michigan Press, 1966.

_____. *John Chrysostom as Apologist*. Thessaloniki: Patriarchal Institute for Patristic Studies, 1987.

_____. "Saint John Chrysostom's Homily on the Protopaschites: Introduction and Translation." *Orientalia Christiana Analecta*. 195 (1973): 167-185.

Schatkin, Margaret A. and Paul W. Harkins. *Saint John Chrysostom Apologist*. Washington, DC: Catholic University of America Press, 1985.

Schlatter, Richard. *Private Property: The History of an Idea*. New Brunswick, NJ: Rutgers University Press, 1951.

Schmemann, Alexander. *The Historical Road of Eastern Orthodoxy*. New York: Holt, Rinehart, and Winston, 1963.

Schoder, R.V. "Saint Chrysostom and the Date of Christ's Nativity." *Theological Studies* 3 (1942): 140-144.

Schoeck, R.J. "The Use of Saint John Chrysostom in Sixteenth Century Controversies." *Harvard Theological Review* 54 (1961): 21-27.

Setton, Kenneth M. *Christian Attitude Towards the Emperor in the Fourth Century.* New York: Columbia University Press, 1941.

Sheerin, Daniel J. *The Eucharist.* Wilmington, Del.: Michael Glazier, 1986.

Sherwig, Walter. *Rich and Poor in Christian Tradition.* London: Burns, Oates and Washbourne, 1948.

Shore, Sally R. *John Chrysostom: On Virginity, Against Remarriage.* New York: Edwin Mellen Press, 1983.

Sider, Robert D. *The Gospel and Its Proclamation.* Wilmington, Del.: Michael Glazier, 1983.

Simon, M. *Verus Israel: A study of the relations between Christians and Jews in the Roman Empire.* Oxford: Littman Library, 1986.

Sladden, J.C. Chrysostome et Confirmation. *Studia Patristica* 11 (1972): 229-233.

Small, Caroline Dermot. "The Understanding of Friendship in the Works of Selected Church Fathers with Reference to Classical Ideas on Friendship." D. Phil. diss., Oxford University, 1984.

Smalley, Beryl. *The Study of the Bible in the Middle Ages.* Notre Dame, IN: University of Notre Dame Press, 1964.

Smothers, Edgar R. "Chrysostom and Symeon." *Harvard Theological Review* 46 (1953): 203-215.

_____. "A Problem of Text in Saint John Chrysostom." *Recherches des Sciences Religieuse* 39 (1949): 416-427.

_____. "Les Texte des Homelies de Saint Jean Chrysostome sur les Actes des Apotres." *Recherches des Sciences Religieuse* 27 (1937): 513-548.

_____. "Toward a Critical Text of the Homilies on Acts of Saint John Chrysostom." *Studia Patristica* 1 (1957): 53-57.

Snee, Rochelle. "Valen's Recall of the Nicene Exiles and Anti-Arian Propaganda." *Greek Roman and Byzantine Studies* 26 (1985): 395-419.

Socrates. *Ecclesiastical History.* In *Nicene and Post Nicene Fathers of the Christian Church.* Second Series, Volume 2, 1-178. Grand Rapids: Eerdmans, 1979.

Soffray, M. "Saint Jean Chrysostome et la Litterature Paienne." *Phoenix* 2 (1948): 82-85.

Sordi, Marta. *The Christians and the Roman Empire.* Norman: University of Oklahoma Press, 1986.

Sozoman. *Ecclesiastical History.* In *Nicene and Post Nicene Fathers of the Christian Church.* Second Series, Volume 2, 179-427. Grand Rapids: Eerdmans, 1979.

Stebe, M. Helene. *La Conversion- Jean Chrysostome.* Paris: De Brouwer, 1979.

Stephens, W.R.W. *Saint John Chrysostom. His Life and Times.* London: John Murray, 1883.

Stevenson, Robert B. "The Reluctant Priests- A study of the growth of the functions and responsibilities of the bishop in the early church. B. Div. thesis, Oxford University, 1975.

Stratmann, F. *Die Heiligen und der Staat. III Athanasius, Ambrosius, Chrysostomus, Augustinus.* Frankfurt: Knecht, 1950.

Swete, Henry Barclay. *Essays on the Early History of the Church and the Ministry.* London: Macmillan, 1918.

Swift, Louis J. *The Early Fathers on War and Military Service*. Wilmington, Del.: Machael Glazier, 1983.

Tanner, R.G. "Chrysostom's Exegesis of Romans." *Studia Patristica* 17 (1982): 1185-1197.

Taylor, R.E. "Attitudes of the Fathers toward Practices of Jewish Christians." *Studia Patristica* 4 (1959): 504-511.

Tavard, George H. *Women in Christian Tradition*. Notre Dame, IN: Notre Dame University Press, 1973.

Telfer, W. *The Office of a Bishop*. London: Darton, Longman and Todd, 1962.

Theodoret . *Ecclesiastical History*. In *Nicene and Post Nicene Fathers of the Christian Church*. Second Series, Volume 3, 33-159. Grand Rapids: Eerdmans, 1979.

Thomas, E. M. "Guilds of Craftsmen and Small Traders in the Ancient World (exclusive of Egypt) from the Earliest Greek Times to the End of the Fifth Century A.D." B. Litt. thesis, Oxford University, 1934.

Thompson, E.A. "Christianity and the Northern Barbarians." In *The Conflict Between Paganism and Christianity in the Fourth Century*. 56-78. ed by A. Momigliano. Oxford: Clarendon, 1963.

Tomlin, R.S.O. "The Emperor Valentinian I." D. Phil. diss., Oxford University, 1973.

Travis, James L. "Confession and the Penitential System in John Chrysostom." M.A. thesis, Southern Baptist Seminary, 1964.

Trombley, Frank R. "Paganism in the Greek World at the End of Antiquity: The Case of Rural Anatolia and Greece." *Harvard Theological Review*. 78 (1985): 327-352.

Tucker, Ruth A. and Walter Liefeld. *Daughters of the Church: Women and Ministry from New Testament Times to the Present.* Grand Rapids: Zondervan, 1987.

Valantasis, Richard. "Body, Hierarchy and Leadership in Chrysostom's On the Priesthood." *Greek Orthodox Theological Review* 30 (1985) 455-471.

Vallianos, Pericles G. "The Attitude of the Three Hierarchs Towards Knowledge and Learning." *Greek Orthodox Theological Review* 24 (1979): 43-57.

Vandenberghe, Bruno H. "L'ame de Chrysostome." *La Vie Spirituelle* 99 (1958): 255-281.

_____. "Chrysostome et Paul." *Vigiliae Christianae* 34 (1952): 161-174.

_____. *John of the Golden Mouth.* London: Blackfrairs, 1958.

_____. *Saint Jean Chrysostome et la Parole de Dieu.* Paris: Editions du Cerf, 1961.

_____. "Saint John Chrysostom on the Priesthood." *Cross and Crown* 11 (1959): 148-164.

_____. "Saint Jean Chrysostome Pasteur des Jeunes Epoux." *La Vie Spirituelle* 89 (1953): 37-56.

Van Ommeslaeghe, Florent. "Jean Chrysostome en Conflit avec l'Imperatice Eudoxie: Le Dossier et les Origines d'une Legende." *Analecta Bollandaina* 97 (1979): 131-159.

Vasiliev, A.A. *History of the Byzantine Empire.* Madison: University of Wisconsin Press, 1952.

Vawter, Bruce. "Creationism: Creative Misuse of the Bible." In *Is God a Creationist? The Religious Case Against Creation Science.* New York: Scribner, 1983.

Vogt, J. "Pagans and Christians in the Family of Constantine the Great." In *The Conflict Between Paganism and Christianity in the Fourth Century.* ed by A. Momigliano, 38-55. Oxford: Clarendon, 1963.

Volz, Carl A. *Pastoral Life and Practice in the Early Church.* Minneapolis: Augsburg, 1990.

Voobus, Arthur. *History of Asceticism in the Syrian Orient.* Louvain: Corpus Scriptorum Christianorum Orientalium, 1958.

Vree, Dale. "Radical Bishops." *New Oxford Review* October, 1984. 22-25.

Wainwright, Geoffrey. *Christian Initiation.* Richmond: John Knox Press, 1969.

Wallace-Hadrill, D. S. *Christian Antioch.* Cambridge: Cambridge University Press, 1982.

Walsh, James and P.G. Walsh. *Divine Providence and Human Suffering.* Wilmington, Del.: Michael Glazier, 1985

Walsh, William and John P. Langan. "Patristic Social Consciousness-The Church and the Poor." In *The Faith that Does Justice.* New York: Paulist Press, 1977.

Ware, Kallistos. "Christian Theology in the East 600-1453." In *A History of Christian Doctrine.* edited by H. Cunliffe-Jones. 181-225. Edinburgh: T and T Clark, 1978.

Watkins, Oscar D. *A History of Penance.* New York: Burt Franklin, 2 vols. 1961.

Weaver, J.A. "Catechetical Themes in the Post-Baptismal Teaching of Saint John Chrysostom." Ph. D. diss ., Catholic University of America Press, 1964.

Webber, Robert E. *The Church in the World.* Grand Rapids: Zondervan, 1986.

Wenger, Antoine. "Homelie de Saint Jean Chrysostome à Son Asia d'Asia."

Revue de Étude Byzantines 19 (1961): 110-123.

_____. "Homilies Patristiques et Hymnes Melodiqoes Jean Chrysostome et Romanos le Melodie." *Revue de Étude Byzantines* 13 (1955): 157-160.

_____. *Huit Catechesis Baptismales Inedits*. Paris: Editiones du Cerf, 1957.

_____. "La tradition des Ouvres de Saint Jean Chrysostome I: Cateches Insonnues et Homelies peu Connues." *Revue de Étude Byzantines* 14 (1956): 5-47.

Westerhoff, John H. and O. C. Edwards, Jr. eds. *A Faithful Church*. Wilton, CT: Morehouse-Barlow, 1981.

Whiteker, G.H. "Chrysostom on 1 Corinthians 1:13." *Journal of Theological Studies*, 15 (1914): 254-257.

Wiles, M. "The Old Testament in Controversy with the Jews." *Scottish Journal of Theology*. 8 (1955): 113-126.

Wilken, Robert L. "The Christian as the Romans (and Greeks) Saw Them." In *Jewish and Christian Self-Definition*. Philadelphia: Fortress, 1980.

_____. "The Jews and Christian Apologetics After Theodosius I *Cunctos Populos*." *Harvard Theological Review* 73 (1980): 451-471.

_____. *John Chrysostom and the Jews: Rhetoric and Reality in the Late Fourth Century*. Berkeley: University of California Press, 1984.

_____. *Judaism and the Early Christian Mind*. New Haven: Yale University Press, 1970.

_____. "Pagan Criticism of Christianity: Greek Religion and Christian Faith." In *Early Christian Literature and the Classical Intellectual Tradition*, ed. William R. Schoedel and Robert L. Wilken, 117-134. Paris: Éditions Beauchesne, 1979.

_____. "Toward a Social Interpretation of Early Christian Apologetics."

Church History 39 (1970) 437-458.

Williams, A. Lukyn. *Adversus Judaeos: a bird's-eye view of Christian Apologiae until the Renaissance*. Cambridge: The University Press, 1935.

Williams, George Huntston. "Christology and Church-State Relations in the Fourth Century." *Church History* 20 (1951): 3-33.

Williams, S.R. "The Household in the Early Church with Comparative Selective References to the Pagan Culture of the Roman World." B. Litt. thesis, Oxford University, 1978.

Wilmart, A. "La Collection des 38 Homelies Latines de Saint Jean Chrysostome." *Journal of Theological Studies* 19 (1918): 305-327.

Wilson, N.G. *Saint Basil on the Value of Greek Literature*. London: Duckworth, 1975.

Wolfson, H.A. *The Philosophy of the Church Fathers*. Cambridge: Harvard University Press, 1956.

Wright, David F. "Homosexuals or Prostitutes." *Vigiliae Christianne*. 38 (1984): 125-153.

_____. "Translating *arsenokotai*," *Vigiliae Christianae*. 41 (1987): 396-398.

Young, Frances M. "Christological Ideas in the Greek Commentaries on the Epistle to the Hebrews." *Journal of Theological Studies* New Series 20 (1969): 150-63.

_____. *From Nicaea to Chalcedon*. London: SCM Press, 1983.

_____. "John Chrysostom on First and Second Corinthians." *Studia Patristica*. 18 (1985) vol. 1. 349-352.

_____. *Sacrifice and the Death of Christ*. London: SCM Press, 1975.

Zosimus. *Historia Nova*. San Antonio, Texas: Trinity University Press, 1967.

INDEX OF JOHN CHRYSOSTOM'S WORKS

GENERAL INDEX

Abel, 33
Abgar, 167
Abiathar, 74
abortion, 187
Adam, 71, 91
Adams, Charles Darwin, 65
Adler, Michael, 219, 220
Albright, W.F., 199
Alexander Severus, 213
Alissandratos, Julia, 65
allegory, 76-77
almsgiving, 152-153
Ameringer, Thomas, 64
Ammianus Marcellinus, 56, 220
Anderson, Galusha, 29, 67
Anthony (Egyptian monk), 27
Anthusa (John's mother), 7, 14
Antioch, 11-14, 37, 214
Antioch- Tax Revolt of 388, 40-42,
    138
Apollo, 10, 32
apologetics, 203f
Apostolic Constitutions, 127-128
Arbogast, 10
Arcadius, 16, 17, 40
Arius, Arianism, 7, 16, 206, 208,
    209, 213
Armstrong, C.B., 220
Athanasius (Archbishop of
    Alexandria), 27, 118
Athanassiadi-Fowden, Polymia, 64
athletic imagery, 107, 156
Attwater, Donald, 29, 210
Aubineau, Michel, 132

Augustine, 22, 34, 199, 235
Avi-Yonah, M., 18, 19, 220
Avila, Charles, 198
Babylas (martyr, Bishop of
    Antioch), 11, 12, 32, 44, 56
Bailey, Derrick Sherwin, 171, 182
Baldovin, John Francis, 23
Bamberger, Bernard J., 219
baptism, 96-98, 115
baptism, deathbed, 97-98
Bardy, G., 23, 134
Barrosse, Thomas, 159
Basil (John's friend), 15, 25, 117,
    146, 151
Basil (Bishop of Caesarea), 22,
    118
Baur, C., 21, 64, 80, 130
Baynes, Norman H., 18, 23
Benin, Stephen D., 183
Bezdeki, Stephanus, 65
Bickersteth, J.E., 132
bishop, 122f
Bobrinskoy, Boris, 132
Boswell, John, 184
Boularand, Ephrem, 100
Bousquet, Joseph, 134
Bowder, Diana, 19, 161
Bowersock, G.W., 47, 64
Breck, John, 82
British Isles, 16
Brooten, Bernardette, 184
Browning, Robert, 48, 220
Bruck, E.F., 102
Burns, Mary, Albania, 65

Fall (first sin of Adam and Eve),
      71, 90, 164
Fee, G.D., 80
Feldman, Hilary, 64
Finn, Thomas, 104, 105
Firmilianus, 9
Flavian Nicomamchus, 206
Flavian (Archbishop of Antioch),
      16, 41, 42, 55, 128
Forell, George Wolfgang, 198
Fravitta, 10
free will, 91-93
Friedrich, Otto, 211
Gagne, Ronald, 162
Ganges River, 16
Geanakopolos, Deno John, 19
Geerlings, J., 80
Generid, 10
Gignac, F.T., 80
gluttony, 194
Goodspeed, Edgar J., 80
Gordon, Barry, 199
Goths, 16, 40, 206
Graef, Hilda, 172
Grant, Robert M., 19, 81, 82
Gratian, 206
Great Church (Antioch), 12
Greek language, 13
Greeley, Delores, 129
Green, Malcolm, 135
Green, H. Benedict, 104
Greer, Rowan A., 182, 235
Grissom, Fred Allen, 219
Haddad, George, 20
Hadrian, 216
Hagar, 14

Hall, Thomas Cuming, 131, 172
Halton, Thomas, 35, 47, 66, 129,
      133
Harjunpaa, Toivo, 22
Harkins, Paul, 20, 22, 34, 63, 99,
      104, 129, 130, 212
Harris, Robbie James, 67
Harris, William V., 149
Hatch, Edwin, 22
Hay, C., 100
Hebrew language, 13, 75, 80
Hellebichus, 41
Henderson, R., 211
Hermione, 109
Hickey, Anne Ewing, 134, 171
Hill, Robert, 21, 78, 79, 81, 82,
      100, 172, 235
Hillel II (Jewish Patriarch), 214
Hillgarth, J.N., 34
Hollinghurst, G.F., 64
homosexuality, 178
Houston, James, 5
Hubbel, Harry M., 64
humility, 153
Hunter, David G., 29, 183
Hussey, J.M., 235
Hyatt, M., 29
Ignatius (Bishop of Antioch), 12,
      31
India, Indians, 16, 203, 204
Innocent (Archbishop of Rome),
      17, 128
Isaiah, 71
Jaeger, Werner, 21
James (Brother of Christ), 123,
      211

DATE DUE

JAN 2 8 1994	NOV 2 5 2008
SEP 1 1994	DEC 5 2007
SEP 1 0 1994	JAN 25 2012
OCT 9 1996	
NOV 1 3 1995	
DEC 1 8 1995	
JAN 9 1996	
FEB 2 4 1997	
FEB 2 3 1997	
AUG 2 0 1997	
MAY 2 8 1997	
MAR 4 1998	
JAN 8 1998	
AUG 1 2 2001	
JUL 1 3 2001	
FEB 1 8 2004	